MAKE WAVES

University of Nevada Press | Reno, Nevada 89557 USA
www.unpress.nevada.edu
Copyright © 2019 by University of Nevada Press
All rights reserved
Cover art by © Andrei Shupilo, © Alexander Potapov, © Dmitry-Fisher
Cover design by Louise O'Farrell

Library of Congress Cataloging-in-Publication Data

Names: Farca, Paula Anca, 1977- editor.
Title: Make waves : water in contemporary writing / edited by Paula Anca
  Farca.
Description: Reno, Nevada : University of Nevada Press [2019] | Includes
  index. | Summary: "Make Waves: Water in Contemporary Literature and Film
  underscores how water is a creatively transformative symbol through
  which we synthesize environmental concerns and a source of cultural and
  political tensions exacerbated by climate change. At its core, Make
  Waves seeks to demonstrate that water is an immense reservoir of
  artistic potentiality and an agent of historical and cultural exchange.
  The goal of this edited book is thus two-fold: to celebrate water which
  is the source of life and a powerful symbol in numerous cultures and to
  raise awareness about global water debates and crises"-- Provided by
  publisher.
Identifiers: LCCN 2019019157 | ISBN 9781948908313 (cloth) | ISBN
  9781948908306 (ebook)
Subjects: LCSH: Water in literature. | Water in motion pictures. |
  Water--Environmental aspects. | Water--Social aspects.
Classification: LCC PN56.W34 M35 2019 | DDC 809.9/336--dc23
LC record available at https://lccn.loc.gov/2019019157

The paper used in this book meets the requirements of American National Standard
  for Information Sciences — Permanence of Paper for Printed Library Materials,
  ANSI/NISO Z39.48-1992 (R2002).

FIRST PRINTING

Manufactured in the United States of America

MAKE WAVES

Water in Contemporary Literature and Film

Edited by

Paula Anca Farca

UNIVERSITY OF NEVADA PRESS *Reno & Las Vegas*

Contents

Part 3: Arid and Awash: High Pollution, High Energy Demands, and High Waters

Introduction

PAULA ANCA FARCA

WHEN NASA CONFIRMED in 2015 that there was liquid water on Mars, many of us immediately thought there was or could be life on Mars. That is because we associate water with life itself. And we know that life originated from water and human beings are more than 50 percent water. In fact, our history on Earth has been a history of and with water. Water sustains and nourishes us, irrigates our crops and produces our food, keeps us clean and healthy, and contributes to our energy needs and various industries. People could potentially survive without fossil fuels, but we cannot live without water, and, unlike coal and oil, water is irreplaceable, and thus priceless. In addition to supporting any life form on our planet, water is also a cultural icon. A rich reservoir of symbolic associations, water is present in many creation myths and it is said to possess purification and regeneration powers. From ancient Greek and Egyptian mythology, to the Bible, Taoist tradition, or Native American practices, water has symbolized life, wisdom, fertility, purity, and even death.

During the twentieth and twenty-first centuries, water's symbolic associations as a foundational life force carried on, but a new layer of environmental issues marked modern times. *Make Waves: Water in Contemporary Literature and Film* strives to capture the cultural aspects of water and the environmental concerns of recent decades; in many situations, these two aspects are intertwined. While water is essential to human survival and prosperity, it also sustains our modern lifestyle through its uses in agriculture, energy production, industry, and manufacturing. Our increasing water and energy demands coupled, with the effects of climate change, put a strain on our even more depleted freshwater supply and water resources. Individuals and communities around the globe have increasingly faced droughts, floods, water pollution, water scarcity, and even water wars. We tend to address and solve these concerns through scientific and technological innovations, but social and cultural analyses and solutions are needed as well. That is why the contributors of this book chose to tackle current water issues in the era of climate change through the lens of recent literature and film. Creating familiar and relatable contexts for their water dilemmas, authors and directors of contemporary literary texts and films present compelling stories on water crises and suggest possible solutions to these crises.

This edited book underscores how water is a creatively transformative symbol through which we synthesize environmental concerns and a source of cultural and political tensions exacerbated by climate change. At its core, *Make Waves* seeks to demonstrate that water is an immense reservoir of artistic potentiality and an agent of historical and cultural exchange. Throughout the book, contributors ask and attempt to answer the following questions: What does water as a symbol entail in contemporary literature and film? How do writers and directors address people's current relationships with water? How does water establish or erode relationships between individuals, communities, and nations? How do water issues intersect with societal and cultural aspects in different regions and countries? What are some of the ecological ramifications of water in contemporary literature and film? Why and how are connections among water, climate change, and people significant? For what reasons do those who control water use it and allow it to be used in different ways? How do we address and solve water pollution? How do individuals and communities respond to water and environmental disasters?

Analyzing novels, autobiographies, poems, nonfiction pieces, video installations, poems written on the stones of a watershed, documentaries, and films, contributors address topics such as: water in industrial landscapes, dam construction, depletion and pollution, water wars, health of river ecosystems, river restoration, interoceanic canals, acequia culture versus prior appropriation, privatization, and ocean activism. Other topics include water symbolism, individual and communal relationships with water, droughts, high sea level, oil spills in rivers and oceans, floods, and temperature rises. Contributors to the collection also explore how global water problems affect local communities around the world and intersect with social and cultural aspects such as health, citizenship, class, gender, race, and ethnicity.

In addition to the introduction, *Make Waves* contains three parts. More theoretical in nature, Part I foregrounds the symbolic and spiritual qualities of water and its potential for cultural change and environmental justice. While Part I focuses on how we view nature and water through culture and art, Part II deals with how water crisis and scarcity could lead to culture clashes and even water wars. This section of the book deals with water scarcity due to climate change—a serious threat in densely populated countries, one that impacts the mental health of vulnerable segments of the population and leaves them exposed and powerless. Part III revolves around connections among water, energy, and industrial development. While climate change effects such as high sea levels and floods impact communities around the world, our high energy demands contribute to oil spills and water pollution. Contributors also look at the future of water as portrayed by authors of post-apocalyptic texts, a future that includes both violence and water wars, but also chances toward new forms of adaptability and humanity.

Despite numerous environmental challenges presented in the book, the tone of the collection is not bleak, as many contributors boldly promise a new water ethics, engaging forms of activism, environmental justice ideas, and fresh ways of breaking down boundaries between human and nonhuman, clean and dirty, or natural and artificial. Water becomes a foundation for life, health, and justice and a sanctuary of creative energies worth fighting and advocating for. The goal of *Make Waves* is thus two-fold: to celebrate water, which is the source of life and a powerful, creative symbol in numerous cultures, and to raise awareness about global water debates and crises.

In the first part of the book, "Water Natures: Culture, Identity, and Creativity," contributors analyze water as a symbol and convey several meanings behind water symbolism. The book opens with an essay whose authors announce a large spectrum of water significations based on the notion of liquidity. "Liquidity Incorporated: Economic Tides and Fluid Data in Hito Steyerl's *Liquidity Inc.*" by Christina Gerhardt and Jaimey Hamilton Faris, examines the literal and metaphorical deployments of water depicted in Hito Steyerl's large-scale thirty-minute video installation called *Liquidity Inc.* (2014). Focusing on the economic tides after the financial crisis of 2008, Steyerl connects water to the economic notion of liquidity but also to weather and climate change-induced calamities. Steyerl also grapples with contemporary technological innovations, including video and art, and engages the liquid circulation of data images, information production, and computer-generated imagery.

As seen above, water and liquidity reveal messages and connections among different fields. The next essay draws even more parallels among water, art, and the environment. In "Material States of Poetry: The Stanza Stones," Emma Trott analyzes Simon Armitage's six poems written on large stones on the West Yorkshire moors, along the Pennine watershed from Ilkley to Armitage's hometown of Marsden. The subject of each poem, which has been assigned its own stone and location, is water in different states: dew, rain, mountain stream, snow, puddle, and mist. Landscape architect Tom Lonsdale and stone mason Pip Hall collaborated with Armitage as key engineers of the project; they all seek to engage the public in its linking of language and landscape. The Stanza Stones also connect water as pure material with site-specific social and industrial histories. Hoping that their readers will create their own environmental ethics, Armitage, Lonsdale, Hall, and their colleagues are working toward a new landscape, which speaks of itself, with the natural forces, human lives, and poetry that shape it.

Contributors in this section also show that water is a mythical surface from which all physical bodies and cultural practices alike shape the daily lives of communities and individuals. Andrew Andermatt underscores such mythical relationships with water in an essay titled "Preying on Water: Hunting Spiritual and Environmental Rebirth on the Kentucky River in Selected Essays from Wendell Berry's *The Long-Legged House.*" Wendell Berry addresses the sense of mystery, magic, and horror the water instills in people and how these feelings lead to a unique religious experience. Andermatt examines how Berry uses symbolism, metaphor, and narration to create the spiritual experience with water. Keeping the symbolism of water in the spiritual realm, Sofia Ahlberg explores water's communication capabilities in her chapter, "'Let everything that binds fall': The Significance of Water in David Vann's Fiction." Ahlberg argues that in David Vann's fiction, water repudiates textuality yet nevertheless communicates and speaks to and through us. As such, water resembles the voice of storytelling.

As previous contributors showed, water alludes to a plethora of significations and symbols and ties together different areas of inquiry. For Irish writers, water usually alludes to island stagnation or emigration. Against this backdrop, Julienne H. Empric proposes an analysis of Colm Tóibín's novel *The Heather Blazing* (1992), which addresses the duality of water in images of erosion and healing. In "Water-Blind: Erosion and (Re)Generation in Colm Tóibín's *The Heather Blazing*," Empric contends that Tóibín uses water imagery aesthetically, to erode the entrenched authority of the protagonist, and he warns that, as in ancient tragedy, catastrophe may be prerequisite to human learning and change.

So far, contributors have focused on water in contemporary literature and film as a rich cultural symbol and a force; they also looked at people's relationships with water and the transformative power of rivers and oceans. Contributors to the second part of the collection, "Water Cultures: Nations, Borders, and Water Wars," delve into intricate relationships that water establishes among individuals, communities, and nations. While water does not respect physical borders between countries, it does influence political, economic, and social relations between neighboring states and nations. The chapters in this section of the book show that limited access to water could lead to political tensions, altercations, and even water wars.

Part II opens with two chapters on the American West and water scarcity. In an essay titled "A Clash of Water Cultures in John Nichols's *The Milagro Beanfield War*," Susan Tyburski explores northern New Mexico's acequia culture and contrasts this communal approach with the dictates of a capitalist legal system based on "prior appropriation." Tyburski discusses Nichols's portrayal of acequia culture, how this co-operative management of water resources contrasts with the competitive adjudication of water rights in the American West, the effect of the publication of *The Milagro Beanfield War* on water rights disputes in northern New Mexico, and the role literature can play in educating readers about issues of environmental justice. The next chapter, "Watershed Ethics and Dam Politics: Mapping Biopolitics, Race, and Resistance in *Sleep Dealer* and *Watershed*," by Tracey Daniels-Lerberg follows the historical development of irrigation and the movement of water resources to serve communities in the American West. Daniels-Lerberg proposes a reading of Percival Everett's novel *Watershed* and Alex Rodriguez's film *Sleep Dealer* in which water is employed as a weapon along predictable and well-worn cultural tributaries. She thus shows that water is a prized resource with a history and a future guided by aesthetic and ethical implications related to race and resistance.

The following chapters discuss social, cultural, and environmental implications of dams and canals. In an essay titled "Thomas King Tells a Different Story: Dams, Rivers, and Indigenous Literary Hydromythology", Rebecca Fullan analyzes connections among water, myth, and action in Thomas King's *Green Grass, Running Water*. The foundational stories about water inspire human action, including building and resisting dams, and these stories caution that water and rivers are forces to be respected not controlled. In 2014, the gates of Mexico's Morelos Dam opened to allow the Colorado River to flow into its delta. This change, Paul Formisano contends in "Shifting Tides: A Literary Exploration of the Colorado River Delta," is also marked by a rich literary tradition about the Colorado Delta that reflects the shifting representations of this place. Formisano traces the values that have drastically transformed the delta ecosystem and argues that the spirit of Mexican-American collaboration contributed to the delta's resurgence as one of North America's great ecological treasures.

Not all collaborations between nations are so environmentally friendly. Jeremy Larochelle, for instance, believes that the building of an interoceanic canal by Chinese Wang Jing in Nicaragua will bring social and environmental unrest. If the canal is built, the people of Nicaragua will no longer be able to fish or drink water from Lake Nicaragua, which happens to be the largest body of fresh water in Central America. In "Poetry and Revolution on the Brink of Ecological

Disaster: Ernesto Cardenal and the Interoceanic Canal in Nicaragua," Larochelle analyzes the poetry of revolution by Nicaraguan poet and priest, Ernesto Cardenal, and the period of optimism across the country in the years immediately following the Sandinista victory of 1979. Cardenal's poetry, Larochelle posits, illustrates the importance of the lake for both the humans and nonhumans that live along its shores.

The topic of the next two essays revolves around water wars. Robert Niemi writes "'Bad for the glass': *Chinatown's* Skewed Rendition of the California Water Wars," a film history piece in which he compares the real events of the California water wars with their film depiction which simplifies the history with a strong element of melodrama. Continuing the portrayal of water wars, Laura Hatry moves the discussion to Latin America. "The Cinematic Portrayals of Water Wars in Bolivia and Ecuador" focuses on the water wars in Bolivia and Ecuador at the beginning of the twenty-first century, as a consequence of the water privatizations that led to massive demonstrations and violent clashes. In her paper, Laura Hatry analyzes how the movies *También la lluvia* (*Even the Rain*) by Icíar Bollaín and *A Dark Truth* by Damian Lee treat the citizens' defiance against neoliberal policies and how the community recovered its common good.

Designed to raise awareness about depleted water supplies due to increased demands from energy and industry sectors and climate change effects, Part III, "Arid and Awash: High Energy Demands, High Pollution, and High Waters," problematizes issues such as energy security, pollution, and people's fragile physical and mental health due to climate change and shifting weather patterns. Here, contributors discuss how our high energy demands contribute to oil spills and water pollution; and how climate change effects such as high sea levels, water scarcity, and floods impact communities around the world and especially affect low-income people.

Two essays on oil and water open up this section. Ila Tyagi argues in "Troubled Waters: Unveiling Industrial Negligence in Three Deepwater Horizon Films" that vision is central to environmental catastrophe because it is harder to care about disasters people do not see. Moving images amplify our capacity to grasp damage disasters like the Deepwater Horizon spill case, persuading us to take effective mitigative and restorative action. Oil disasters are unfortunately present in other parts of the world, including Niger Delta, a beautiful area destroyed by oil extraction, pollution, and violent ethnic conflicts. Idom Inyabri argues in "The River as Character in Niger Delta Poetry" that water in the form of rivers and streams has been significant to the life of ecosystems in Niger Delta and the cultural practices of this place prior to the discovery and exploitation of crude oil. The paper interrogates the imagery of rivers in the poetry of third generation Niger Delta poets such as Ibiwari Ikiriko, Ebi Yeibo, Ogaga Ifowodo, and Joe Ushie and critically negotiates the connectedness of humans and nonhumans in the fate of the rivers within the context of mindless oil exploitation in the Niger Delta.

Part III ends with two essays on eco-thrillers and post-apocalyptic novels. Giulia Miller considers three British eco-thrillers and concludes that irregular weather patterns and environmental crises such as floods, drought, and storms contribute to the protagonists' deteriorating mental health. In "Water and Mental Health in Three British Climate Fiction Novels," Miller claims that the environment's impact on mental health dictates both the behavior of the protagonists and the direction of the plot. In the last essay, "There Will Be Blood: Water Futures in Paolo Bacigalupi's *The Water Knife* and Claire Vaye Watkins's *Gold Fame Citrus,*" Paula Anca Farca looks at the future of water as portrayed by authors of post-apocalyptic novels, a future that includes both violence and water wars, but also chances for new forms of adaptability and humanity. She discusses water in connection to survival, tragedy, and violence and underlines people's immense capacity for adaptation and creativity in the face of disaster.

The goal of *Make Waves: Water in Contemporary Literature and Film* is simply to celebrate water as a life foundation and cultural icon and raise awareness about global water issues and crises around the world. The book includes critical inquiries about water in all its forms, whether as sea, oceans, snow, rain, dew, lakes, or moisture, and raises awareness of recent water challenges around the world.

PART 1

Water Natures

Culture, Identity, and Creativity

Liquidity Incorporated

Economic Tides and Fluid Data in Hito Steyerl's *Liquidity Inc.*

CHRISTINA GERHARDT *and* JAIMEY HAMILTON FARIS

> You must be shapeless, formless, like water.
> When you pour water in a cup, it becomes the cup.
> When you pour water in a bottle, it becomes the bottle.
> When you pour water in a teapot, it becomes the teapot.
> Water can drip and it can crash. Become like water my friend.
>
> —Bruce Lee

> There are reasons to consider "fluidity" or "liquidity" as fitting
> metaphors when we wish to grasp the nature of the present, in
> many ways *novel*, phase in the history of modernity.
>
> —Bauman (2)

> Water is the lifeblood of human survival, *liquidity* is
> fundamental to corporate vitality.
>
> —J. P. Morgan

LIQUIDITY CONNECTS to and expresses our most cataclysmic contemporary crises: be they financial asset fluctuations or climate-change-induced sea level rises. Through metaphors of water, filmmaker, artist, and essayist Hito Steyerl's large-scale 30-minute video installation *Liquidity Inc.* (2014) connects topics such as late capitalism, precarious labor, climate change, and data circulation. In particular, *Liquidity Inc.*

thematizes the economic tides after the financial crisis of 2008. The first epigraph above, quoting Bruce Lee on water, opens the video and appears as a refrain throughout the installation. Spoken over recurring images of waves, diagrams of liquid assets, storm systems, and other idiosyncratic visuals of water, the video offers a renewed engagement with Lee's statement. What does it mean to be water, especially in the twenty-first century?

This essay examines the literal and metaphorical use of the concept of water in Steyerl's *Liquidity Inc.*, focusing on the following four concerns. First, water, like the installation's very title, obviously puts forward the economic notion of liquidity, that is, the degree to which a financial asset can be accessed or brought onto the market; and the fluidity associated with financial transactions. Second, in the contemporary economic world of fluid and ever-changing labor conditions, individuals swim in the fluctuating waters of economic tides and need to be flexible to flow in the river of capital. Thus, the video engages liquidity as an articulation of precarious labor. Third, the video considers water as weather. It discusses water as climate change–induced tsunamis, as clouds, as torrents, as rain, as storm, and as flood. Reporters in balaclavas, invoking the Weather Underground but with a contemporary climate change and computer cloud referencing twist, also appear.[1] Fourth, Steyerl attempts to engage the liquid circulation of data, of information production and dissemination, of computer-generated imagery (CGI) and of animation.

These four concerns are clear in retrospect, but the rhythm and sequencing of the video itself mixes them all together like a brewing storm in the ocean: segments are intercut in faster and faster waves, crashing down on other segments; frames generate within frames. By the video's end, the viewer is awash in sounds and images of water, building the perception that a particular message does not need to be understood by the viewer, but rather a virtual superstorm of clichés about liquidity needs to be felt and absorbed. Steyerl's work, here and elsewhere, is intentionally nonlinear and playful in her engagement of key issues in contemporary politics, economics, environmental studies and informatics. Her keen attention to recurring deployments of water aims to expose how the poetic coincidence of "liquidity" across domains might actually operate as a veil for the integration, implementation, and catastrophic consequences of neoliberal power. Ultimately, this essay seeks to articulate the video's claims that politics, economics, environment, and informatics now flow through each other and thus must be read together.

Liquidity Inc. opens with what seems at first to be fairly straightforward exploration of economic liquidity learned through the lessons of the Lehman Brothers bankruptcy. Its first main sequence features a TV magazine–style story about Jacob Wood, a Vietnamese American stockbroker-cum-martial-artist. Wood is an empathetic protagonist who had been working for Lehman Brothers at the time of the stock market crash of 2008. For the camera, he retraces the day he lost his job, how he felt, as well as his efforts to rebound by making a living as a mixed martial arts (MMA) fighter and announcer. Wood's explanation, replete with Bruce Lee's watery metaphors about learning to adapt gracefully, seems to minimize and naturalize Lehman Brothers' role in the financial crisis. In the video, Wood looks to the camera and says:

> There were purges every year because of the economy. Especially large financial companies have had a lot of pressure, for more earnings, for their stock price to increase, and so it's normal, kind of purging every year to lay off a certain amount of people. That's why you've got to position yourself to be defensive, to be ready for those shocks . . . to have a shockproof portfolio. You've got to adapt to whatever is happening in the market . . . You've got to adapt to your situation. It's very fluid. It's kind of like fighting.

As Wood describes the pressuring and purging forces of the economy, questions arise for the viewer. How is it that Wood (despite hard-hitting exposés like *Inside Job*, 2010) *does not* blame particular people, corporations, or governments for his financial straits? How is it that Wood even empathizes with Lehman Brothers because it was under "pressure" to perform? As the video repeats his words along with pictures of storms and water, it cultivates sensitivity toward and curiosity about how the economy is naturalized through water metaphors.

To understand the context for Wood's point of view, it is instructive to review how watery metaphors emerged in economic thinking in the first place. The notion of the economy acting like a liquid "under pressure" has its origins in the seventeenth century, when new discoveries of hydraulic power and blood circulation were at the forefront of technological, political, and economic thought. Blaise Pascal and others described how the pneumatic properties of water multiply force and William Harvey revolutionized medicine when he described the human pulmonary system as hydraulic—blood pumping both away from and back to the heart in a ceaseless and elegant cycle (Harvey 48). Economic and political thinkers of the day quickly seized upon these paradigms. Thomas Hobbes, for example, made it a key theme of his 1651 treatise *Leviathan*:

> Money . . . goes round about, nourishing, as it passeth, every part thereof; in so much as this concoction is, as it were, the sanguification of the Commonwealth: for natural blood is in like manner made of the fruits of the earth; and, circulating, nourisheth by the way every member of the body of man. (118)

As scholar Kath Weston argues in "Lifeblood, Liquidity, and Cash Transfusions," metaphors of circulation and flow gained momentum when Adam Smith wrote in his 1776 *The Wealth of Nations* about "the free circulation of labor and stock, both from employment to employment and from place to place" (57). Indeed, the concept of circulation undergirded the whole of Smith's argument—that the natural and automatic forces of the free market should be able to self-regulate.

Recurring motifs of economic circulation were broadened by the literal link between water and wealth in the Age of Empire. The health of nation-states depended not only on rain, irrigation, and riverside mills but also on rivers, canals, ports, and transoceanic crossings of a far-flung trade system. Water became a primary metaphor for the "natural" state of the economy. Yet, despite the seeming fluidity of the world trade system represented by Smith, a need already existed in the early years of the stock market to establish mechanisms by which money could be shifted from one account to another and hence used to hide and absorb over-extended investment and debt.[2] Two centuries later, John Maynard Keynes was the first to use the term "liquidity" in a scathing critique of such practices. In his 1936 *The General Theory of Employment, Interest, and Money*, Keynes argued:

> Of the maxims of orthodox finance none, surely, is more anti-social than the fetish of liquidity, the doctrine that it is a positive virtue on the part of investment institutions to concentrate their resources upon the holding of "liquid" securities. It forgets that there is no such thing as liquidity of investment for the community as a whole . . . The actual, private object of the most skilled investment today is "to beat the gun," as the Americans so well express it, to outwit the crowd, and to pass the bad, or depreciating, half-crown to the other fellow. (155)

Reflecting on the lessons of the Great Depression, Keynes insisted that liquidity was really a shell game played by investment institutions and that ultimately, it was usually the citizen and community who bore the brunt of speculation. Yet over the course of the twentieth century, the orthodoxies of liquidity have come to dominate the computerized probability-driven system of futures trading and hedge funds. As J. P. Morgan asserts in its marketing brochures, "Water is the *lifeblood* of human survival, *liquidity* is fundamental to corporate vitality." It celebrates the power of the corporation to concentrate global cash flow and further claims that "web technology enables active, automated liquidity and investment management."[3] Yet the average consumer's confidence in these seemingly fluid and automated systems, as many have argued, actually hid the calculated activities of firms like Lehman Brothers, who knowingly bundled subprime mortgages that led to the 2008 crash (Langley; Pasanek and Polillo). As this brief overview shows, the laws of hydro-physics do not govern economics: economics has simply drawn on its language.

Steyerl's *Liquidity Inc.* emphasizes the confusing build up of liquid and water metaphors in Wood's language by pairing them with visual montages of CGI waves, water drops, texts referencing water, clouds, tsunamis, and more. As these images begin to break up the narrative, they also challenge the viewer's understanding of the 2008 financial crisis and of Wood's interpretation of it. The video's approach is both radical and subtle in that it eschews an exploration of the cause and effect of the crisis (as other documentaries have done) for an exploration of the persistent metaphoric and affective use of "liquidity." This visual strategy of exaggerating the simple juxtaposition of economic operations to the natural pressure systems of waves comments on how the notion of the economy as a "natural" ecology of water is instrumentalized throughout the cultural sphere, used, in effect, to displace and disguise the human forces at work.

Steyerl also brings home this point narratively at the very end of the opening documentary sequence by also inserting some found footage of a folksy-looking nineties financial advisor wearing a cream colored turtleneck who explains the virtues of liquidity for the individual investor. This short clip plays in a box at the upper right corner of a larger screen in which Wood spars with another fighter. The expert investor's voice is privileged while Wood fights silently. In the clip, the investor explains how simple it is to convert certain assets (a home mortgage or stocks) quickly into cash before, as he puts it, "financial disaster strikes." This scene within a scene brings the contradictions of Wood's situation to the fore. Even Wood, himself a stockbroker, did not have enough economic liquidity to avoid the market "shocks" of 2008. This reminds us of Keynes's comment on "liquidity"—that there really is no such thing at the individual or community level. Even at the corporate level, Lehman Brothers did not escape bankruptcy. Still, if the construct has any applicability, it is for corporations who are "too big to fail" (like J. P. Morgan and Bear Stearns) and can rely either on huge global networks of cash flow or government tax-payer "bail outs." Lacking financial liquidity, Wood's only option is to "be fluid" in his changing work situation.

Not only the economy but also labor, upon which the economy relies, is framed in terms of liquidity. Labor—as such an asset in a neoliberal free market economy—needs to be ever more fluid and flexible, in order to accommodate the changing tides of capital. "Meet Jacob Wood," the text on a glass of water in *Liquidity Inc.*, reads: "After years of training to fight and swimming through my seas, he has developed the strength and endurance to travel freely to Vietnam and in around 150 milliseconds and returning [sic] to Los Angeles in roughly the same time." Jacob Wood is strong, has endurance and is malleable, manifesting neoliberal labor and its attendant "flexibility strategies."

The term "precarious labor" describes flexible labor and working conditions. As Ben Trott states: "The term 'precariat' first came into widespread use among activists at once interested in organizing around 'precarious' working conditions—and the way their emergence was intertwined with broader social, political, economic and cultural dynamics—while simultaneously convinced traditional forms of workers' organisation were insufficient for building effective forms of resistance and counter-power" (406–7). The term was first used in conjunction with a May Day Parade that took place on May 1, 2001, in Milan, Italy. Alex Foti coorganized the event and the subsequent EuroMayDay network, which mobilized "young temps, partimers [*sic*], freelancers and contract workers, researchers and teachers, service and knowledge workers" (21). The terms *precariat* and *precarious labor* have since come into common usage to describe Post-Fordist working conditions (Guy Standing).

After World War II, a global economy was established based on free market principles, such as competition and individualism, and in particular after the 1973 oil crisis and recession and the challenge to developed nations mounted by the New International Economic Order (NIEO), flexible labor formed a key component of it (David Harvey, Prashad). Characterizing the impact of these shifts, "the temporary contract," as Lyotard wrote in *The Postmodern Condition*, "is in practice supplanting permanent institutions in the professional, the emotional, sexual, cultural, family and international domains, as well as in political affairs . . . the temporary contract is favored by the system due to its greater flexibility, lower cost" (66). This cheaper labor is often not unionized labor. As Joseph Stiglitz argues, "Market forces have also limited the effectiveness of the unions that remain" (64). He continues:

> Part of the conventional wisdom in economics of the last three decades is that flexible labor markets contribute to economic strength. I would argue, in contrast, that strong worker protections correct what would otherwise be an imbalance of economic power. Such protection leads to a higher-quality labor force with workers who are more loyal to their firms and more willing to invest in themselves and in their jobs. It also makes for a more cohesive society and better workplaces. (65)

The increased flexibility or liquidity of the labor market is, according to Stiglitz, in part responsible for the growing economic inequality. The precariat is at once *the outcome* of this liberalization but also *the source* of a new organizing principle due to the gutted traditional forms of workers' organization, that is, unions.

Relatedly, the elite's ability or need to transcend both space and time has become more malleable in this arrangement. In *Liquid Modernity*, Zygmunt Bauman characterizes this era as follows: "We are witnessing the revenge of nomadism over the principle of territoriality and settlement" (13). "In the fluid stage of modernity," he continues, "the settled majority is ruled by the nomadic and exterritorial elite. Keeping the roads free for nomadic traffic and phasing out the remaining checkpoints has now become the meta-purpose of politics" (13). Movement, Bauman underscores, needs to be as unimpeded for the elite as it is for their finances and for the trade on which it relies.

Labor has also experienced an increased mobility—not always necessarily by choice but also due to (economic) force. Workers are *obligated* to be constantly on the move with impacts on relationships, on family life, and on a sense of home and of community. In *Liquid Modernity* Bauman states:

> Any dense and tight network of social bonds, and particularly a territorially rooted tight network, is an obstacle to be cleared out of the way. Global powers are bent on dismantling such networks for the sake of their continuous and growing fluidity, that principal source of their strength and the warrant of their invincibility. And it is the falling apart, the friability, the brittleness, the transience, the until-further-noticeness of human bonds and networks[,] which allow these powers to do their job in the first place. (14)

Thus, the liquidity of labor also renders the networks—of home, relationship, community, home city, homeland—as liquid, so that they can bend to the aforementioned needs of capitalism.

In Steyerl's *Liquidity Inc.* this fluidity manifests in Jacob Wood's journey. "I am in your veins. I am in your eyes. I am gushing through your heart, plumbing and wires," the video's voiceover narrator states, intercut with shots of Wood gearing up for and competing in an MMA match. Liquidity incorporated. Not only is the water part of our body.

The very notion of liquidity is incorporated, as the title tells us, gushing not only through our hearts but also our plumbing and wires. Liquidity constitutes us figuratively and literally. Wood, in what seems to be his bedroom, tells us: "So it was the moment when I putting my tie on, literally, when I got a call from my boss and HR, that I was getting laid off." While the visuals cut to him in the MMA match, he continues on with the voice-over narration cited in the previous section: "There were purges every year because of the economy . . . so it is normal purging every year to lay off a certain amount of people . . . That's why you've got to position yourself to be ready for those shocks." "You have got to adapt to whatever is happening," he continues, "It's very fluid." He has absorbed entirely the precarity of labor as the situation to which the laborer has to adapt. About the layoffs or purges, as he calls them, he says: "It is normal." The onus, in his estimation, is clearly on the worker and on his or her adaptability. Neoliberalism imbibed.

Wood goes from working at Lehman Brothers to serving as commentator for the matches. A close-up shot focuses on a sheet of paper with the MMA fighters' names and photographs on it. Suddenly, one photo morphs into a video, which then fills the screen as the voice-over states: "When you have liquidity, you're in control." It is the aforementioned found footage advertisement for loans: "The important thing is to have cash when you need . . . you can put food on the table if you don't have an income. You can avoid financial disaster." But liquidity and adaptability do not always mean control—as Wood being laid off showed. It is the myth of the modern flexible labor market that if one is adaptable then one is in control. It is the myth of the loan, never named as such, above, the liquidity of "cash when you need it," which in reality is debt. And debt is never about control—on a personal or national level.

As the video progresses, Steyerl weaves the discourse around liquidity related to economics and labor together with weather, using the latter to open up onto a range of further notions.[4] In the opening sequence, the sentence "I am liquidity incorporated" stands starkly alone on the screen, running along the bottom; then, the following words, as if generating a word "cloud," start to appear on and eventually fill in the screen: "ice, stream, flood, leak, tsunami, rainbow, cloud, wave, flow, tears, weather, polygons, sweat, twisters, stream, capital, torrent, numbers, statistic distribution." In *Liquidity Inc.* water imagery flows between "capital, torrent, numbers, statistic distribution" and "polygons"—between data distribution and finances, on the one hand, and "ice, stream, flood, leak, tsunami, rainbow, cloud, wave, flow, tears, weather, . . . sweat, twisters [and] stream" or nature and weather, on the other hand.

In talking about the weather, Steyerl eschews the approach of recent cinema on climate change, presenting it less as a scientific phenomenon to be explained in terms of causes and consequences. That is, the video does not consider the environmental impact of oil drilling or of felling rain forests to make way for megafarms. Instead, Steyerl takes an affective route to critique financial capitalism. She considers and presents the mindset of the worker to reveal how she or he explains her or his economic condition as natural, thereby erasing the structural or systemic inequity from view. Yet precisely herein lies her reread of finance and climate change. What drives, *Liquidity Inc.* asks, the intertwined forces of economic liquidity and superstorms? Early on, Steyerl's video connects the liquidity of neoliberal labor, finance, and superstorms visually. Shortly after the video computer generated imagery states that Jacob Wood can (technologically) move to Vietnam and back to Los Angeles in a millisecond, slow meditative music plays and a close-up shows moving water. The image cuts to a shot of Wood's flat-screen television, in his room, showing footage of a massive storm and surging waves, perhaps of the 2004 tsunami in the Indian Ocean, which hit Indonesia. Quick crosscuts feature talking heads narrating the storm conditions, cyclones, again shots of the surging waves, and then satellite images of cyclones, showing the massive size of the storm. Then, the video cuts to a shot of a smartphone on a table at Wood's home, playing a video of Bruce Lee stating "water can flow or it can crash." This visual bridge—of a surfer riding a wave, appearing on the flat-screen at the MMA match, on the flat-screen in Wood's bedroom, on his smartphone and on the phone held by his colleague at the MMA match, and then, again on the flat-screen television in his room—connects the images of water, as something that can flow or crash, and the various spaces the video associates with liquidity.

The sequence cuts to the weather report, presented by "weather underground." The weathercaster dons a balaclava and sports a T-shirt with the owl of Minerva emblazoned on it. As Laura Poitras puts it in a conversation with Hito Steyerl, "I . . . had a look when you were installing, and this tense relationship between representation and reality was palpable. I was surprised to see the Weather Underground, for instance, channeled in a very funny, surreal way" (307). Steyerl explains:

> Of course, today, the Weather Underground is the name of a corporate weather forecasting website. At one point it stated explicitly that they took the name from this radical organization. In my video, reporters supposedly from the Weather Underground—played by a young girl and two adult performers—come onstage to announce the weather, but the weather is a strange mixture of man-made weather, political weather, affective weather, all sorts of catastrophes, going crazy: climate change, financial, geopolitical. There are storms brewing everywhere, different bits and pieces mixed up in one continuous tsunami.

Indeed, the weather report that unfolds presents a history of politics, economics, colonization, and imperialism. "The trade winds," the weatherman announces, "are blowing people back to their homes, blowing goods back to their factories, blowing factories back to their countries, blowing the countries back to their assumed origins" as a medium shot presents South America and Africa, then a medium shot presents southeast Asia, and the camera zooms out to a long shot that includes Africa and Europe. Countries are labeled as "imaginary states, self-declared state, bipolar country, uncontrolled, multiple kingdoms within a country, commonwealth, nonterritorial sovereign entities, unrecognized state, non-autonomous, collapsed state, autonomous areas." The shot pans right to and across Africa and then continues to Asia. Trade winds, trade routes, and the entire map is "unwound," spatially and temporally or historically, panning to the northwest, to wind things back "to their assumed origins" or Europe.

The video cuts back to shots of the tsunami on the flat-screen television in Wood's bedroom. The waves unfold and surge forward. The trade winds wind back. Many people would recognize that the structure of the image references Paul Klee's *Angelus Novus* (1920), which appears in Walter Benjamin's "Theses on the Philosophy of History" (1940): the angel's face turned toward the past, and with ruins and wreckage resulting from history, being hurled at and piling up at its feet in the future:

> Where we perceive a chain of events, he sees one single catastrophe, which keeps piling wreckage upon wreckage and hurls it in front of his feet. The angel would like to stay, awaken the dead, and make whole what has been smashed. But a storm is blowing from Paradise; it has got caught in his wings with such violence that the angel can no longer close them. This storm irresistibly propels him into the future to which his back is turned, while the pile of debris before him grows skyward. This storm is what we call progress. (257–58)

Sure enough, a second later, Paul Klee's *Angelus Novus* appears on the screen. Indirectly, therefore, the video connects the history, politics, and economics of colonialism, imperialism, and neoliberalism with the storms of climate change and beyond. Yet Steyerl also inverts the reference, as a girl weathercaster dressed similarly in a balaclava and owl of Minerva T-shirt appears and states: "The storm is driving from hell; driving us back into the past."

As Poitras pinpoints, Steyerl connects these dots affectively. In a closing sequence, the weathercaster announces:

> This weekend this weather will be a dream. Not only over the weekend! The weather will be just as you thought it would be. To be more precise, it will be exactly as you imagined it to be. Or even more precisely what you are feeling not inside but outside in the stratosphere.

The weather is presented either as the externalization of what one feels or as the internalization of what lies outside. Either way, in the segments on weather (and throughout) affect plays a large role to connect notions of liquidity informing finance, labor, and storms—be they personal, historical, political, economic, or climate change-induced.

Through the liquid circulation of data images and computer-generated imagery (CGI), by the video's end a palpable sense of confusion emerges about which economic, political, and environmental pressure systems have caused which catastrophes. In this complex and fluid system, cause and effect cannot easily be understood in a linear and logical fashion. For this reason, Steyerl instead emphasizes, even dramatizes, eddying or circling around of liquid metaphors to such a degree that their redundancy overwhelms the viewer. The rhythm of imagery informs Steyerl's method of explication. Most of the motifs consist either of found footage of waves and storms or of CGI renditions of water created in C4D—a common software used in video game development for modeling, animation, and motion graphics. CGI manipulations of waves, drops, and watery text are intercut and overlaid on the relatively straightforward documentary featuring Jacob Wood and the surreal weather forecast, which, in turn, uses blue screen technology.

The watery aesthetic of the video speaks to a consistent concern in all of Steyerl's work: the affective force of digital images disseminated across the internet to reinforce dominant ideological narratives and metaphors. Over the course of the last decade, in both her videos and her writing, Steyerl has explored the new agency that images have gained in the digital network revolution. In particular she has addressed their unbounded capacity to multiply, to circulate, and also to create our reality. In one of her regular essay contributions to *E-flux*, "Too Much World: Is the Internet Dead?" she unfolded part of her long-standing argument. Leveraged by her provocative title, she claims polemically that the internet is *not* dead, indeed, it is more powerful than ever. She suggests that the expansion of the internet has facilitated a digital infrastructure in which images not only proliferate within the screen but now also have the ability to move through the screen into reality (Steyerl 6). Steyerl is fascinated by the agency images have in their accumulative power to incapacitate the viewer emotively, materially, and affectively in such a way that they obfuscate an understanding of complex interrelationships between, among other things, economy and ecology, as well as entertainment and politics.

In the next part of "Too Much World," Steyerl explores how images circulate. Here, she shifts toward metaphors of water and more specifically "the cloud"—this time leveraging the naturalization of the digital and virtual into terrifying scenes of connected catastrophe:

> We thought [the internet] was a plumbing system so how did this tsunami creep up in my sink? How is this algorithm drying up this rice paddy? And how many workers are desperately clambering on the menacing cloud that hovers in the distance right now, trying to squeeze out a living, groping through a fog which may at any second transform both into an immersive art installation and a demonstration doused in cutting-edge tear gas? (6)

Environmental degradation, art, and war are all linked through the algorithms of big data and Tumblr. Ultimately, the arc of the essay insinuates that the cloud is not the merely convenient user interface it may at first appear to be but also a globally connected server infrastructure that hides the more insidious aspects of global capitalism. The cloud accumulates metadata and search histories that can be used and sold by the corporations who own the servers; it allows corporations to exploit labor beyond national borders; and it makes offshore money laundering as easy as a few keystrokes.

Steyerl wrote "Too Much World" while she was working on *Liquidity Inc.* so the text and the video are informed by similar ideas. In the video, over snippets of the weather forecast and scenes of Wood boxing, drawings of various diagrams and charts of the cloud begin to appear. At first, they seem like simple demonstrations, like those in financial experts' webinars, showing how uploads to cloud storage eases the cause of corporate "service" and "security." But by the end of the demo, the last chart spells out an explicit critique of the cloud as the "new territory" of big data capitalism. With instant access of information, corporations can virtualize and outsource labor, while at the same time distract viewers with new memes and photo streams.

The cloud makes possible the condition of what Steyerl calls consistently throughout her writing "circulationism." Parallel to the naturalized metaphor of blood circulation to describe the economy, she argues that the "cloud" has come to be regarded as a naturalized system of image and information distribution and redistribution. The capitalist complement to Stalinist "productivism," circulationism impels consumers to work for capitalism through their leisure acts of sharing, posting, filtering, and sorting. Likes, interests, opened files, and clicked pages: all of this information contributes to "State scopophilia, capital compliance, and wholesale surveillance" (Steyerl 7). Sometimes the dystopic digital world Steyerl depicts is pointedly fantastic, but more often than not she strikes very close to the reality of how data and images actually operate to obfuscate abuses of power that we would not otherwise tolerate.

Liquidity Inc. attempts to highlight the phenomenon of digital circulationism not simply by illustrating it as a "cloud" in the narrative. It also creates a metacommentary by showing the conditions of circulationism undergirding the very production of video itself. Steyerl sets this up gradually, first by simply emphasizing the fact that the video was made on the computer. The entire opening sequence is actually a video capture of a CGI environment being made on C4D software. As viewers, we see the frame of the video as it is constructed by toolbars that again frame the image of an ocean as it is being layered, tile-by-tile, over a blue and green perspectival grid, to meet the horizon line of a serenely beclouded sky. We literally follow the cursor through this process. With a click of a button, the sky turns dark. With another click, the ocean is put in motion, then algorithmic "moonlight" is added.

Throughout the video Steyerl uses a similar self-consciously amateur style. She even embeds clips of tutorials she ostensibly used to guide her creation of "gorgeous displaced animated water." The CGI animations have the feel of an enthusiastic novice experimenting with every function of C4D at once. Water fonts are dragged around the screen in exaggerated wave patterns, while ripple effects are used indiscriminately. Small screens—televisions, phones, or just boxes—become displays for new movies or animations shown within the main screen. In the first usage, the technique is inventive and surprising. But by the sixth or seventh time, one wonders what it really adds to the already overwhelming stream of images on the main screen. Likewise, the Jacob Wood segments use every affective ploy of TV docudrama possible: electronic music drones throughout. Reenactments of innocuous events, such as Wood getting ready for work the morning he was fired, are edited to lend the video a very artificial feeling of suspense. In the weather report sequences, the obvious swap of weathercasters—from woman to man to child—in front of the blue screens unsettles.

About a third of the way through the video, Steyerl shows email correspondence from people she met on CGI forums in which they discuss segments of the video she has outsourced to them. With this new information, it suddenly becomes clear that the aesthetic of the video is the result of throwing together multiple image sources from multiple people; it is the very condition of the cloud she critiques through the plot points of the video. As the imagery and production of the video show, the internet forms an integral part of the liquid economy and weather matrix Steyerl describes. Moreover, the viewer comes to understand that Steyerl's own artistic production as a self-conscious "circulationist" video is potentially complicit in this process. Yet she also obviously holds out hope that if liquidity—as a dominant metaphor in the economy, the environment, and digital creativity—cannot be unthought, it can at least be reinvented or rerouted. This seems to be the ambition of *Liquidity Inc.*—to put the liquid metaphor into such an intense circulation of feedback loops of information and images that it could potentially burst the clichés.

On the surface, the consistency with which the metaphor of liquidity flows across seemingly isolated domains of economics, labor, weather, and the internet in the video installation *Liquidity Inc.* can be explained simply by understanding water as a conceptual or metaphoric source domain (Davidko). Of course, water has often been used as a metaphor and in many different contexts to explain complex operations. Yet Steyerl pushes to explore the ways that image and concept circulation are ever more connected because these domains do, in fact, literally flow into each other. The internet's capacity to link information systems has transformed capitalism. The internet affects our access to the world. And, yes, that leads us to make choices within our economic system that do in fact cumulatively impact the weather. As Steyerl put it in a 2015 interview with Amelia Goom, the video addresses the complex interpenetrating domains of political reality as "a wide-ranging continuum: a military-finance-art-entertainment-real estate complex. It ranges from indentured labour to logistics, security, branding. So the system is much more vast than it seems and there is a lot of inside to it" (121). In trying to chart this larger systems ecology of liquidity in the twenty-first century, Steyerl may have come up with a rather conspiratorial video. It is not conspiratorial in the traditional sense of singling out and exposing a hidden culprit, but in the sense that it actively demonstrates how and why we constantly disguise the complexity of interpenetrating human-controlled power-knowledge systems with the elegant natural language of capital flow, labor flow, water flow, and image flow.

Economy as "liquid" does not have a basis in physics or hydraulics; yet its unnatural forces have changed both our mood and the weather. We can see how they are caught up in each other's ecologies. Ultimately, the video poses the useful question of how metaphor might mask our desire for understanding these conspiring, albeit ever-more-entangled, forces. The video's last and perhaps most important message is that as much as we can be seduced by the representational or metaphorical power of "becoming water," we should not forget the agency, the weight, and the force that water has to lash back at us.

Notes

1. The "Weather Underground" refers at once to a contemporary weather monitoring site <https://www.wunderground.com/> and to a left-wing armed struggle group in the US. See also Jeremy Varon, *Bringing the War Home: The Weather Underground, the Red Army Faction, and Revolutionary Violence in the Sixties and Seventies* (U of California P, 2004).

2. The so-called South Sea Bubble of 1720 had early on threatened the solvency of the English government, which had invested heavily in colonial infrastructure and trade in South America, despite the War of Spanish Succession. As Nina Boy argues in "Sovereign Safety," only through the establishment of the national securities markets, through which joint stock companies could liquefy the government's debt through loans, was the problem mitigated.

3. J. P. Morgan brochure, "Liquidity: Lifeblood of Corporate Survival," downloaded on 30 December 2016, https://www.jpmorgan.com/cm/BlobServer?blobtable=Document&blobcol=urlblob&blobkey=name&blobheader=application/pdf&blobwhere=jpmorgan/cash/pdf/liquidity-lifeblood.

4. See also Kath Weston on the entanglement of late capitalism, affect, precarious labor, and climate change. Kath Weston, "Political Ecologies of the Precarious." *Anthropological Quarterly*, vol. 85, no. 2, Spring 2012, pp. 429–55.

Works Cited

Bauman, Zygmunt. "On Being Light and Liquid." *Liquid Modernity*. Polity Press, 2000, pp. 1–15.

Benjamin, Walter. "Theses on the Philosophy of History." *Illuminations*. Trans. Harry Zohn. Schocken, 1969, pp. 253–64.

Boy, Nina. "Sovereign Safety." *Security Dialogue*, vol. 46, no. 6, December 2015, pp. 530–47.

Davidko, Natalya. "The Concept of 'Water' in the Metaphorics of Economic Discourse." *Verbum*, vol. 3, 2015, pp. 39–50.

Foti, Alex. "Mayday, Mayday: Euro Flex Workers Time to Get a Move On." Precarity Issue, *Greenpepper Magazine*, vol. 2, 2004, pp. 21–27.

Harvey, David. *A Brief History of Neoliberalism*. Oxford UP, 2008.

Harvey, William. *On the Motion of the Heart and Blood in Animals*. George Bell and Sons, 1889.

Hobbes, Thomas. *Leviathan*. Routledge, 1982.

Keynes, John M. *The General Theory of Employment, Interest, and Money*. Macmillan, 1973.

Langley, Paul. *Liquidity Lost: The Governance of the Global Financial Crisis*. Oxford UP, 2015.

Lyotard, Jean-François. *The Postmodern Condition: A Report on Knowledge*. Trans. Geoff Bennington and Brian Massumi. U of Minnesota P, 1979.

J. P. Morgan brochure, "Liquidity: Lifeblood of Corporate Survival," downloaded on 30 December 2016, https://www.jpmorgan.com/cm/BlobServer?blobtable=Document&blobcol=urlblob&blobkey=name&blobheader=application/pdf&blobwhere=jpmorgan/cash/pdf/liquidity-lifeblood.

Pasanek, Brad, and Simone Polillo, eds. *Beyond Liquidity: The Metaphor of Money in Financial Crisis*. Routledge, 2013.

Prashad, Vijay. *The Poorer Nations: A Possible History of the Global South*. Verso, 2013.

Smith, Adam. *The Wealth of Nations*. Penguin, 1982.

Standing, Guy. *The Precariat: The New Dangerous Class*. Bloomsbury, 2011.

Steyerl, Hito. "Too Much World: Is the Internet Dead?" *E-flux*, vol. 49, Nov. 2013, pp. 1–10.

Steyerl, Hito, and Laura Poitras. "Techniques of the Observer." *Artforum International*, vol. 53, no. 9, May 2015, pp. 307–17.

Steyerl, Hito. "Interview with Amelia Groom." *Discipline*, vol. 4, 2015, pp. 112–25.

Stiglitz, Joseph. "Markets and Inequality." *The Price of Inequality: How Today's Divided Society Endangers Our Future*. Norton, 2012, 52–82.

Trott, Ben. "From the Precariat to the Multitude." *Global Discourse: An Interdisciplinary Journal of Current Affairs and Applied Contemporary Thought*, vol. 3, no. 3–4, 2014, pp. 406–25.

Varon, Jeremy. *Bringing the War Home: The Weather Underground, the Red Army Faction and Revolutionary Violence in the Sixties and Seventies*. U of California P, 2004.

Weston, Kath. "Lifeblood, Liquidity, and Cash Transfusions: Beyond Metaphor in the Cultural Study of Finance." *Journal of the Royal Anthropological Institute*, vol. 19, May 2013, pp. 24–41.

Weston, Kath. "Political Ecologies of the Precarious." *Anthropological Quarterly*, vol. 85, no. 2, Spring 2012, pp. 429–55.

Material States of Poetry

The Stanza Stones

EMMA TROTT

IN A 47-MILE LINE along the Pennine watershed from Ilkley to Marsden in Yorkshire stand six large stones, each inscribed with the text of an original poem written by Simon Armitage. The subject of each poem is water, in each case in a different state: beck, puddle, dew, mist, rain, and snow.[1] The poems' thematic and stylistic coherence form a thread running across geographical distance, creating what the project's landscape architect Tom Lonsdale calls "the watershed story" (*Stanza Stones* 99). The connective thread is not linear, however, but ecological. Armitage, Lonsdale, and stone mason Pip Hall worked closely together as the key engineers of the project: in *Stanza Stones* (2013), which features firsthand accounts from the three team-members, Armitage writes that the project "was not in any way the work of a single mind, but endlessly collaborative in nature" (*Stanza Stones* 16).[2] The processes of collaboration extend beyond Armitage, Lonsdale, and Hall to include public funding bodies, landowners, and local groups. Armitage has led creative writing sessions for young writers in the Leeds area, and guide materials published online feature detailed directions, maps, and difficulty ratings for the walks to each stone.[3] The local bioregion and its communities have made key contributions at each stage of the project (Ilkley Literature Festival was responsible for the first ideas relating to the project, while Marsden is Armitage's home village) and the stone-poems continue to engage their audience in site-specific, mutually creative ways. Armitage premiered the group of poems at the

2011 Ilkley Literature Festival with the title *In Memory of Water*, which speaks to the Stanza Stones' various allusions to interplay—between the imagination and the physical world, between history and futurity, and between language and landscape.

The relationship between what is produced (poems and stone-poems) and the ways in which it is produced (planning, writing, and carving) in this project is brought into relief by an awareness of materiality. As Jane Bennett writes, "Human culture is inextricably enmeshed with vibrant, nonhuman agencies" (108), and the Stanza Stones appear to function with an understanding that creativity may be both human and nonhuman, organic and inorganic. Further, the certainty of each of those categories appears to be challenged when the self, the text, and the world are viewed from a perspective of *material* encounters. In this essay, I will identify key ways in which the audience's experience of the stone-poems is informed by the stones' materiality, explore the material nature of the poems, and make notes toward an account of the audience's experience. I will provide an example of art's capacity to help us (briefly and incompletely) approach an understanding of another organism, ecosystem, or element's experience. Artists' observations and tactile experiences of water are passed on to the reader in creative narratives that tell the water's "story" — and the reader might gain insight into the nature of the element or ecosystem and be able to articulate a more thoughtful environmental ethics. Each reader enters the stone-poem into dialogue with an indefinite number of feelings, memories, ideas, and other imaginative processes, producing a varied ecology of perspectives on the water. The audience experiences the water as an element that is continually in flux, and is touched by the agency of history, industry, and living creatures, and by the transformative agency of the stone.

First, I will explore the influence of the material—the landscape, the elements, and the body—on the writing process, to demonstrate how the language that describes water, flora, and fauna has been directly shaped by the physical world to which the poems refer. The stone-poems are not preconceived impositions on the landscape, but responses formed from thoughtful material engagement. Armitage accounts for his poetic production in terms of an exploratory journey: "I've said on many occasions that if a poem, once written, is exactly the same as its author first imagined it would be, then it is almost certainly a failure, and that artistic success must always involve a process of transformation" (*Stanza Stones* 9). Poetic material accumulates over time, and the "process of transformation" necessary for the release of creative energy can be seen both in notes on the poetry's generation and in the definitive (final) forms of the poems. The project is a significant one, wide-reaching and long lasting, and Armitage is aware of the responsibility he is shouldering, as he describes in the self-conscious account in *Stanza Stones*. He explains his labors in detail, from the "first inclination . . . to write a sestina," to the acknowledgment that, "as so often with a poem, the plan had to change" (*Stanza Stones* 13–14). While the capacity of the poet to build, alter, and redirect is clearly essential, nonetheless the openness of the remit is challenging, and the poet must labor to produce work with definition. Armitage has described his tendency to set his word processor to the Faber font and page size when writing poetry for traditional collections. "The visual element is part of it," he says in an interview with the *New Statesman*:

> [*New Statesman*:] So sometimes you've lost words or changed a rhythm just to fit the Faber page?
> [Armitage:] Yeah. In some ways that might seem odd but we all work to some kind of template; even a synthetic size can push your mind into territories that you might not have taken it when left to your own devices.

This physical language—"synthetic," "push," "territories," "devices"— describes a creative process that is highly influenced by the practicalities of composition. A similar sensitivity to the relationship between the poetic self and the material world is evident in Armitage's account of writing the water poems, which reveals a creative mind that is deeply engaged with elements and physical features of the landscape, particularly groundwater and precipitation. Composition of the poems began when the foundations of the project were already in place, including the team of collaborators, the funding, the legal permissions, and the stones and sites. If Armitage finds that the framework of Faber's technical specifications shapes his creativity in a positive way, it follows that the "pages" of the Stanza Stones (collaborations, permissions, sites, stones) might also provide a useful structure within which to work. The stones present a different set of restrictions and opportunities, but the principle is similar: that creativity flourishes when the imagination is required to adhere to a predetermined set of rules. In some instances, the sonnet form, for example, might provide a firm enough springboard to allow a poet to generate truly novel work with language. For Armitage, the pressures of the project's limitations present him with a canvas on which to work.

The understanding that freedoms can be limiting and restrictions can be inspiring is not unique to Armitage, but he negotiates the challenge in a way that affords us an insight into the creative processes bearing on the project as a whole. The raw material for the poems is eventually discovered through a *material* experience:

> After another visit to the hills, this time in lashing rain, I came back with a different idea and a single purpose. To let water be the overall subject: the water that sculpted the valleys, the water that powered the industries, the water we take for granted. (*Stanza Stones* 14)

Here, creativity is embodied in the moorland: the rain is a physical muse, landing on the poet's skin and then (metaphorically) getting inside his body—which includes his imagination. The poetic creation story is evident in the text of "Rain," where the raindrop is a seed:

> And no matter how much
> it strafes or sheets,
> it is no mean feat
> to catch one raindrop
> clean in the mouth,
> to take one drop
> on the tongue, tasting
> cloud-pollen,
> grain of the heavens,
> raw sky.[4]

The raindrop is made organic, and the sky is made material—both are transformed into poetic potential and are defamiliarized for the reader. Like the landscape itself, Armitage's course is shaped by water.

The poetic self and the material world are (to borrow a phrase of Karen Barad's) *intra-active*:

> in contrast to the usual "interaction," which assumes that there are separate individual agencies that precede their interaction, the notion of intra-action recognizes that distinct agencies do not precede, but rather emerge through, their intra-action. (Barad 33)

The sensation of rain on skin, experience of water's mutability, and pre-existing knowledge of water's social landscape in the region converge and form poetic raw material, material which is thus generated out of an understanding of the cocurrent codependencies of those elements. From this spark of inspiration follows a period of heightened creativity:

> To me this is always the most engaging phase, where the internal, abstract concept of the poem is attempting to materialize externally, where the mind is in negotiation with the world through the medium of language. (Armitage, *Stanza Stones* 15)

The displacement of agency elicited by the suggestion that a significant part of the creative process occurs in the unconscious, where (it appears that) the poem uses the poet as a means of coming into being, seems to afford the poet with some freedom from the parameters of his mind. The pleasure felt in these "most engaging" moments is produced by the poet's acknowledgment of his mind's transformative "negotiation" with external material reality, which blurs the boundary between consciousness and the phenomenal world. Such a destabilization of well-established categories poses a challenge to a hard distinction between life and nonlife, where the elemental is an "actant" in dialogue with the poet's imagination. For Armitage, language occupies the space between the self and world where defined categories such as "active" and "inert" become less concrete: at times, the living mind's role is passive and the nonliving water is active. With this in mind, I want to consider the nature of the other principal element in the project: the stone.

With the stones selected, the sites identified, and the texts of the poems formulated, the next stage was for stone mason Pip Hall to carve the poems into the rock. The inscription transmits agency to the stones, but that is not to suggest that in their preexisting incarnations the stones were lifeless or inert. On the contrary, the stone is a compound of organic and inorganic particles and processes, and a thoughtful observer may "read" parts of such a narrative, as Serpil Oppermann explains:

> Semiotic materiality is not confined to biological organisms. . . . Elements, cells, genes, atoms, stones, water, landscapes, machines, among innumerable others, are embodied narratives, repositories of storied matter. (Oppermann 58–59)

Oppermann identifies parallels between the functions of elements and material bodies that are vastly different in size, scale, range, and situation: similar processes occur on landscapes as within atoms. She also demonstrates that the capacity to communicate does not depend on intention. Material qualities articulate an experiential narrative, which is both history *and* the very agency with which that history can be communicated to the informed observer. With preexisting knowledge, Armitage can observe the bioregional water cycle and articulate histories of human intervention and industry alongside the water's behavior and material presence. A close study of a sample of water might reveal the kinds of rock it has passed through, pollution it has come into contact with, and the temperature and other environmental factors that have affected it. In a similar way, stone "is a perfect material archive for stories" (Oppermann 66), and may be read, even if there remains much that can never be revealed to the observer. Oppermann quotes Jeffrey J. Cohen:

> Most any pebble is full of carbon microfossils such as acritarchs, the cysts of ancient algae. Such data burgeon with narrative, for story is a process of relation making, and thereby inherently ethical. (66)

The sense of buried histories that Oppermann describes is identifiable in the Stanza Stones in the stone (naturally occurring) as well as in human experience (socially performed). Both are what they are because of what has come before. If "story is a process of relation making," then it is possible to identify in the stone-poems, which reveal or generate relationships between poem and stone, human and moorland, people and place, a form of narrative that tells a material history in which these forms were organized very differently. The Stanza Stones team are conscious of the social and ecological responsibility that they are taking on. Lonsdale writes of the "very confident ethical stance for the project" and the group's "guiding principles, by which we could justify to future generations that the 21st century has a worthy entry to make in the 'Book of the Land'" (*Stanza Stones* 24–25). The resistance of stone, the chosen material for the *pages*, influences the language of this entry, as Armitage explains:

> The moment that you start cutting into stone you are automatically involved in something elegiac. You can't help but have an association with commemorative, monumental inscription. The process of creating those poems brought a kind of diction forward in me that I hadn't necessarily used before. . . . I guess the poems might be longer lasting than some of the other things that I've produced, just by virtue of being carved rather than printed, so I steered away from noun objects or phrases which are overtly of their time . . . technical equipment, branded goods, that kind of thing—things that I normally like to deploy in poems. (Interview, January 2018)

While in poems for print media, colloquialisms and (often mundane) cultural references are employed by Armitage as a means of engaging a wide audience, in *In Memory of Water*, the same concern to sustain accessibility requires different self-imposed linguistic limitations. It is interesting to appreciate that the apparent concentration of subject in the poems, on the water and its immediate bioregion, comes not from a turn away from the human, but from a sustained engagement with culture and audience that extends past the poet's own lifetime. Writing in response to an as-yet-unborn audience is a performed process of "relation making" (Cohen) where the future is imagined as the present and the present is imagined as the past, which generates an ethics of responsibility for the cultural and material environments that reaches beyond the stones. For Armitage, the project's environmental ethics is also expressed in terms of futurity, though rather than imagining a future observer looking back, his perspective is grounded firmly in the present:

> I saw an opportunity to draw on the often commemorative nature of monumental-masonry and engraving by making an unspoken connection with environmental themes and concerns about climate change. Perhaps I was thinking ahead, pessimistically, to a future where the Stanza Stones still existed but on a planet that had either drowned or boiled dry. (*Stanza Stones* 14–15)

Concern about environmental degradation produces an elegiac mode where the stones are transformed into *grave*stones, memorializing a natural habitat, or water itself. But here, elegy functions by inversion: whereas a gravestone respectfully faces the past, the Stanza Stones perform an act of warning, pointing to a speculative future. The potential of material (i.e., nonlanguage) narrative to coalesce with the artists' (projected) creativity produces continually renegotiable, relational modes of knowledge. As a response to climate change, the irreversibility of this kind of transformation seems quite logical.

I have demonstrated some of the ways in which the poems and the stones are archival objects that consist of complex meshworks of material, environmental, social, and imaginative influences and affects. A key point about this kind of creativity is that it refutes the notion of the object being static. As well as the formative past, both stone and poem are always changing, however minutely or however invisible to the naked eye: stone is eroded by water, wind, and temperature fluctuations, while the poem takes on new life as it enters and takes root within the mind of the reader. The Stanza Stones, of course, play with the ever-changing nature of art (as well as matter) in an explicit way, by carving the language into stone and rendering it up to the elements. The poems were inscribed on the stones by a skilled stone mason, Pip Hall, who kept an open dialogue with Armitage and the team throughout the process. One of Hall's tasks was to design a suitable lettering style: she and Armitage "agreed right at the start that it should be common to all poems, that it would play an important role in connecting the Stanza Stones across the Pennines" (*Stanza Stones* 107). The poems appear on fragments of stone arranged at distances from each other, but, as the consistency of font suggests, their narrative is an ecology of relations and interconnections. Hall notes that the common font was created to be "neutral" rather than active (*Stanza Stones* 107), which affords the act of inscription a significant degree of creative freedom that is nevertheless balanced by a number of restrictions. Hall writes of the considerable effort taken to choose stones that would work with the language, the landscape, and herself as technician: the stones needed to offer the right level of resistance to her tools, have a smooth surface for legible lettering, and also "fit" with an appropriate site. Lonsdale writes that the Puddle stones "offered natural 'pages' for the poem but their precise position had to be carefully chosen," a decision that was at once pragmatic and aesthetic (*Stanza Stones* 89). Elsewhere, stones are imported "where the existing rock wouldn't offer enough of a 'page'" (Lonsdale, *Stanza Stones* 29). The idea of the landscape as a page or canvas is articulated in the descriptive accounts in *Stanza Stones* and in the poems, as we find in "Snow":

Snow, snow, snow
is how the snow speaks,
is how its clean page reads.

The snow's visual blankness does not translate into a lack of agency or meaning. The inorganic is *intra-acting* with the creative observer, who reciprocates through his or her act of perception: the snow is both an active "speaker" and a "text" to be read. The stone collaborates with the artists in different but related ways. In her project diary, Hall makes notes on the Dew stone, which is in two parts:

The uniformly flat carving surfaces of these 2-metre-high megalithic [have] echoes of the printed page . . . . it would be good if the lettering helps to connect these machined "off-comedens" with their intended home, [so] I shall keep in mind the distant rolling hills and the irregular courses of drystone walling of the Rivock Edge site. (*Stanza Stones* 81)

The letters engage the stone with the language of the poem, connect Dew with the other stone-poems, and enhance the connection between the stone and the landscape. These integrations take place both literally and imaginatively. The poems speak of the water, but they also have an agency in a different direction: a speaking *to*. The Mist stone was chosen despite its having a delicate fissure down the middle, and it broke into two as it was being moved to its new site. Hall writes of "trying to reassure the mortified team that I was truly thrilled," since she no longer needed to negotiate the tricky job of carving over the crack (*Stanza Stones* 70). Hall begins to see the stones as visually analogous with an open book, which informs her organization of the words on the stone "page." She "intra-acts" with stone, elements, and landscape, writing: "I engage with the environment on many levels, and I naturally draw inspiration from my surroundings: this influences my designing and decision-making in subtle, unconscious ways" (*Stanza Stones* 81). What the audience reads in the stone-poems, then, is materially different from the poems they would read on the page, even if the language is identical. The lettering *style* is as "neutral" as possible, but the ways the letters are made manifest on the stone are directly produced by Hall's responses, not to a generalized landscape and rock surface but to specifics of the respective stone, water, and site.

Negotiating with the material of the Beck stone shaped the corresponding poem in a different (but related) way. Hall describes days spent working at the surface of the stone in full waterproof clothing, the water gushing over her after high levels of rainfall in a "watery onslaught that was to mark the wettest carving experience of my career" (*Stanza Stones* 100). Tactile experience of the water sparks her creativity, and just as Armitage found inspiration in the "lashing" rain, Hall senses something dangerous that is close to the sublime: "I arrived in dry weather, thrilled and alarmed in equal measure on seeing the wildness of the beck" (*Stanza Stones* 101). The exhilaration evident in Hall's account is clearly influenced by the threat posed by the surprising force of the water. The wild, then, is brought into contact with the human imagination in conscious as well as "subtle, unconscious ways." The energy of the beck creates an artist's studio, which in turn becomes the venue in which the audience experiences the work. The nature of that artwork is the stone-poem *in the context of* the movement of the water.

Intra-action with water, therefore, has significant material and imaginative impact on the project's development, and there is a related agency at work in the stone. Challenges Hall faces while carving the Beck stone become opportunities and push the poem in new directions: "This rock, more than the others, creates ... a new template for the poem. Repositioning words to avoid the crumbly bits, there is a rewrite: this not only frees up some space, but also tightens the poem" (*Stanza Stones* 102). The stone's material qualities influence not only the layout of the words on the "page," but also the qualities of the poem's language, which itself shapes the stone and is in turn shaped by it. This reciprocal, organic process can work at a slower pace, where the poet's ideas for change come a few days later:

> 23 April. . . . A call from Simon this morning about another alteration. He thought it would make things easier for me if 'over' were replaced with "at" (". . . water unbinds and hangs at the waterfall's face . . ."). I was pleased about a shorter word which would certainly help with the space issue; and far from compromising the poem, it is, as Simon explained, "more active; visually and aurally lighter; gives it more tension." (*Stanza Stones* 103)

Form and content are inextricably connected (or, we might say, intra-connected). The stone's resistance and fragility become part of the poetic narrative. There is a comparison with Armitage's way of working with the Faber page size, but the stone's capacity to change once carving has begun means it is an active participant in the creative process. Crucially, the pressure to edit the poem produces *positive* effects: a tightening of the stone around the poem, and a deeper integration between the materials, the artists, and the audience. In a transfer of agency from material to mind, the imagination absorbs properties of the stone and works them into a new creative output, which is expressed by further changes to the stone.

The tension between practical and aesthetic considerations is a highly productive one. As Hall and Armitage continue to collaborate on the production of the stone-poems, the boundary between material stone and material language is made less distinct, and the drives to create a good poem and a good stone are the same work. The restrictions of the stone invigorate the language by affording it qualities that enhance the audience's *physical* experience of reading. The reader feels the "tension," sees and hears the "light" quality, and can sense movement: the beck creeps into the audience's mind with physical presence. The image

FIGURE 2.1. Dew stones, Rivock Edge

or idea of a momentary snapshot of water is presented throughout the poems, where the water is always changing and always moving away. The stone, far from being a static antithesis to water's mutability, allows the artists even more opportunity to articulate their experience of water.

The stones have a performative agency that transforms the language with which they are brought into encounter. The reverse is also the case: clearly, the inscription of the poems alters the physical form of the stones, and this is also true in a metaphorical sense. The language of these poems has the potential to change *both* the way the stone appears *and* the way the stone is seen by the audience, which is not quite the same thing. In her account of the Puddle stone, Hall writes:

> I am struck by the way the words I'm drawing encourage a particular way of seeing the stone. I chose the stones for the poem, and yet the stones, with their rusty remnants and hoof-imprinted surfaces seem to be adopting the poem. (*Stanza Stones* 91)

As the poem is embodied in the stone's surface, Hall's inscription infuses it with agency, the ability to actively "adopt." While this agency is imagined by Hall, the stone is brought to life in a way that opens up the observer to the complex narrative of the stone's history, encompassing both abrasions from recent encounters with animals and elements, and a much longer history of sedimentary rock formation. Without ever directly addressing the material they are laid into, the poems nevertheless defamiliarize the stone, demanding that the audience see it afresh. The poetry also defamiliarizes the rain, beck, snow, mist, puddle, and dew. Focusing on ways in which the poems describe water in states of flux, I will now consider language's capacity to re-vision and make strange the principal subject of the poems: water.

Armitage represents water in six different states, creating an effect that is not fragmentary but ecological, due to a stylistic consistency of brevity, directness, and tonal clarity. The interrelations between material subject (water), material substance (stone), embodied language, and the imagination of the audience constitute a literary ecology. Particulars of the bioregion are central to the project: the language of water is generated in relation to landscape, air, sky, flora, and fauna. The poet encounters water with an understanding that it exists in a continuous process of intra-action with its environments, which include the West Yorkshire landscape and the poet's creative consciousness. There is no chronology within the group of poems, however: each state of water exists concurrently with each of the others, but nevertheless the reader is exposed to unseen processes of change as he or she moves through the poems, imagining the rain falling to the ground and forming a puddle, which evaporates and condenses into mist. These links are not made explicit, but a tendency toward transformation runs through the poetry. Serenella Iovino and Serpil Oppermann write that "the true dimension of matter is not that of a static and passive substance or being, but of a generative becoming" (77), a kind of creativity that is at the heart of the Stanza Stones project. It is when change occurs to the stone that its nature becomes most apparent, and in a related way, the transience of each state of water is, paradoxically, what most powerfully defines it.

The Stanza Stones poems thus evade static descriptions, and privilege the transformative potential of water and stone. In a related way, the poems explore a world of bodies and material substance that do not exist independently. Timothy Morton's notion of the *ecological thought* "realizes that all beings are interconnected. This is the mesh. The ecological thought realizes that the boundaries between, and the identities of, beings are affected by this interconnection" (94). Identity

FIGURE 2.2. Puddle stones, Rombalds Moor

depends on external elements for its definition (what is "me" if there is no "not-me"?), yet the impossibility of a hard boundary also makes the concept of "me" necessarily multiplicitous. Poetry is able to speak of matter's connective quality in a unique way, thinking the ecological thought through metaphor. An image in "Puddle" demonstrates a complex meshwork of elements:

> The shy deer
> of the daytime moon
> comes to sip from the rim.

Wild deer live on parts of the Pennine Way, so a reading from this perspective places the puddle in its bioregional context. However, an alternative reading which is contradictory yet—crucially—not mutually exclusive exemplifies Armitage's ability to generate metaphor that, with both "this" and "that" occupying the same space, destabilizes the very oppositions that enabled them in the first place. The doublings here work as follows. On the one hand, "shy deer" is the primary subject in an image of an animal, bathed in sunlight, drinking from a puddle of rainwater, evidence of an ecosystem at work. The "shy deer" is a meta-phor for the primary subject which is the Sun, or "daytime moon": as a deer might gradually reduce the puddle by drinking, the Sun evaporates it. The deer and the sun are partnered opposites, as are day and night ("daytime moon"). However, in some hunting circles it is believed that the moon's phases influence deer's movements and mating behavior, so the modes of influence between deer, sun, and moon appear more com-plex in the light of bioregional knowledge, and the relationships between *apparently* discrete elements demonstrate that material boundaries as we might conceive them are always subject to scrutiny.

It is important to note, however, that the recognition of the inter-play of matter is not equivalent to a homogenization: the intra-action of elements does not write out difference. "Dew" plays with a form of doubling in elemental transformation that may be destructive as well as creative. The subject is implicated in contexts of darkness and light, sexual passion and battle imagery, where dramatic change is always imminent:

> The tense stand-off
> of summer's end,
> the touchy fuse-wire
> of parched grass

Doubles appear in a connective vocabulary of burning ("fuse-wire," "flame," "torch," and "fire-star") as oppositional to the water. This is a kind of poetic negative creation, where the dew, which only emerges in the second stanza, is defined in opposition to what it is not. In other poems in the set, too, the water emerges *from* ecological proximity to other elements. For example, the "Mist" comes into being *in relation to* the aspects of its environments that it touches. The poet asks: "What does it mean, / such nearness"—the meaning of mist is defined by what it is *not* as well as what it *is*. In a related way, Armitage writes about "Rain" *in relation to* the sea, the self, and the sky, and the picture of the "Puddle" emerges in relation to the Sun, the moon, and the deer. In the case of "Dew," we are aware that when water is poured on fire, of course, the fire is extinguished. When heat (fire) acts on water, however, the effect is not to destroy it but to change its form—in evaporating, the water does not cease to exist, but merely changes into a different state. So the fire in "Dew" does portray water's vulnerability, but it also reveals water's potential to change, as a material that endures even while it is in flux.

Water's capacity for change is also central to "Beck." What I want to draw attention to here is the way the poetic consciousness plays with the materiality and texture of the water. The poem represents a beck, but it is also a beck *as it is experienced by the poet.* The stream is figured in material terms as a type of cloth, invoking the industrial history of textile manufacture and trade in the West Yorkshire region. "The unbroken thread / of the beck" reaches a change in terrain and briefly becomes a waterfall:

> and just for that one
> stretched white moment
> becomes lace.

The physical continuity of the stream is paralleled with the "unbroken" legacy of the industry on which the urban communities in the area developed, in terms of both economy and the waterways (Leeds-Liverpool canal) on which trade was made possible. The transience of the poem's "moment" acknowledges the decline of that industry, but also plays with the poet's capacity to historicize, elegize, and recall. The "stretch" is both a quality of the fabric and an acknowledgment that, for the poet, time does not seem to run at a regular pace. The poet is not seeking meaning in the beck by itself, but rather a composite image that is created by the encounter between the poet and the water. The states of water are experienced and recorded in fine detail, but it is a *poetic* recording where, through metaphor and engagement of the audience's visual imagination, the language communicates an element of what an encounter with the water might feel like. What necessarily comes with this poetic "truth"—a getting to the "nature" of things— is, paradoxically, an obscuring of the water's primacy. The poet deepens the reader's understanding of the world, yet the poet's perception clouds as much as it reveals. A transformation occurs whereby the water changes state—here not with heat of the fire, but under pressure of poetic consciousness, with the capacity of poetic language to connect the poet's visual sense with that of the reader. What is produced is a *poetic* phenomenon that is neither purely physical world, nor creative imagination, but a composite mix. This embodied encounter suggests that the water in the poem is both the element on its own terms and a chronicle of the creative self. The poet's description of the water is read as a text that on the one hand reveals a powerful (though not impartial) account of the element, and on the other hand functions as a deep (though incomplete) illustration of the poet's mind. What is interesting about the Stanza Stones project is that the audience—which, like the poet, has its own capacities for enhancing information gathering and obscuring insight—engages not only as a reader, but also as an intra-active, material participant.

I have identified a number of ways in which we might call the language in these poems material. I have suggested that the poems articulate a narrative of water's tendency to transform, in response to its environments (temperature, weather, geology, creaturely life). I have suggested that such collaborative creativity is paralleled with the meeting of water and the poetic consciousness, which react together to produce a new state of water, that in one sense *is* the water passing through the West Yorkshire moors, and, at the same time, is something quite different from that water. In the final section of this essay, I will identify a third parallel process of creative collaboration, involving the audience, by drawing out ways in which the audience's 'reading' of the Stanza Stones is a materially embodied experience. If the landscape is a book, then the landscape is an open book that is continually revised and extended by a host of collaborators, which include the elemental/non-life (wind, rain), the organic/nonhuman life (moss, horses), and human life (intentional visitors and unsuspecting passersby). The stone-poems have been situated close to established pathways so the project will not bring about a degradation of vulnerable terrain. The Stanza Stones are a significant, material entry into the landscape's history book, but the artists are thoughtful about the nature and range of their impact. Yet the artists have relinquished control of the stone-poems, which are entered into a new, mutually creative collaboration with members of the public who look at, touch, walk past, and imaginatively engage with them. The stones are subtly altered by people coming into their vicinity, and the people take away an impression, which they may pass on to others who may or may not visit the stones themselves. In terms of the stone-poems' futures and the actants that will come to bear forces on them, the distinction between life and nonlife is *immaterial* (a word used ironically because these actants are very much material). Once the stones are situated and inscribed, they take on new life as participants in a complex mesh of material intra-actions.

I have discussed the ways stones and landscape present themselves to the artists as pages, and have demonstrated that a thoughtful observer can always access a form of creative agency in what appears first as a merely blank surface of stone or snow. I want to briefly return to "Dew" for an illustration of a further way in which the landscape can be read. There are several plants identified by name in "Dew": "grass," "bulrush," "reed," and "bog-cotton." The last of these is the official county flower of Greater Manchester, and its presence is often seen as an indicator to hikers of potentially dangerous deep peat bogs. Thus, the plant hints at the risk invoked by "stand-off" and battle imagery, and sets up a tension between human presence and nonhuman environment, where the landscape can be dangerous (where there is a risk of sinking into a bog), but also offers evidence about how such danger can be avoided. A knowledgeable walker can "read" the signs (bog-cotton) and process the information to act accordingly (by giving the bog-cotton a wide berth). In this way, the moorland ecosystem can function like a text. The audience may "read" the Stanza Stones in two ways: assuming they know the dangers of ground that bog-cotton grows on, they may read the plant when out walking, and when reading the stone-poem they will understand that this process of walking/reading is what the poem is referring to. The lack of *intention* on the part of the bog-cotton does not mean that there is a lack of *agency*, and the difference is crucial. The walker's drawing an interpretation of what the plant signifies (unsafe terrain) by no means indicates that the organic world deliberately communicated the information, or that it exists *for* the human observer in any meaningful way. Although the walker is able to respond to his or her environment, the bog-cotton exists before and without the walker. Yet without the walking subject, the bog-cotton's capacity to signify (to human beings) does not exist. The bog-cotton's communicative function comes into being as the plant and the creative human mind are brought together in physical and sensory encounters. The reader will see how "reading" the land parallels the reading of any text, which, once distributed to an audience, takes on a new life with each imagination it encounters.

Thus, we are starting to see how the act of reading cannot, in the case of the Stanza Stones, be extricated from the movements of the body. The physical effort required to access the stone-poems is explorative just like the movements of the mind in reading. Armitage writes: "It may seem ironic but it is also of great significance that sacred or artistic gestures like these should appear in such a high, remote and inaccessible location, appealing for the most part to an audience of nobody" (*Stanza Stones* 13). The words of the poems are, of course, a very important part of the Stanza Stones, but they are not all of it. The project speaks of materiality in literal terms, but also in non-linguistic and less direct ways. If poetry is supposed to make the reader *work*, with dense language, multiplicities of interpretation, and delayed transmission of meaning, then it appears that the Stanza Stones do function in this tradition, but in a radical way. A writer of public poetry, which is akin to a performance, can be expected to have different priorities from a poet writing for traditional publication. The water poems demonstrate a refined use of language but are relatively unadventurous in form and content. When reading or listening to poetry being recited, body and imagination are engaged in various ways. In the case of the Stanza Stones project, the audience's embodied experience occurs differently. The audience's engagement with the complexities of metaphor is only one stage in the reading process: the imagination also "reads" the geography of the moors and the surfaces of the stones. What is generated is a genuinely material poetics where walking to, from, and around the stones—whether they are encountered intentionally or not—is part of the reading experience. The walk away from the stone is colored by the language, and that walker-reader's perceptions and physical exercise—the movements of their body—continue the collaboration between landscape, language, and imagination. The site of the poetry is not only the language and not only the stones, and the stones' being situated in "high, remote and inaccessible location[s]" is not arbitrary, but fundamental to the engaged, multilayered poetic experience.

We have gained valuable insights into the nature of a particular kind of collaborative, intra-active creativity. This discussion demonstrates the unique contribution to our understanding of matter that is made not only by poetry and by landscape art, but also by landscape poetry. The Stanza Stones animate their audience's thinking about material nature, producing increased sensitivity to nonorganic agency. Further, the project encourages our understanding that the ways we physically move about in the world are intra-active processes that are never isolated. The response is a sense of responsibility that can influence even day-to-day behaviors that are usually performed without thinking. The Stanza Stones show us that sensitivity to the material world we are enmeshed with might be valuable not only to our environments but also, directly, to our cognitive lives. The stone-poems are examples of matter that can be read in a very explicit sense, but we have also seen how they are able to lead us to knowledge and understanding that is available when we know how to turn our curiosity to objects, landscapes, and modes of thinking that we might have previously overlooked. The material the stone-poems invites us to read extends beyond the edges of the slabs of stone: the audience "reads" the water's connections with ecosystems, industry, and history, and individual, phenomenal experience. Such encounters with water produce fresh understandings of liquid materiality, the landscape of the Pennine Way in the past, present, and future, and the human body, which, with a developed understanding of the "vibrant" embodiment of human beings in their environments, becomes neither as special nor as solitary as we might have thought. If the environmental crisis propagates a radically redefined concept of selfhood, in which the very notion of a hard boundary between self and other, inside and outside, is repudiated, the political, ecological, and societal potential may be significant. Art is able to show us what this might look like.

Notes

1. "Beck" is a Northern English word for a stream, often one that runs through a narrow or stony valley. With etymological roots in Old Norse, the name is used in parts of the North that were occupied by Norse settlers in the Early Medieval period. "Beck" is often used in literature (See *beck, n.1*).

2. As well as brief essays from Armitage and Lonsdale, diary entries from Hall and extensive color photographs, the book gives the texts of the poem.

3. The Stanza Stones Poetry Trail Guide is downloadable from the Ilkley Literature Festival Website: http://www.ilkleyliteraturefestival.org.uk/wp-content/uploads/2012/05/Stanza-Stones-Trail-Guide.pdf.

4. There is a strong thematic connection with Psalm 78, from which the concept of "manna"—signified spiritual good—seems to be taken:

> Yet he gave a command to the skies above
> and opened the doors of the heavens;
> he rained down manna for the people to eat,
> he gave them the grain of heaven. (Psalm 78: 23–24)

Works Cited

Armitage, Simon, et al. *Stanza Stones*. Enitharmon Press, 2013.

Armitage, Simon. "Beck." *Stanza Stones*, p. 97.

——. "Dew." *Stanza Stones*, p. 77.

——. Interview by Alice Gribbin. *New Statesman*, 12 January 2012, http://www.newstatesman.com/blogs/cultural-capital/2012/01/simon-armitage-poetry-arthur. Accessed 25 January 2017.

——. Personal interview. 18 January 2018.

——. "Mist." *Stanza Stones*, p. 67.

——. "Puddle." *Stanza Stones*, p. 87.

——. "Rain." *Stanza Stones*, p. 55.

——. "Snow." *Stanza Stones*, p. 41.

Barad, Karen. *Meeting the Universe Halfway: Quantum Physics and the Entanglement of Matter and Meaning*. Duke UP, 2007.

"beck, n.1." *OED Online*, Oxford UP, January 2018, www.oed.com/view/Entry/16756. Accessed 6 February 2018.

Bennett, Jane. *Vibrant Matter: A Political Ecology of Things*. Duke UP, 2010.

Iovino, Serenella, and Serpil Oppermann. "Material Ecocriticism: Materiality, Agency, and Models of Narrativity." *Ecozon@*, vol. 3, no. 1, 2012, pp. 75–91.

Morton, Timothy. *The Ecological Thought*. Harvard UP, 2010.

Oppermann, Serpil. "Material Ecocriticism and the Creativity of Storied Matter." *Frame*, vol. 26, no. 2, 2013, pp. 55–69.

Stanza Stones Poetry Trail Guide. Website, http://www.ilkleyliteraturefestival.org.uk/wp-content/uploads/2012/05/Stanza-Stones-Trail-Guide.pdf. Accessed 10 April 2017.

Preying on Water

Hunting Spiritual and Environmental Rebirth on the Kentucky River in Selected Essays from Wendell Berry's *The Long-Legged House*

Andrew S. Andermatt

While modern environmentalism, inspired in part by Rachel Carson's controversial 1962 publication *Silent Spring*, did not fully develop into a formal discourse until the 1970s, the seeds for an "environmental conscience" were firmly planted by essays such as those found in Wendell Berry's 1965 collection, *The Long-Legged House*.[1] Despite its continued relevancy to contemporary environmentalism, Berry's collection of philosophical and anecdotal essays about his beloved Port Royal, Kentucky, is largely unrepresented in literary scholarship. Each of the groundbreaking essays in this collection share Berry's perspective for how we should rightly live with the land while combating the strain that industrialized societies have had on our relationship with nature.

The environmental conscience that drives modern environmentalism depends largely on an understanding of our ethical responsibility to nature. As stewards of the environment—preservationists, conservationists, and responsible enjoyers of nature—it is our perception of our moral obligations to protecting the environment that dictates how we treat nature. Because Berry's *The Long-Legged House* was published just three years after Carson's pioneering work, the notion of a formal environmentalism would have only been in its infancy. Therefore, as works of contemporary environmental writing, Berry's guidelines for how we best reconnect morally and spiritually with the environment were well ahead of their time.

In the mid-nineteenth century, transcendentalist writers such as
Ralph Waldo Emerson and Henry David Thoreau tasked themselves
with providing such a sublime picture of nature in their writing that
gone were the days of looking upon the dark and mysterious forest with
abhorrence.[2] By the early twentieth century, influential voices such as
Aldo Leopold, John Muir, and Gifford Pinchot shaped our views of rec-
reational outings in the environment. While the writings and teachings
of these individuals often made access to nature appear much more fea-
sible, it is clear that by the mid-twentieth century that easier access to
nature and "wilderness" areas risked leaving nature lovers complacent
toward the environment. Berry, not unlike many of his contemporar-
ies, recognized the loss of our ability to become intimately acquainted
with the physical features of the land. To illustrate this loss, Berry describes a man fishing on the banks of the Kentucky River. The fisherman is on the shoreline working the quieter areas of the river, hardly
turning himself over to the magic that Berry witnesses from his own
canoe. The river, for the fisherman, is ordinary. Berry says, "Here was a
man who made a daily thing of it, and went to it as another man would
go to an office" (103). Where does this leave us in modern times? Have
we lost our faith in the beauty and mystery of the river? Is nature just
another location for us to carry out our daily activities? And if this last
question should be the case, how do we go about preserving the sublime experience that writers such as Emerson and Thoreau promised?

It may be impossible to answer these questions; however, in an effort
to shed some light on them and to provide a relevant twenty-first-century
reading of Berry's essays, I turn to sociologist Fred Kniss and his 2013
analysis of the problems with mainstream religion. In "Against the Flow:
Learning from New, Emergent, and Peripheral Religious Currents,"
Kniss problematizes mainstream religion by creating a metaphor that
compares religion to a river.[3] He argues that sociologists have focused
too much on conventional religion, thus failing to see how it is a product of multiple beliefs, cultures, and experiences. However, if we look
deeper into what the term "religion" entails, we see that it is made up
of many complex theories and philosophies, denominations, and histories. Each of these divergent elements add to the characteristics of what
"mainstream religion" means to us as a whole.

To develop the river metaphor, Kniss compares the differing beliefs and philosophies that fall under the heading of "mainstream religion" to tributaries, eddies, and crosscurrents. He likens tributaries to new religions that have "flowed" into the mainstream beliefs of a given culture or location, eddies as new ideas that have developed or emerged out of existing beliefs within the mainstream, and crosscurrents as alternative (or peripheral) beliefs that challenge an established religion. He argues that all of these categories go against the established flow of mainstream religion, but that their influence reshapes the character of religion given geographical and historical contexts.

Kniss's metaphor is so compelling that applying it to Wendell Berry's observations of the people of Port Royal, Kentucky, and the Kentucky River seems obvious. My analysis calls for a rereading of these essays through the lens of the river metaphor, which allows readers a contemporary application of the spiritual, cultural, and economic implications of an early twenty-first-century environmentalism. Moreover, my analysis allows readers to draw parallels between Kniss's approach to understanding mainstream religion and Berry's approach to presenting a heightened awareness for why we interact with the environment the way we do. Using Kniss's metaphor of religion as a river offers a tangible way to engage with Berry's call for a new relationship with nature before modern-day environmentalism was formally established. Since I am using a river metaphor in this analysis and the Kentucky River is the centerpiece of the essays in *The Long-Legged House*, I will focus only on those essays that directly place human beings in contact with the river.

Like Kniss who spends ample time problematizing attitudes toward mainstream religion, it is important that I spend time problematizing the attitudes toward nature that Berry observes in his essays. In his 1993 essay, "Christianity and the Survival of Creation," Berry says that we "are holy creatures living among other holy creatures in a world that is holy," and that this sense of holiness is "not compatible with an exploitive economy," it is not compatible with "economic practices that daily destroy life and diminish possibility." Like Kniss's argument that the tributaries, eddies, and currents are "branches" of a larger meaning of religion, Berry's descriptions demonstrate how our own personal environmental awareness is made up of many "branches" of lived experiences, beliefs, and desires. However, it takes the equivalence of a profound religious experience to awaken that awareness. Kniss argues that "we should think instead of religion as a confluence of disparate influences, bringing together a variety of ideas, traditions, practices, and institutions—having a relatively persistent shape and course over time, to be sure, but also in constant motion, with the ever present potential for significant shifts in course" (352). As Berry urges his readers to refine, and perhaps adopt, their own environmentalism by finding themselves within nature in the face of increased industrialization, he advocates, as Kniss does with religion, for a flexible and intimate understanding of the natural world.

"The Rise," arguably the most pivotal essay in the collection, offers a deeper explanation of why humanity struggles to establish a positive understanding of and relationship with nature and a potential solution to getting humanity back on moral ground. Harold K. Bush Jr., in his article "Wendell Berry, Seeds of Hope and the Survival of Creation," asserts that "Berry desires to reestablish a similarly wild and primal connection with nature. And like the transcendentalists, Berry wishes to recover a view of nature as a place of moral authority and insight" (302). Much like transcendentalist Ralph Waldo Emerson's suggestion that humans must go into the wild to have an "original" relationship with the universe, Berry's original relationship with the universe is realized when he turns back to the Kentucky River.[4]

Through the use of Kniss's metaphor, we, too, can see how Berry establishes the river as a divine, spiritual entity that has the power to change our industrial-driven attitudes toward nature. I will address the "mainstream" attitudes toward the environment that Berry observes by establishing the following metaphors: Berry's tributaries are the experiences and influences of those individuals who temporarily escape the industrialized city and converge on the Kentucky River; his eddies are our philosophies toward the treatment of the environment that are complicated in the presence of nature; and his crosscurrents are the potential dangers and unpredictability of nature that upset the established norms of our current environmentalism. These three metaphors work together to illustrate that modern environmentalism is more than just a mainstream belief: it is made up of an intricate fabric of complex influences.

Our own modern-day views of how we should regard the environment lies in the "lived experiences" we bring to nature. These lived
experiences include our upbringing, home life, education, religion, and
values, just to name a few, that impact our individual ethics for living
rightly with the environment. In Berry's Port Royal, Kentucky, it is industrialization that appeared to have the greatest impact on the people
who directly interact with the Kentucky River. Berry's depiction of
those individuals seeking the banks of the Kentucky for recreation may
be best read within the context of Kniss's tributary metaphor. Like a
tributary that provides smaller bodies of moving water to enter a larger
river or stream, Kniss argues that new or immigrant religions impact
mainstream beliefs and influence religious movements. Moreover, paying attention to religious tributaries allows us to provide new insights
into "old" questions. In short, recognizing these tributaries allows us
to understand the variation and complexity of our mainstream beliefs.

The tributaries that make up our approach to the ethical treatment
of the environment are heavily influenced by the increased disappearance of nature. When modern industrialization poses new challenges
to the preservation and conservation of nature, we must adjust some
of the basic approaches of our accepted environmental policies and
behavior. These basic approaches, which make up our mainstream understanding of environmentalism, are heavily influenced by the more
intricate underlying experiences and advances in development. Berry
is explicit in acknowledging that the people he sees recreating on the
river are there to escape the hectic city life. With their escape from
the city, they bring their fast-paced lifestyle, frustrations, and anxieties
into the environment. Individuals seeking the Kentucky River as a refuge from the city impose their modern inventions—engines for their
speedboats, radios that chase away the maddening silence, and trash
that is better off placed in the river where it can be whisked away to another location—on the river banks. As Berry notes, the river can wash
away our trash, but it can never eliminate it. The river can provide
an escape from the city, but it cannot necessarily eliminate the conveniences of industrialized living. Rather than dismissing the people that
come to and actively pollute the river, Berry tries to understand the
intentions they have when they arrive at the river.

The reality that Berry recognizes upon observing these nature seek-
ers is that in their zealous attempt to leave the city behind, they are not
particularly keen on seeing the river beyond what is on the surface. The
takeaway message from Berry's collection appears at the end of the essay
"The Nature Consumers" when he says, "What I hope—and it is not an
easy hope—is that people will begin to come into the countryside with a
clearer awareness of why they come, of what they need from it and of what
they owe it. I assume—and it is not an easy assumption—that the world
must live in men's minds if men are to continue to live in the world" (42). Is
it *really* possible for humans to coexist with the environment? Is it possible
to *fully* understand why we seek the solitude of a secluded forest or quiet
body of water in the country when our hectic day-to-day lives become too
overwhelming? And, is it possible to ever fully comprehend our place in
and impact on the natural world? These are some of the "old" questions
that Berry's essays attempt to readdress, but without an understanding of
how industry and the city have influenced the individuals who have come
to the river, we cannot begin to discuss them.

According to Berry, an escape from the industrialized cities means
bringing motorized boats, loud music, and unending amounts of refuse to the riverbanks. It is not about scenery, per se, or even the peaceful wilderness that draws visitors: it is the freedom that one feels when
racing down the river in a motor boat. In "The Nature Consumers," the
final chapter of part 1 of Berry's collection, he addresses people's overall
lack of connection with nature, and more specifically, the river. Berry
shares the story of a man and his wife who spend four days camping
on the riverbank. At first, Berry admires the fact that the man uses a
rowboat to maneuver on the water and that he is using old-fashioned
fishing equipment to hunt for his dinner. However, Berry quickly observes that the man grows impatient, moving quickly from location to
location without much success. The next day, the man shows up with
a rented speed boat, and when the motor fails to operate correctly, the
family packs up and leaves. While seeking out a quiet, natural place
to vacation, Berry notes that the man had stayed as "remote from the
place he had come to as if he had never left the city where he lived"
(32). Though the frustration of living without the conveniences of the
modernized world negatively affected the family, the man remains

significant to Berry. He says, "He has become a symbol, to me, of an alienation from the world that I believe to be common among us, and on the increase" (32). This symbol is significant in that well before serious conversations about human disconnectedness with nature became commonplace, Berry, through his own casual observations, sees the escalation of potentially catastrophic relationships with the environment.

Much of Berry's analysis of the Port Royal community's relationships with nature reaches beyond just the behavior they exhibit on the banks of the river. In addition to their own lived experiences influencing how they perceive the environment, it is equally important to look within themselves as they interact with nature. This part of the argument will benefit from an application of Kniss's eddy metaphor. Kniss defines an eddy as "an emergent form, a swirling, or backcurrent that occurs when water collides with an obstacle or when two distinct currents collide" (358). New movements form in response to new problems or issues, and these new ideas reshape the mainstream. Kniss argues that "[e]ddies provide energy and movement that can shake up the normal course of events. If we focus our attention on emergent movements within conventional religion, we will find challenges to the dominant narrative of decline in the mainstream" (361). Our interactions with nature have the power to shape our spirituality, philosophy, and appreciation for nature. For this, Berry calls for an intimate relationship with nature by recognizing the multiple perspectives from within the river. By physically immersing oneself in the river and allowing for an eye-level perspective of the surface of the water, new beauty is easily recognized.

The opening paragraph of "The Loss of the Future" offers a definitive articulation of the problems Berry sees with humanity. He begins his chapter with the following proclamation:

> We are a remnant people in a remnant country. We have used up the possibilities inherent in the youth of our nation: the new start in a new place with new vision and new hope. We have gone far toward using up our topsoils and our forests and many of our other natural resources. We have come, or we are coming fast, to the end of what we were given. The good possibilities that may lie ahead are only those that we will make ourselves, by a wiser and more generous and more exacting use of what we have left. (45)

The fact that Berry uses the word "remnant" in this passage suggests that humanity has indeed become a simple "leftover," trying to make use of what has already been long overused and nearly consumed: the land. In order to realize the "good possibilities" that exist, we need to create them ourselves by reinventing our relationship with nature. To do this, Berry turns to faith and spirituality found nowhere else other than in the water he calls home: the Kentucky River.

The power and deeper mysteries of the river, to which I will refer as eddies, provide Berry with challenges that reshape his own philosophy of nature. Many of the observations found both within Berry's stories, promote a respect for the power of the river. Berry reminds his readers that the Kentucky River represents life, survival, and uses the water and the riverbank as symbols. Unlike the many stories of other people's experiences in nature, Berry sees the rich life that the river affords. Without the river, no life exists. Berry notes that "it has been a long time since this was a 'natural river'" (32), but he goes on to describe the life that he has taken the time to appreciate. "Its wonders are commonplace and shy. Knowing them is an endless labor and, if one can willingly expend the labor, an endless pleasure" (33–34). Berry asserts that "the pleasure of Americans can be destructive in the same way that their work has already proved to be" (34). He says later that "propelled at twenty or thirty miles an hour by a roaring engine, one can only experience the country only as 'scenery'—a painted landscape without life or sound" (40). These observations are important because like the image of mainstream religion that Kniss creates, Berry's "characters" only see the Kentucky River from the comfort of the riverbank or their speed boat. They are not fully emerged in the river to experience the complexity and unpredictability of the water, and perhaps more importantly, to realize the life-giving qualities of the river—the many "tributaries" or "eddies" of lived experience and philosophies necessary for survival.

Berry represents the power of the river during a rise, but his narration translates the physical power of the river into a figurative power of faith and spirituality. However, it is not enough to witness the rise from our mainstream perch on the river bank; we must meet the river head-on at eye level, submerged without the human-made power of a motorized boat. Berry says, "There is an exhilaration in being *accustomed* to a boat on dangerous water. It is as though into one's consciousness of the dark violence of the depths at one's feet there rises the idea of the boat, the buoyancy of it" (97). It is not until we are submerged in the river, as Berry himself becomes eye-level with the water, do we become aware of its "bigness" (99).[5] And, of course, while observing the river's "bigness," the water's unpredictability is never far from Berry's mind.

The water's instability during a rise allows Berry to see the world change. "At the water line, when a rise is on, the world is changing" (95). Without willingly becoming intimate with the river, we never fully realize the diverse qualities of the river. "What the canoeist gets, instead of an impression of the river's speed," Berry argues, "is an impression of its power. Or, more exactly, an impression of the *voluminousness* of its power" (98). The overall power of the river is significant. It gives life (and later we address its power to take life), it offers pleasure and relaxation as well as a sense of adventure, and it offers us the opportunity to see our surroundings from a different angle. But, we must quickly move from the riverbank in order to fully grasp the meaning of our experience with the river. We have to be willing to venture out on the river in a canoe and become vulnerable to the river's power. He concludes that "once the connection with the shore is broken, the journey has begun" (96). The journey, in this case, is the beginning of our spiritual and environmental awakening, and because of the unknown that this journey promises to expose, many people are content to simply engage it from the safety of the shore.

Much like redefining our own religious beliefs by recognizing the many cultural eddies that Kniss points out, we need to reestablish our perceptions of our relationship with the river, or more philosophically, our place in the world, by venturing away from what we have always known. Kniss argues that, "Exclusively focusing on the mainstream slows down the progress of knowledge in our field. Ignoring the tributaries, eddies, and crosscurrents means we are missing much of the important variation in the phenomena we are studying" (353). The river, as Berry concludes and as Kniss would likely concur, is a world with which we have not fully been acquainted and our senses "must begin to live another kind of life" (96). Being on the river has the power to change our perspective, to see what we ordinarily would not see from the safety of the shore or the safety of our current mainstream beliefs. Berry mentions that he is on the water in December, a time when many people may not be. So, the perspective he has at a time when the leaves are off the trees is something most would not see. The river, like mainstream religion, is often used when it is convenient or "needed." Acquainting ourselves with the river when it is cold and lacking life seems to emphasize the point that we cannot rely on part-time religion or environmentalism to survive.

Perhaps more daunting and challenging to accepted beliefs than tributaries and eddies are the crosscurrents. Kniss argues that "[i]f we want to understand religion in any particular place and time, we need to pay attention to the forces running counter to the mainstream" (363). How do these events shape our perspective and view of the river?

The adventure of leaving sure footing is not simple, however. Since focusing on the mainstream will only serve to skew our understanding of religion as a whole, as Kniss asserts, we must be willing to accept our vulnerability and take on the river more intimately (358). The strength of the current, Berry realizes, has the ability to bring us in several directions. Here, again, we return to Kniss's discussion about changing our perspective of mainstream religion. The religious tributaries, eddies, and crosscurrents are at work in shaping a newly realized religion. He explains that eddies occur when the water meets obstacles or when two currents collide and that these eddies can vary in size and significance and may persist over time (358). While his metaphor exists within the context of reformed religious thought, one can make an easy connection to the beliefs fueling modern environmentalism. Like in religion, when new problems present themselves one must adjust his or her perceptions and beliefs. "Eddies provide energy and movement that can shake up the normal course of events," Kniss argues. "If we focus our attention on emergent movements within conventional religion, we will find challenges to the dominant narrative of decline in the mainstream" (361). Likewise, if we are afraid to venture into a new conversation about environmentalism and our attitudes toward nature, we run the risk of doing more harm to nature than we had ever intended.

The concept of embracing and respecting the river's power is evident when Berry and his companions embark on the Kentucky in their canoe. He states, "We kept our direction by *intention*; there could be no dependence on habit or inertia; when our minds wandered the river took over and turned us according to inclinations of its own. It bore us like a consciousness, acutely wakeful, filling perfectly the lapses in our own" (97). The importance of simply allowing the river to direct them is clear. This passage allows readers to see the coexistence of the river and the intentions of the men. Kniss concludes that if we are to understand religion we must examine the major arguments or "currents" that run against it (363). The same can be said of our own attitudes toward respecting the environment. Understanding views we did not know existed or those with which we may not agree, are a necessity to understanding the larger movement.

The river's power and perhaps our increased vulnerability by interacting with it intimately heightens the mystery of the water and challenges our views of the river. The magical experience that one could potentially have on the water, without all of the "necessities" of modern life, increases the necessity of realizing a sixth sense, Berry claims. Taking new perceptions and angles into consideration will allow us to see the environment in a renewed way. Berry experiences a moment of clarity after giving himself over to the river. "The force that mattered, that surrounded us, and inundated us with its sounds, and pulled at or shook or carried everything around us, was the river," he asserts (98). Power and magic come together. We do not have the power to remember its wild and unpredictable characteristics. "It would take a god to watch it as it changes and not be surprised," Berry concludes (99). This conclusion underscores the significance of Berry's experience. Simply put, there is always an element of awe and surprise.

This awe and surprise with the appreciation of the river's power and the majesty and mystery it embodies, however, also comes with an element of horror and darkness. The vulnerability of accessing and analyzing our faith, religion, spirituality, or in Berry's case, moral responsibility to the environment, is that we might see and learn more than that with which we are comfortable. There is the potential that we may become too powerless for our own liking and at any given moment the very entity that we cherish and trust with our lives could destroy us. Berry reminds us that the river only exposes its dangers to us through selected, piecemeal events. While we can use the river for pleasure and "ride on its back in boats," we cannot easily get off the river should we make a mistake. If a mistake should be made by becoming too comfortable with the river, "why then it will suffer a little wrinkle on its surface, and go on as before" (100). Whether or not this "wrinkle" is in reference to the river's ability to easily correct a mistake or the ability to recover should we make a fatal mistake ourselves is left to the reader's imagination. The river is more adaptable than we think. Our recollection of the events that weave together the fabric of our faith and spirituality are simply momentary events. We do not often have the entire picture in front of us. There are always hidden secrets in the reveal, yet we hunt for the adventure.

Berry reflects on a situation where a man he knew from his boyhood capsized on the river. The people who live along the banks, in the safety and comfort of the "mainstream," know that something has happened on the water. They can hear the man yelling for help, "but it makes them uneasy. Whether or not there *is* somebody out there, the possibility that there *may* be reminds them of their lot; they never know what may be going by them in the darkness. And they think of the river, so dark and cold" (101). Knowing the river's power, or to continue our metaphor, the power of deeper religious thought or the revelation of what we are doing to the environment, we may be unprepared to address the potential darkness that can be revealed.

It seems that part of Berry's intent with his metaphor is to persuade people to acknowledge the need for a change in the way we see the environment on a local level. In doing so, it is important to make environmentalism the religion that establishes a strong moral code of behavior when interacting with nature. If we reflect back on the essay, "The Nature Consumers," Berry makes a compelling statement about the condition of our environmental and spiritual thought. He says, "It raises, still, all the old answerless questions of origins and ends. It asks a man what is the use and the worth of his life. It asks him who he thinks he is, and what he thinks he's doing, and where he thinks he's going" (41). Once it is attended to, admitted into the head, one must bear a greater burden of consciousness and knowledge—one must change one's life. Perhaps the most compelling part of the above passage is the point that once we recognize and learn about the full picture of what we are encountering—whether it is religious understanding, environmental degradation, or ordinary human behavior—we have the responsibility of answering to it regardless of whether or not we are ready. For some, this "darkness" or "mystery," is simply too much to handle. Later, Berry concludes that people are comfortable strewing their garbage on the face of the water and speeding down the river as fast as they can. He says, "Pursued into the wilderness by questions he is afraid even to ask, no wonder he finds his comfort—to his bewilderment, surely—in what he thought he wanted to be free of: crowdedness and commotion and hurry and mess" (41). The spiritual awakening that occurs on the river is powerful and so uncomfortable to some that they are perfectly content returning to the very conditions from which they had hoped to escape.

It is much too easy to say that human beings in the twenty-first century need to have a clearer awareness of their environmental footprint. It is equally dismissive to say that a spiritual connection with the environment will lead to a heightened desire to protect it. There are consequences for those of us who are comfortable to stay within the safety of the riverbank or within the familiarity of our homes without fully immersing ourselves in the river.

Are there dangers with being *too* acquainted with the river? Before human-made floods and roads, Berry contends, people turned toward the river, but they do not seem to do that as often anymore. Has modernization also detracted us from our own spirituality? Perhaps, we have either answered too many uncomfortable questions about our moral obligation to the environment, or better yet, perhaps we are afraid to fully answer any of them.

Notes

1. For a full discussion of the development of modern environmentalism, see Hal Rothman's *The Greening of a Nation? Environmentalism in the United States Since 1945.*
2. Roderick Nash, in *Wilderness and the American Mind*, provides an excellent overview of the historical and philosophical progression of environmental thought from exploration to the late twentieth century.
3. Kniss's essay served as the Presidential Address of the Association for the Sociology of Religion at the August 2013 Annual Meeting in New York City.
4. Emerson provides a full interpretation of what it means to have an original relationship with nature in his 1836 essay "Nature."
5. To demonstrate what Berry means about becoming "eye-level" with the river, he references George Caleb Bingham's painting of trappers on the Missouri. In these nineteenth-century paintings, Bingham captures American life from the perspective of the viewer looking at the trappers in their canoes from the surface of the water.

Works Cited

Berry, Wendell. *The Long-Legged House.* 1965. Shoemaker & Hoard, 2004.

———. "Christianity and the Survival of Creation." *CrossCurrents*, vol. 43, no. 2, Summer 1993, pp. 149-63. *JSTOR*, http://www.jstor.org/stable/24460004.

Bush, Harold K. Jr. "Wendell Berry, Seeds of Hope, and the Survival of Creation." *Christianity and Literature*, vol. 56, no. 2, 2007, pp. 297–316. *Sage Journals*, doi. org/10.1177/014833310705600206.

Carson, Rachel. *Silent Spring.* 1962. Houghton Mifflin, 2002.

Kniss, Fred. "Against the Flow: Learning from New, Emergent, and Peripheral Religious Currents." *Sociology of Religion*, vol. 75, no. 3, 2014, pp. 351–66. doi: 10.1093/socrel/sru020.

Nash, Roderick. *Wilderness and the American Mind.* Yale UP, 1984.

Rothman, Hal. *The Greening of a Nation? Environmentalism in the United States Since 1945.* Wadsworth, 1997.

"Let everything that binds fall"

The Significance of Water in David Vann's Fiction

SOFIA AHLBERG

IN ONE VERSION of the Greek myth of Medea and Jason, Medea helps her lover Jason flee after his attempt to overthrow her father King Aeëtes of Colchis. Having murdered her brother Absyrtus, Medea then distracts her father by flinging parts of Absyrtus's dismembered body into the water, knowing her father will stop to retrieve the parts to give his son a proper burial. In David Vann's 300-word short story "Ink," the narrator describes the water as it receives the forearm of her brother: "Dark wood in darker water, a sea of ink, and pattern felt but unseen, quartering waves caught only in glimpses" ("Ink"). Medea then implores the water itself: "Dark one," she says, "Let everything that binds fall. Let all that is known be confused. Let all that we are die. Let me be most hated of all women, and most true." For David Vann, an Alaskan author, what struggles to find expression among his most harmed or harmful characters especially, is beset by water's unbinding power. The role of the ocean in Vann's writing is to repudiate the enduring structure of "everything that binds" though formlessness is not Vann's only goal. Water is all-encompassing in Vann's biographical *A Mile Down: The True Story of a Disastrous Career at Sea* (2005), it recurs in the inlets and estuaries in the novella "Sukkwan Island" from *Legend of a Suicide* (2008) as well as the lake in which the island of *Caribou Island* (2011) becomes the stage for the murder-suicide that erases a marriage. Vann's characters do not just live on, in, or near water, but water is also the way they—or usually we, Vann's readers—discover meaning. For Vann, the stricture of familial destiny is often traceable to its roots in Greek tragedy ("David Vann: An Ode to Literary Tradition"). In Vann's most recent novel *Aquarium* (2015), the formlessness of water brings a welcome liberation from the determinism that constrains families endlessly to relive the past.

Water can at times be a soothing balm for Vann, though it is also capable of a destabilizing effect that may provoke shocking or revelatory new associations. Although early environmentalist scholars and educators such as David Orr often point to the similarities between water and poetics, particularly the beauty of language, its flow and metaphorical reach (54), Vann does not emphasize water's beauty in any of these ways. Instead, in his fiction water literally and figuratively both joins and separates. In the face of water's pervasive unbinding power, in Vann's writing individual lives are nevertheless written and circulate even over vast distances. Water subtly mediates the distribution of human stories, not directly, through properties intrinsic to it, but rather through the ubiquitous spread of its provocation to give life's fluidity an enduring form—to narrate. Of course, form can also be seen in the burden that human life places on the environment. It stabilizes law and custom, technology and commerce, and it also presently allows a misguided notion of progress to endure beyond its long-term effectiveness. Here, water's ceaseless renegotiation of all contracts becomes a plus. Although the fate of humanity may seem to be circumscribed by the pressures endured by nature, Vann also shows how this limit can dissolve, offering readers (if not characters, who are often tragically bound) access to a far more spacious and compassionate understanding of the desperate situations that recur in his fiction. He provides water with the staying power that narrative form alone can bestow and by virtue of this distribution, water itself can be said to signify.

Vann's fiction insists on a deep accord between water and literary invention that for me calls to mind Walter Benjamin's "magical correspondences" ("Mimetic Faculty" 334) by which material things in themselves first manifest meaning. Benjamin develops this idea in "On Language as Such and on the Language of Man" as well, asserting that what is communicable through language's "magical community with things" (67) conveys an immediacy between the human and the natural world, that "communicates itself *in* language and not *through* language" (63). In "Ink" Vann has Medea seeking a fatal fame by way of an intentional alliance with the destructive aspect of water. As she requests of the sea to endure traces of her actions that will make her "most hated of all women" ("Ink"), she is as much in water as she is, in Benjamin's words, "*in* language" ("On Language as Such" 63). When Medea looks down at the surface of the water, something more than her distraught face is reflected back at her. A paradox in Vann's writing that is central to this essay shows up when human narrative intersects with a formless riposte to language that may yet, as Benjamin writes, "give birth to the language of things themselves . . . soundlessly, in the mute magic of nature" (69). In the original myth, to protect Jason, Medea brutalizes her brother's body, thereby blaspheming against the burial rites. What I want to emphasize is that in Vann's rendition of the myth, Medea's act has inflicted something of water's formlessness on that sacred form, and her crime at the same time garners some of the immortality attached to writing. It is as though water's unwritable rebuke to writing, its endless capacity to dissolve "everything that binds" ("Ink") has itself become immortalized, just as if it had been written. Vann has Medea inscribe herself beyond the present moment, thereby entering language not just as a figure in literature but as an example of how a life can become readable to others long after death. Vann's Medea wishes to be freed from her humanity, a creature of pure instinct that is as free and unleashed as water that overflows and cannot easily be contained or regulated. The ocean and Medea's incantation are both the ink of his story's title. This is because, as Sarah Wood asserts, "to read is to enter writing" (88) as though reading could be an act of submersion.

In his autobiographical text *A Mile Down: The True Story of a Disastrous Career at Sea*, Vann chronicles his pursuit of a dream that nearly kills him just as it killed his father: to live on and make a living off the sea. Because Vann could not get a full-time job as a professor of literature, and because of his disenchantment with the education system more generally as well as his thirst for autonomous living, Vann's plan is to create his own "university on the water" (*Mile Down* 8) by offering cruises on the Mediterranean with higher education classes thrown in. Stubbornly, Vann persists with the enterprise of building his own luxury cruise ship for this purpose despite suffering just about every misfortune possible, ranging from corrupt ship outfitters in the ports of the Mediterranean to freak weather incidents. The great strength of this piece of writing is Vann's humbling ability to self-reflect. At no point does he delude himself into thinking of his project as anything but madness and yet he is compelled to see it through. Since the beginning of his authorship, Vann recognizes that when stories attempt to tell of the natural world, they are as resonant as any myth. Vann's reality becomes the stuff of myth: "I sometimes felt like Oedipus, running and running and escaping nothing" (167) and later, "I really felt like Oedipus trying to run from his fate" (215).

Like Oedipus but not the same as Oedipus because, after all, Vann's fate is not written in stone but on water, allowing him to hope for some latitude. Nevertheless, as Vann reflects on his predicament at sea ("Different ocean, different year, different business plan, different rudder even, but the same problem" [215]), he is at first tempted to see his adventure as following in the wake of his father's life which ended in his suicide (79). The boat that figures in *A Mile Down* has something in common with the *Argo* and thus has some resonance with Vann's evocation of the Jason myth in "Ink." In the myth of Jason and the Argonauts, Jason and his crew were condemned by the gods to sail the ship *Argo* whose certain destruction had been prophesied. According to the myth, to circumvent this doom they ingeniously replaced every bit of the ship so that they ended up with an entirely new vessel that was exactly the same as the original. As narrated in *A Mile Down*, Vann's own vessel *Bird of Paradise* ends up similarly patched, if not to that extreme. It sustains multiple damages in stormy weather and about as many repairs, and, as with the *Argo*, Vann's crew and Vann himself live to tell the tale long after the vessel itself sinks. Their physical survival is no doubt due to the rescue operation carried out by the US Coast Guard, but also the narratives that continue to surface after *Bird of Paradise* is lost testify to a more enduring form of buoyancy.

In stories of individuals teetering on the edge of sanity, Vann shows us how to reroute rather than squander creative energies via a renewed alertness to water's signifying power. The ship *Argo* communicates, in

Roland Barthes's account, "not by genius, inspiration, determination, evolution, but by two modest actions (which cannot be caught up in any mystique of creation): substitution (one part replaces another, as in a paradigm) and nomination (the name is in no way linked to the stability of the parts)" (46). The ship thus takes on qualities and properties of water through this process of (in principle) endless substitution predicated on the name "*Argo.*" Water, as an intriguing composite of medium and message, keeps Vann afloat insofar as he applies water's principle of substitution to the terms of what would otherwise have been his own fixed destiny. While he seems fated to fail in his sea enterprise, like his father, nevertheless, water ensures that there is something that is not known, that cannot be known. My point here is that for Vann, water's restless, tempestuous energy, inseparable from its refusal to be bound to a single form, offers a chartless escape route from any notion of a tragic fate that is for all time written in the stars. Vann's journey at sea is formally the same as his predecessors', but *A Mile Down* ultimately shows that what is written on water's shifting page of substitutions will bear new meaning with each new attempt.

Sometimes this new meaning takes the form of a cathartic emptying out of an earlier, older meaning. Toward the end of *A Mile Down*, Vann's own plight as his disabled boat is being rescued can be seen throwing an inverting reflection back at the much-discussed "green light at the end of Daisy's dock" that seemed to assure Gatsby of a future that in Fitzgerald's novel is forever withheld. Arguably, the culmination of this motif in the closing lines of *The Great Gatsby* has been so widely and deeply considered for its significances pertaining to the American Dream that there is little more to be said:

> Gatsby believed in the green light, the orgastic future that year by year recedes before us. It eluded us then, but that's no matter— tomorrow we will run faster, stretch out our arms farther . . . and one fine morning—
> So we beat on, boats against the current, borne back ceaselessly into the past. (Fitzgerald 188)

In *A Mile Down*, a "green light stick" attached by the US Coast Guard to the throwing line for hauling in the tow rope becomes the focus of Vann's contemplation of his situation. He writes, "I stood there for a while staring absentmindedly at the green light shining through the messy pile of their heaving line," and I could believe Vann also has Gatsby's fate in mind as he reflects in painful detail on what besets anyone's aim of ever reaching a goal by water:

> One thing about being at sea is that you don't really get to stop.
> . . . Until you arrive in port, you're stuck, and conditions can always worsen, the boat can always break in new ways, whether you're prepared or not. Even in port, you can slip anchor, blow against other anchored boats in crosswinds and currents, or run aground. In a marina, battering, chafing, and electrolysis are still possible, as are . . . all the expensive things you can run into and crush. A boat simply does not allow for genuine rest. Its essential nature is peril, held in check only through enormous effort and expense. (*Mile Down* 218)

For Vann, the green light is no invitation to hope in "an orgastic future" that we may or may not attain if we "beat on, boats against the current," despite being "borne back ceaselessly into the past" (Fitzgerald 188). No such ideal, questioned or upheld, applies to this green light. Rather this light is something to "stare absentmindedly" at as he and the *Bird of Paradise* are towed not back but forward by the US Coast Guard. However, in keeping with Barthes's account of the salvation of the *Argo*, Vann draws on water itself as a literary resource as well as a physical medium where stuff actually happens, allowing its substitutive possibilities to inform the core of his narrative. The green light remains, but rather than signifying the ineluctable pull of the past, this light is attached to a life-line sent by strangers who tow his vessel to relative safety away from the past and the fate of his father. Same light, same ocean, different meaning. Vann escapes his fate through the use of another language of his own making. Water speaks, impossibly and hopefully, not by staying fixed but through its porous boundaries and reshaping potential. As such, it resembles life which is in itself, as Vann's concluding remarks suggest, "a work of art, constantly melted away and reshaped" (*Mile Down* 240).

In Vann's collection *Legend of a Suicide*, *Argo*'s principle of substitution enables Vann to rework and reimagine the most disturbing aspects of his past. In "Sukkwan Island," Vann's most acclaimed story from that collection, the lives of father and son are hemmed in by the forbidding Alaskan waters. The novella depicts the father Jim as highly unstable and when he produces a .44 Magnum, the reader feels certain of the outcome, especially since Vann's actual father's suicide is well known even to a newcomer to Vann's fiction who can read of it on the book's back cover. All the more shocking than that, in place of the father it is the son Roy, Vann's alter ego, who kills himself, and for the rest of the novella, the father goes on the run (always keeping the liquefying corpse of his son with him) as he fears he will be accused of his son's murder. At the outset of his journey, Jim leaves the island on an inflatable boat with Roy's corpse in a nylon sleeping bag. Finally, he pays two smugglers to take him down to the coast to Mexico, but on their way, he is attacked by them, thrown overboard, and left to drown. In place of a tragic fate, however, the father experiences a final moment of benediction to which I return below. Vann recognizes the pull of the past and is heavily influenced by Greek tragedy in his own work. Nevertheless, stories such as "Sukkwan Island" do not present the past as an absolute determinant, nor do they strive to make amends with it. Instead, in Vann's careful dialoguing with the natural environment the tragic hero's limited scope is exchanged for a set of narrative improvisations that even include redemption.

For Vann, stories he knew from the age of thirteen and for twenty years until the publication of "Sukkwan Island" were particularly dark as he grew up in the shadow of his father's suicide (Cooke). But with "Sukkwan Island" Vann determines to rework those old stories and in doing so he strives to remake himself. In a daring substitution, rather than retell his own history, or even invent an altogether different fiction, Van creates a dark reflection of the facts. In this story, a young boy takes his life leaving the father bereft and in search of answers. In this version, it is now the father who is left with regrets, condemned to search for clues on the sea's surface, wondering if taking his son sailing around the world instead of living in remote Alaska would have been a better choice (158). On a ferry to Haines, Jim tries to make sense of the shock of his son's suicide by studying the trace of his own progress in the water:

He stared at the wake. Though it trailed away and spread and
dissipated, it remained exactly the same from his viewpoint. It
would never catch up with the boat nor would it ever be lost. It
seemed like this might mean something, but then Jim was only
wondering what his life was now, and not knowing. (194)

Meanwhile, Roy's corpse is decomposing to a liquid mass inside the
sleeping bag and soon, "some of Roy leaked out through the tears in the
bag" (166). Without much hope of understanding Roy's death or what
possible future there could be after his passing, Jim turns to the landscape, specifically water, for salvation. Vann suggests that it is possible
to disengage oneself from the gravitational pull of a violent past and
that, moreover, a narrative reformed in accord with water's shape-shifting power is well suited to this task. This is contrary to the dialectical
way of reading violence suggested by other critics, such as Watts, who in
another context argues that violence is both structured and structuring:

> structured because the idea of violence results from historical events,
> stored as the memory of past deeds, of past encounters, of past frus-
> trations; and structuring because the idea of violence informs human
> actions, determines the acceptability, even the banality of violence,
> if not the ability to erase the scandal of its occurrence. (277)

Vann's fiction certainly supports this suggestion that violence structures human experience, but his narratives also indicate that there is
room for other influences to transform a life rather than simply building on the past. Most importantly, he imputes much meaning to the
landscape of his native southeast Alaska ("American Inferno"). Thus,
I see in "Sukkwan Island" traces of Benjamin's "magical correspondences" by which the unwritten forms of the natural world shape our
lives and their narratives ("Mimetic Faculty" 334). Vann's affirmation of
meaning in landscape echoes the assurance of a more primitive form of
communion with nature that Benjamin offers:

> "To read what was never written." Such reading is the most an-
> cient: reading before all languages, from the entrails, the stars,
> or dances. Later the mediating link of a new kind of reading, of

runes and hieroglyphs, came into use. It seems fair to suppose that these were the stages by which the mimetic gift, which was once the foundation of occult practices, gained admittance to writing and language. (336)

Here, Benjamin begins by citing his contemporary, the poet Hoffmansthal, then he proceeds to situate the inaugural literary gesture not in an act of writing but in a reading prior to all writing, of the actual things that take place around us. The actuality of water—its promise of deliverance from the past, its perilous unpredictability—is for Vann the urtext that subsequently informs and deforms his own writings.

Of significance in the conclusion of "Sukkwan Island" is the juxtaposition of two distinct images: one of extreme violence and the other of a personal transformation. As he is drowning, Jim has an out-of-body experience in which he sees himself as an infant: "He was a tiny golden infant shrunken inside himself with strings reaching out to each part of this larger body, pulling in. He was vanishing" ("Sukkwan Island" 208). This curious case of drowning as an infant suspended within while separate from one's adulthood offers author and reader, albeit not Jim to whom it is all too late, a glimpse of redemption. As already mentioned, "Sukkwan Island," as with just about everything Vann writes, is in part autobiographical writing. By distinguishing between two kinds of writing, one that happens and is lived bodily, not unlike the "entrails" or the "dance" Benjamin refers to above, and the other retrospective, distanced and autobiographical, Vann is able to gain sufficient perspective to enable the artistic substitutions that constitute his fiction. He can reconcile himself with his father's suicide by writing about it, not verbatim as it happened, but through a reversal of roles played by father and son as well as by swapping his father's suicide for a death resonant with insight.

It is this second writing, the one that reads, and renews, the past as "what was never written," that is redemptive. I am suggesting that the glowing image of the suspended infant is a hopeful vision of a writing that does not seek to escape out of the scene of its painful birth but rather, which heroically endures within that scene and triumphs when its narrative substitutions can exert a gravitational pull of their own. In

Vann's story, substitutions suggest that what was written by the body as that which actually happened in life is not as important as the second kind of writing, the literary posthumous version that is born within the bloody horror of the other. There is redemption in the fact that "Sukkwan Island" becomes the raft made of the pages of Vann's life through a magical, transformative correspondence between the past things and events, and their later narration. Toward the end of the harrowing novella, Jim's drowning is imaged as a reverse birth. If read as what was never written, the past need not return to us as how it once was, but "transformed into something that never was" (Heller-Roazen 1). I think Benjamin's exposure to the horror of a genocidal war made a compelling argument for what his idea of magical correspondences has to offer. The idea affirms that literature has power to create real distance from real trauma while retaining the courage to look steadily at the most painful subjects when refracted through a language that was forged in that trauma.

Benjamin's fascination with the magical way that natural things come close to the condition of being words sheds light on the minimal distance Vann sets up between the actual traumatic fate intrinsic to the human condition and his darkly luminous staging of the same, made different through narrative. We can see the beginnings of this approach to narrating the human condition and Vann's preoccupation with the physical aspect of language mediated by water in his first novel, the family tragedy *Caribou Island*. In this novel, the role of water is that of the storyteller in a tale of family life becoming utterly fragmented, while only the story endures. In *Caribou Island*, Irene is a newly retired schoolteacher who lives with her husband Gary. Their children have moved out. Plagued by mysterious headaches, Irene becomes addicted to very strong painkillers to help her cope with memories of a tragic childhood and also complications, though it is not clear exactly what these are, in her relations with her husband. Much of *Caribou Island* is told from the point of view of Irene as she helps Gary build a cabin on Caribou Island in the middle of a remote Alaskan lake that to Irene is a "metaphor for self," an unending series of selves, like waves, or tides, "each new version refuting all previous" (*Caribou Island* 129). Water does not simply reflect the state of mind of characters in *Caribou Island*, it also speaks them. In this novel, human beings are passively told as stories, as though everything is story. However, this is not to say that his characters know where storytelling comes from. Their tragedy—an inescapable condition, like fate—is that they cannot fathom the grounds of their own story.

Both Irene and Gary attempt to read their place in the natural world, specifically in relation to water. This can be seen as a "reading before all languages," as Gabriel Levy puts it, discussing Benjamin's language myth that situates human affairs in analogous relation to events in nature (Levy 31). Thus, as Irene succumbs to heavy sleep induced by painkillers, she has the impression of diving under the surface of the water. She imagines the "ocean with a heartbeat, slow waves of pressure, water compacting but no edge to it" (*Caribou Island* 70), and her identification with the ocean seems fatal as it shows Irene's unawareness of her own boundaries. Indeed, the full scale of the tragedy of *Caribou Island* becomes apparent when the characters discover that they are doomed because they cannot read their place in the world. Stories come from somewhere, but Vann suggests that it is not for human beings to know where. Both Gary and Irene feel certain that the secret of their being is connected to water: "The world of air a world of myth only, storms and lightning and sun. The only reality the density of the water, the coolness of it, the pressure and weight of it" (70). Irene's sense of homelessness and lack of self-knowledge, in particular, is traced back to her Icelandic heritage and the uprooting of her sense of belonging to that culture: "She had lost the stories, also, children's tales. Her memory now was only of figures in landscape. She had lost their movement and words, their purpose. A figure in the forest, the sense of that forest, frightening, or a figure on the sea, some kind of small boat, an ancient ship" (147). After having lost the ability to speak Icelandic around the age of ten, Irene is also bereft of the stories that formed her attachment to place.

To be in the dark, not knowing how things are connected, or what might still connect lives that are dissolving, this is what pushes Irene over the edge of sanity. We might say that this is the result of a profound failure to find or hear the voice of water as storyteller and instead to be inundated with a meaningless noise suggesting either possibility, or else, paralyzed with the fear of possibility. While our lives are narrated

as stories, this does not mean that everything is readable to us. There
are things that escape understanding and these constitute the limits of
language. At that limit, Vann deploys water as a setting that dissolves
limits while at the same time it inscribes a fluid freedom from fate. As
such, the words of Irene's life move like water itself even if they go beyond her ken, leaving her dizzy and desperate for a pattern that eludes
her. Instead of any assurance, by reading the water that surrounds the
island, which (this much she grasps) is the metaphor of self, she must
only concede to its transience and unexpected impermeability (129).
Gary fares no better than Irene. Like her, he is attempting to read what
was never written, thinking that his purpose on earth will reveal itself
if only he tries to merge with the water and become one with its purity,
"to be swept clean of thoughts" (219) by it. Drenched by waves, Gary
yells in ecstasy only to find that the feelings the water communicate to
him are impermanent:

> That expansive feeling, that sense of extension, of connec-
> tion, could moments later feel smaller, hard and cold, and
> Gary didn't know how this worked. The moment was over,
> before he had ridden it as far as he would have liked, and if he
> stayed here now, it would not come back. He knew that. But he
> stayed anyway, because he didn't like that rule. Was it a rule of
> the world, or just a limitation of self, and how could you ever
> know the difference? (219)

As with Irene, Gary is left with an overwhelming feeling of loss, of
being sidelined in his marriage and of not understanding the limits
of language and the writing and reading of self. At the mercy of the
powerful waves the ocean throws at him, Gary suspects his inability to
discern the world is due to his own inadequacies and so he challenges
the waves to return and speak to him once again. At other mom ts
in the novel, Gary imagines himself a "new kind of fisherman, a pros-
pector, almost, prodding at the deep to find what could be unburied"
(250). His is the ultimate dream of mankind to be the master over nature: "The Lake Man, they'd call him, and he'd find everything that
had ever been forgotten" (250). Shortly before the shocking conclusion of *Caribou Island* that sees Irene hunting Gary down, killing him,

and then herself, only for her daughter to discover her parents' bodies, Irene makes another desperate attempt to read the meaning of her existence via the water. Irene feels that the whole island is

> rolling, slowly turning over, capsizing. She had to keep her feet moving fast to stay upright. The island born long ago at lake bottom, rising to the surface on some kind of stalk, and now that stalk had been severed and the island was top-heavy, the hills of rock, the trees, and it would roll over until its slick flat underside was facing upward, wet and dark and known for thousands of years only to the lake, new to the sky. (283)

The desperation to make legible what refuses to represent is striking in this image of a capsizing island. In her imagination, the lake submits to her will and bares a clean page, another "slick flat" surface for the sky to read. Despite this, the story of her life that she wishes to tell will not be told and Irene is doomed to live out what was never written. Thus, unable to be the creator of her own story, she becomes its destroyer. Both her life and the life of her husband are sacrificed in the process. And the life of her daughter now seems destined to be a repetition of her mother's, given the way she, like Irene, falls victim to her mother's violence.

Vann's recent *Aquarium* marks a departure from the form of his fiction to date insofar as, unlike his other stories and novels, this is not a tragedy. On the contrary, despite its harrowing content, it presents the possibility of reconciliation and forgiveness within the family. At the heart of *Aquarium* is the question of trust in what is always subject to change. Mothers change into monsters, monsters change into angels of mercy, a bad father becomes a possible grandfather, everything metamorphoses. Nevertheless, there is no tragedy because if everything is subject to change, nothing is predetermined or immutably fixed. Vann captures two contradictory depictions of formlessness via his representation of water in *Aquarium*. It has emancipatory, even utopian, qualities, suggesting some relief to prepubescent Caitlin from the immense pressure of having to assume any particular form, this at a time when she feels her body changing and she is developing sexual feelings toward her best friend Shalini. Caitlin envies water for its formlessness and the shape-shifting qualities of fish, wishing she could morph into them (*Aquarium* 83). The seadragon symbolizes just this kind of freedom through which "you could imagine trees coming alive, entire forests waking up" (62). To Caitlin, who narrates her coming-of-age story retrospectively as an adult woman, "metamorphosis is the greatest beauty," and the creatures she studies in the aquarium "can become corollary to anything, unlimited, not held to any base, able to transform beyond the imagination" (63). Water becomes the symbol of this beauty of endless discovery and hope because "[w]e're still finding new shapes in the ocean" (63), and continues to do so even after Caitlin is grown up. On the other hand, there is a downside to all this fluidity. Despite the emphasis in *Aquarium* on the possibility of trust even in fickle and mutable circumstances, by having Caitlin tell her story from the perspective of the future her childhood self could only guess at, Vann shows that there is indeed much to fear from formlessness.

It was always difficult for the young Caitlin to feel confident in the face of events as they unfolded around her. Now, as an adult, she says, we "know so much more . . . about ocean acidification" (52) and we also know something about the destructive impact this is going to have on our own survival. As a child, Caitlin has a premonition of the uncertainty of humanity's survival by reading the water and the creatures that inhabit it. When her grandfather shows her the mackerel that have a hole going through them from "their mouths to the water behind" (126), the girl panics and as an adult she tries in hindsight to make sense of that confusion and fear:

> What I saw was every part of a fish wandering the oceans on its own. One of these gaping mouths straining through endless water with no body attached, a tail like a boomerang flinging itself through blue empty space, an eye floating alone. What if everything was unfinished? What if everything was made incomplete? (126)

What is bothering Caitlin the adult narrator at this moment is a profound and unsettling insight into biological reality. In fact, evolution does not have an end. Lacking purpose or telos, every life continually morphs and evolves into something else. As a twelve-year-old, Caitlin understands this as both freedom and as a worrying forgetfulness.

At the same time, Vann's novel recognizes the functional ordering of water as in the fishing industry centered around the port of Seattle where the novel is set, as well as in the compartmentalized bodies of water and sea life in the aquarium itself. This is a structure in which Caitlin finds "worlds within worlds all within reach" (61). However, neither architectural form nor scientific taxonomy can ever ultimately contain human life and give shape to its uncertain trajectory on what is becoming in our age a path toward self-destruction. Caitlin hears an expert at the aquarium predict that in the future "most of the fish might be gone, and we might be back to only jellyfish" (51). What she can only feel as a child, she fully comprehends in its full magnitude as an adult:

> We know so much more now about ocean acidification, and I should hate the jellyfish as a sign of all that we've destroyed. In my lifetime, the reefs will melt away, dissolved. By the end of the century, nearly all fish will be gone. The entire legacy of humanity will be only one thing, a line of red goop in the paleo-oceanographic record, a time of no calcium carbonate shells that will stretch on for several million years. (52–53)

What at one level can be felt as a form of liberation from destiny becomes a profound problem when taking into consideration humanity's own evolution and therefore our commitment to preserve the natural world, including the oceans. There is no assurance that human lives are the pinnacle of evolution. Indeed, the indeterminacy of our fate is made fully apparent when compared to the jellyfish, whose survival, despite the poisoning of the oceans, is guaranteed because of their potential for transformation and endless reconstitution. To the young Caitlin, whose own mother becomes a Medea-like woman attempting to tear the family to shreds, change does not induce trust. While Caitlin survives the unpredictable and violent rage of her mother, and hers is a (relatively) happy ending, the first happy endings that Vann has written so far, she nevertheless has no reason to consider humanity as a whole in any positive light.

Thinking about the destruction we have caused our oceans, Caitlin feels only that the "sadness of our stupidity is overwhelming" (53). Still, the formlessness does bring with it hope so long as endless potential for change endures. Ultimately, what the novel tells its readers is something about forgiveness. The idea that the process of evolution has no end gives grounds for withholding moral judgement, on actions or characters. Paradoxically, formlessness becomes the foundation for a steadfast refusal to pass judgment on the fluctuating fates of human subjects. Significantly, in this novel, the aquarium, in which the creatures of the deep are so carefully taxonomized and displayed, also gives form to water itself. This suggests that hopeful mutability is based on a way of dealing with water's formlessness and of harnessing it.

Reading what was never written resists the apparently ineluctable, which is to say tragic, terms of the human condition. When her grandfather asks Caitlin what the fish would say if they could talk, she predicts their simple message would be: "Come back . . . Join us. Watch out" (41). The invitation by the fish, as imagined by Caitlin, says something very important about the narrative perspective of the novel. To "come back" refers then to the hindsight that allows readers to relive their beginnings with added compassion. This capacity to relive beginnings reminds readers that the signifying power of water in Vann's writing is to generate its own correspondence free from bondage to the letter of the law. "Let everything that binds fall," says Vann's Medea in a gesture from within her tragedy that is a way to go beyond tragedy ("Ink"). Here, the signifying power of water begins not with a written text, but first with a reading free from prior readings. To Vann this bare response to things is the foundation of the potential for reflexivity. Later, a symbolic perspective is built on this inaugural narrative gesture.

I have said that Vann makes water his urtext. He reads in its actual fluidity a palpable indeterminacy or a literal formlessness that speaks to him of the associated risks of life on the sea and the perils of crossing it. His interest does not end there, however, since the notion of a crossing entails for him the possibility of shelter on a further shore. That unbinding capability of water is not Vann's only goal, it allows him to depart from the ineluctable outcomes of classical tragic form without renouncing form completely. As seen in *Aquarium*, this enables the achievement of an adult perspective on childhood, when narrative makes a break with what went before followed by a subsequent reconstitution that qualifies, ultimately, as forgiveness. At the same time, it is a perspective that confers more responsibility on us as subjects of history. Arguing against the inevitability of history, Bernstein notes that history is not a single line, rather it is a question of various choices, as well as accidents and possibilities, parallel narratives that sadly are largely obliterated by the course of events (21). The role of water in David Vann's fiction is recuperative, it offers a second chance at what could have happened but did not. In the light of the adult Caitlin's dismal reflection on the future of life on earth, perhaps this troping of latitude in Vann's work might lend forgiveness and tolerance to debates over environmental degradation and pollution. The present deterioration of the natural world is often overwhelming and, when this does not lead to denial, tends to produce paralysis or inertia at the inevitability of an impending catastrophe. However, in an age that seems shackled by natural law to the physical consequences of the past, the unbinding quality of water present in Vann's work supplies our imagination with a narratively performed freedom from such overdetermination.

Works Cited

Barthes, Roland. *Roland Barthes by Roland Barthes*. Translated by Richard Howard, U of California P, 1994.

Benjamin, Walter. "On the Mimetic Faculty." *Reflections*. Translated by Edmund Jephcott, edited by Peter Demetz, Schocken Books, 1986.

———. "On Language as Such and on the Languages of Man." *Selected Writings 1913–1926*, edited by Marcus Bullock and Michael W. Jennings, vol. 1, Harvard UP, 1996, pp. 62–74.

Bernstein, Michael André. *Foregone Conclusions: Against Apocalyptic History*. U of California P, 1994.

Cooke, Rachel. "David Vann: 'I was filled with rage. For three years I said my father had died of cancer.'" *The Guardian*, 2 January 2011, https://www.theguardian.com/books/2011/jan/02/david-vann-caribou-island-interview.

Fitzgerald, Scott F. *The Great Gatsby*. Penguin Books, 1981.

Heller-Roazen, Daniel. Introduction. "Editor's Introduction: 'To Read What Was Never Written.'" *Potentialities: Collected Essays in Philosophy*, edited by Giorgio Agamben, Stanford UP, 1999, pp. 1–23.

Levy, Gabriel. "Prophecy, Written Language, and the Mimetic Faculty: Benjamin's Linguistic Mysticism as Cure of the 'Language Myth.'" *Epoché: The University of California Journal for the Study of Religion*, vol. 26, 2006, pp. 19–48.

Orr, David. *Earth in Mind: On Education, Environment, and the Human Prospect*. Island Press, 2004.

Vann, David. "American Inferno." *The Guardian*, 14 November 2009, https://www.theguardian.com/books/2009/nov/14/david-vann-cormac-mccarthy?INTCMP=SRCH.

———. *Aquarium.* The Text Publishing Company, 2015.

———. *Caribou Island.* Penguin Books, 2011.

———. "David Vann: An Ode to Literary Tradition." *The Wheeler Centre: Books, Writing, Ideas,* 27 February 2014, http://www.wheelercentre.com/broadcasts/lunchbox-soapbox-david-vann-an-ode-to-literary-tradition.

———. "Ink." *Shortlist,* http://www.shortlist.com/entertainment/books/ink-by-david-vann.

———. *A Mile Down: The True Story of a Disastrous Career at Sea,* Windmill Books, 2005.

———. "Sukkwan Island." *Legend of a Suicide: Stories.* Collins Publishers, 2010, pp. 36–134.

Watts, Michael. "Petro-Violence: Community, Extraction, and Political Ecology of a Mythic Commodity." *Violent Environments,* edited by Nancy Lee Peluso and Michael Watts, Cornell UP, 2001, pp. 189–212.

Wood, Sarah. *Without Mastery: Reading and Other Forces.* Edinburgh UP, 2014.

Water-Blind

Erosion and (Re)Generation in Colm Tóibín's *The Heather Blazing*

JULIENNE H. EMPRIC

REPRESENTATIONS of water have served literary art across cultures for millennia—in realistic images that add texture to settings and landscapes, and as metaphors and symbols, enhancing events and characters with the resonance of universal themes such as power, threat, purification, obliteration, passage and rites of passage, life and death, infinity and eternity. This dual function of water in literary contexts has singular and longstanding relevance to island nations, as apparent from the epics and tragedies of ancient Greece and the ocean voyage narratives of early England and Ireland. More recent Irish literary masters like Lady Augusta Gregory, John Millington Synge, William Butler Yeats, and James Joyce have built upon this tradition, deploying seascapes and marine elements to channel mythological power, ballast concepts of emerging Irish nationhood, and plumb psychological complexity. The sea circumscribes and in many ways defines Ireland, a relatively compact island that has for centuries endured trials of colonization and postcolonial division, of romanticizing and exploiting, an island where threats of isolation and stagnation vie with the perils of hemorrhaging emigration, to stunt potential regenerative forces. Contemporary authors and critics continue these originary models and critique them, often enabling marine elements to illuminate life in the twenty-first century, when pressing awareness of water as an endangered resource inscribes itself upon these traditional tropes. In the postmodern world, the luxury of imagining

water as an infinite resource—a fantasy supported by the apparent vast-
ness of the sea—is chastened by increasing awareness of its scarcity and
commodification. The lament of Coleridge's Ancient Mariner, stranded
at sea and finding "Water, water, everywhere / Nor any drop to drink,"
today takes on apocalyptic significance.

The fiction of contemporary Irish author Colm Tóibín resonates
with images of the sea and marine elements. He sets several of his
works, in whole or part, along the coast of County Wexford in southeast Ireland, a seascape he knows intimately, as he himself was raised
there and regularly returns (Tóibín, Interview). This coastline, like
Tóibín's prose, is "sparse, understated, . . . deceptively simple" ("Tóibín,
Colm"). Even at its roughest, the Irish Sea at Cush is never breathtak-
ing like the open waters off Ireland's west coast. Instead, "there is a sort
of mildness in the landscape. There are no vast and dramatic conflicts
in the way the waves break or the wind roars" (Tóibín, "No One").
Such a seascape suggests a natural world that is stable and unthreaten-
ing, where change can go unnoticed, and environmental threat can be
ignored. The cliffs rising along a part of this shoreline are composed
of marl and sand, not of limestone, as in the west, making them softer,
thus more vulnerable to erosion by waves, wind, and rain. This coastal
strand, providing a view of the gray sea and horizon on one side and
arching cliffs with their continuously eroding surfaces on the other,
recurs in Tóibín's fiction, and is key to understanding the centrality of
water as an agent for recognition and regeneration in his work.

In Tóibín's novels, the vast open sea functions ambiguously. In *The
South* (1990), the central character exiles herself from Ireland, in an
effort to cure an unspecified *malaise*, only to be drawn home years
later. In the more recent *Brooklyn* (2009), also a feature film (*Brooklyn*,
2015), a young female protagonist sets sail for America in hopes of a
better life, but on a brief return home, finds herself emotionally paralyzed, unable to leave. In these works, the sea, as a literal aspect of setting, offers freedom from insularity, while at the same time fracturing
families, communities, and identities. Ironically, despite the promise
attached to going abroad, insight always waits upon a return home.

The narrow strip of sea hugging the Irish coastline at Cush, while
much smaller, carries far greater significance in Tóibín's work. On the

surface, although its gray cold might repel strangers, it offers its natives familiar comforts. It rewards the stamina of the solitary swimmer, willing to brave its bone-chilling temperatures, and it releases the inhibitions and fosters the romantic union of couples seeking its sensual pleasures. On a deeper level, the sea at Cush and its elements—waves, sea wind, rain, and erosion—are catalysts for hardship, loss, and disturbing realizations. In this, Tóibín's use of marine elements channels and transforms the power of ancient Greek tragedy, where a flawed human subject confronts cosmic forces, then submits and usually succumbs to the clarifying experience of trauma, and in the process attains wisdom. While Tóibín explicitly appropriates ancient tragedy in his recent retelling of the cursed family of Agamemnon, *House of Names* (2017), even his earliest novels feature protagonists who closely resemble Greek tragic heroes, powerful and privileged figures who harbor a hubris and complacency that blinds them to the need for humility and human responsiveness. Like their Greek forebears, they endure intense suffering, but in Tóibín's rendering, pain and recognition ultimately give rise to insight that opens the way to redemption.

The power of the sea to generate change and renewal is particularly significant in Tóibín's first two novels *The South* (1990) and *The Heather Blazing* (1992), works he himself calls "a diptych" ("Afterword" 246). Time and memory imbue both books and, in each, alternating chapters juxtapose present with past in a palimpsest that elucidates experience. Katherine Proctor, the central character in *The South* is an artist who abandons Ireland, her Irish husband, and young son for Spain. As an artist, she is particularly sensitive to what she sees, so the narrative consciously elevates visual aspects of setting. Before leaving Ireland, Katherine suffers from an unspecified frustration, evident in her attempts to paint the River Slaney as seen from the window of her ancestral home, "knowing that no matter how intensely she watched this scene and studied it ... she would never get it right" (Tóibín, *South* 37). While she paints, a woman—possibly a beggar—passes haltingly in the distance. Katherine's response likens her to a figure from Greek tragedy, dwarfed by the setting: "She looked back at the watercolour to see if she could include the figure of the woman, but the scale was too small, the figure could only be a brushstroke, a fleck" (Tóibín, *South*

37). The mysterious woman, in fact, becomes the harbinger of tragedy when Katherine's husband brings a lawsuit against her, an act that precipitates Katherine's abandonment of Ireland. But this early attention to scope and scale is prescient. Although this novel seems like a mosaic of small watercolors, surfacing at regular intervals is a cosmic canvas, broaching the age-old question about the proper place for humans in this universe. In Greek tragedy—in the outdoor theatre at Delphi, for example—the human figure would appear dwarfed against the immensity of the mountains and sea, establishing a perspective that the tragic hero would eventually be forced to concede, where human supremacy with its control over others, human and inhuman, is a dangerous illusion.

In Tóibín's novel, Katherine flees to Barcelona and the Pyrenees for more than a decade but, despite the sunnier climate, to her the mountain landscape appears gargantuan, dark, impassive: "She noticed more and more how the colour of the stone in the houses matched the colour of the rock almost exactly. . . . The houses could have been caves, so closely were they related to the surrounding rock" (Tóibín, *South* 72). Human structures and the civilization they represent seem to stand in only temporary relief from the stone, pending inevitable disintegration and oblivion. While there is no sea in Katherine's experience of Spain, her time there is framed by repeated episodes of being kept awake by "the sound of water rushing rushing from the small hills above them down into the valley" (Tóibín, *South* 81). The apparent indifference of nature is oddly comforting; however, the rushing water keeping her awake also prepares Katherine for an awakening, when she hears her lover finally divulge the brutality used by both fascist and anti-fascist forces—himself included—during the Spanish Civil War, a decade earlier.

Shortly after this disturbing revelation, Katherine imagines a similar vision of human cruelty. Coming upon a simple scene of workmen felling trees, she feels an "unsettling of nature at its source. . . . What was left behind resembled a battle scene: stumps of trees, blocks of wood, . . . an oasis of hurt" (Tóibín, *South* 92). As she contemplates painting this scene, her memory connects it to images of First World War art, "pictures of landscape as wreck, as a place where men died brutally and cruelly, . . . in which the violence was done to the natural order, to animals, to birds and insects, to fields and flowers" (Tóibín, *South* 92). Before now, Katherine has managed to distance herself from feeling, something typical of Tóibín's central characters. Her life as an artist and as one of the privileged class has insulated her from involvement and responsibility. In this moment, what arrests her is the demise of humans overlaid by the ravaging of the natural order, and through this biocentric realization—that humans are no more valuable than any other living thing and that only they are guilty of conscious cruelty— Katherine's path to insight begins. When her lover Miguel goes miss- ing, she has a further realization: "He was another being amongst all the life out there, a small element, as important as a tree in the grand sweep of things. Neither his consciousness nor hers were of any signif- icance" (Tóibín, *South* 157). This acknowledgment of human insignif- icance effectively reduces Miguel, Katherine—*all* humans to "a brush stroke, a fleck."

Soon after, Miguel and their young daughter die in an accident and Katherine is slowly drawn back to Wexford. If the mountains of Spain precipitated her enlightenment, only the "dull grey light on the gun- metal sea" of home (Tóibín, *South* 208) can make it permanent. Tóibín actually entitles the chapter of Katherine's homecoming "The Sea," and she abandons herself to it as to a lost friend. She compulsively paints this sea, walks along it for miles, plunges into it despite the cold, tests who she is against it. And along its shore, in a climactic confessional moment, her longtime friend and compatriot Michael Graves reveals to her that she, too, is complicit in the violence that humans perpetrate. She lives in unacknowledged fear of those unlike her, those of the un- derclass—those like him, an impoverished Irish Catholic who narrowly escaped death from tuberculosis, the typical plight of the Irish poor. As she internalizes this, Katherine recalls the woman of long ago, whom she excluded from her landscape as only "a brushstroke, a fleck," not worth changing the scale of her painting for.

In Tóibín's understated prose, Katherine has this recognition only obliquely. But afterward, as she stands before the sea at Cush, she *sees* differently, and she channels this new insight into transforming her art. Compelled to paint in ways she has never before imagined, she moves beyond safe window views and lucrative watercolors and, like some Lady of Shalott who gazes upon reality but lives, she is driven right onto the shore, to confront the sea and to paint it in oils on an immense canvas. In Spain's mountains Katherine had a biocentric vision of the equality of all living things and the relative insignificance of humans. In a return to Ireland, she is empowered to accept personal responsibility for engaging with the world. Her cultural and class blindness undergoes a ritual cleansing on the shores of the Irish Sea, and she sees—as if for the first time—directly, without filters. This new vision manifests in gigantic paintings (six feet by four) that foreground her insignificance: "'I want you to stop saying I'm working on too large a scale,'" she tells Michael Graves. "'I know I'm working on too large a scale'" (Tóibín, *South* 210).

Katherine has a gallery show in Dublin the following spring, featuring sixteen of these immense paintings. In a downstairs wing, she hangs some of her earlier watercolors, now described as "the small modest images of sand, sea and sky, muted, almost colourless. They made no statement, they tried nothing new, nobody could dislike them. They were competent; they had ease" (Tóibín, *South* 225–26). These watercolors are no match for Katherine's recent paintings of the Irish Sea and of the River Slaney. Now she paints

> as though she was trying to catch the landscape rolling backwards into history, as though horizon was a time as well as a place. . . . Dusk on the Slaney and the sense of all dusks that have come and gone in one spot, in one country, the time it was painted to stand for all time, with all time's ambiguities. (Tóibín, *South* 220–21)

These oil paintings capture for her a new freedom and the responsibility to see better, to accept the "other," to own the human violence symbolized by war and logging, but also to act in the world through the integrity of her art. Tóibín here explicitly foregrounds the dawning of an ethical sense of history. But such a realization and the positive human agency it spawns are also intimately bound to a relationship with an implacable and disinterested environment, the instrumentality of which his characters and even the author seem far less conscious of.

The same stretch of shore at Cush Gap in County Wexford that engenders Katherine's enlightenment in *The South*, recurs in Tóibín's other

Wexford works, especially its companion piece, *The Heather Blazing*. In this second novel, water imagery is dominant, captured in unforgettable images of erosion, immersion, cleansing, and healing, leading again to new perspectives, insight, and agency. Here, the main character, Eamon Redmond, is a High Court judge of retirement age, whose life has been blindingly successful, and who has a love/hate relationship with the sea. Like the cold he persuades himself to endure before his swims become pleasurable and revitalizing, the sea from the first requires that Eamon disrupt comfortable patterns to engage the potential for genuine renewal. Through the ordeal of Eamon, Tóibín suggests that such disruption is essential for life to continue and flourish. For most of his sixty-odd years, disruption has held limited sway in Eamon's life, shaped as it was under the careful management of his father—a history teacher, a quiet authoritarian, and a political activist, whose expectations of his son are prescriptive and absolute. The geographical setting of the novel reinforces this containment, restricting Eamon's world to one small triangle of Ireland: the southeastern town of Enniscorthy, where Eamon and his father live; the coastal village of Cush, where they spend summers; and Dublin, where Eamon later works. The novel's alternating chapters suggest parallels between his years as a studious, sheltered boy and young man, and his years as a judge to whom people defer. Dublin is the emblem of his success—at university, as a young attorney, and now as a High Court judge. The summerhouse at Cush, with its strand along the Irish Sea at Cush Gap, will become the site of his vulnerability, the locus for traumatic disruption.

Still more than in *The South*, instances of water and water-related phenomena imbue this novel, all the more apparent, given the remarkably few examples of other nature imagery. The first images in the novel are of water, as Judge Redmond gazes out from his Dublin chambers at the dark and muddy river, a clogged artery in the city's center. Even as he braces himself for a challenging day in court, with a weighty judicial opinion to deliver, his mind wanders to his journey later that day to the seaside at Cush for the summer recess. Rain or drizzle are always occurring or threatening, and related images tinge the light, the air, and the land: dark clouds, dampness, mist, haze, wetlands, dikes, a silted harbor. The rivers of these settings—the Liffey and the Slaney—are granted recurring importance, though no names. They are, however, entities marking boundaries and serving human purposes—navigable, bridgeable, especially by comparison to the monolithic significance of the open sea at Cush, a site that Tóibín himself holds as dearly as does his protagonist (Tóibín, Interview).

Early in the novel, Eamon is informed that a house near his family's cottage at Cush has suffered the shearing away of an entire wall, the result of encroaching erosion. Like much else in the novel, Tóibín draws this detail from real life, as he notes in a nonfictional piece on Wexford:

> There is the line of strand that stretches down the east of the county. . . . There is nothing dramatic about this landscape; there are no rocks or crashing waves. It varies and becomes softer as you move south, the marly cliffs become sand dunes.
>
> ... There is erosion here, the soil is soft and ready to dissolve, just as the line between the sea itself and the horizon seems soft and ready to dissolve. ("No One")

Many critics acknowledge erosion as a significant motif in Tóibín's work, most often symbolizing historical necessity and personal consciousness. Oona Frawley, for instance, sees coastal erosion as standing for gaps in history and memory, undermining certainties of the past, both cultural and personal (74). Neil Corcoran associates it with a society losing permanent hold of cherished ideals (98). Mary Fitzgerald-Hoyt connects it with the instability of the images and language that shape history—the Irish republican narrative that Eamon cherishes, and that he uses to conceal his own "eroding sense of self" (118). Liam Harte sees Tóibín's shifting landscapes as emblematizing ambiguity, projecting a way to explore what Ireland might become, if freed from the "calcified ideologies" of its nationalistic past (339). The sea and the eroding cliffside, images that recur in this novel, are clearly more than literal aspects of setting. While their most obvious metaphoric tenor might be the sloughing off of fossilized mythic, historic, religious, and legal narratives, given the ubiquity of water references and the dominant role of the sea, the imagery deserves environmental scrutiny as well.

By Tóibín's own admission, he intended the sea in *The Heather Blazing* to be viewed as an *actual* element in Wexford, and erosion at Cush as a naturally occurring process, *not* as a metaphor ("Afterword"

247). However, global concern for the environment—a process already gaining momentum when Tóibín began writing—prompts consideration of how an ecocritical perspective might inform a reading of this novel. First, regarding the actual facts of erosion at Cush: to whatever extent Tóibín knew this, the gradual disappearance of cliffsides on the Cush coastline is not primarily the result of the sea. In 1989, three years before the publication of *The Heather Blazing*, coastal environmentalist Bill Carter explained erosion as inevitable, given the glacial composition of the Irish coast, naturally vulnerable to wind and waves. However, he also noted that much of the erosion of the past century has been caused by humans—specifically, in Cush Gap, from roof run-off producing gullying, and from human activity such as pedestrian trampling, resulting in dune degradation (411–12). These facts complicate how erosion may be understood in the novel. On a grand scale, the phenomenon of erosion is a slowly ongoing natural system. However, the destructive and threatening aspects of accelerated erosion at Cush—beginning with nineteenth-century land reclamation "protection" schemes for Wexford Harbor, and increasing with the post-war leisure industry of transient vacationers and mobile home parks (Carter 407)—are due to oblivious, inept, or self-serving *human* activity. Aside, then, from its value as a historical metaphor, erosion and the water-related images associated with it can point quite directly to present and future environmental awareness. And metaphorically, the dominant imagery of eroding cliffs and the resulting wounds in the land that Eamon confronts in *The Heather Blazing* come to stand for his purgatory, even as the sea will generate his enlightenment, and his new agency in a world desperate to outgrow its blind ways.

It is specifically upon the human agency of a powerful but flawed male figure that Tóibín trains his spotlight in *The Heather Blazing*. As the novel opens Judge Eamon Redmond is at the apex of his power. Alternating chapters, however, reveal how the young Eamon, shaped by an intense familial past, is increasingly entrapped by success. The voice of the patriarchy that he is groomed to inherit is univocal, representing the authority of a single parent, and a family with a single allegiance to republican Irish ideals and Roman Catholic beliefs. Eamon is as good at internalizing this voice as he is at being the best student in school.

Among the many ironies in the novel is that the product of a rebel family is this docile boy who toes the party line. As he listens to the retelling of his family's dramatic history, he seems to have lived it—the nationalist insurrections, evictions, internments, and subterfuge arsons of Ireland in the early twentieth century. The result of his unquestioning loyalty to this narrative is the evolution of Eamon as a person without agency, and a High Court judge unable to authentically listen before judging.

As Tóibín structures the novel, Eamon's lack of agency emerges, ironically, alongside his judicial decisions, the site of his power. In fact, the first mention of erosion in Cush occurs as Eamon publishes a judgment in a controversial court case, in which he has concluded that the state has no ultimate responsibility for the medical welfare of a handicapped child (Tóibín, *Heather* 6–8). Precisely as he nervously considers his progressive family's reaction to this ruling, his wife mentions that the front of their neighbor's house at Cush has just fallen into the sea (Tóibín, *Heather* 30–31). Eamon listens absentmindedly. His position and self-importance frees him from the need to be troubled with the affairs of others. Given the advancing cliff erosion responsible for the incident, their own summerhouse is genuinely at risk, but Eamon's wry quip dismisses the news: "Our house is next" (Tóibín, *Heather* 31). Unlike his neighbors' houses, Eamon's is only a vacation home; he is insulated from the threat of homelessness, and does not trouble himself about the causes or consequences of this erosion for others or for the natural world. That afternoon, he ventures out for a walk and comes face to face with the damage:

> . . . The entire front of the house was missing. The land around jutted out on both sides. . . . It was strange too how the small house had been singled out by the erosion. It seemed unlucky and hard to understand. . . .
>
> It had been so gradual this erosion, a matter of time, lumps of clay, small boulders studded with stones becoming loose and falling away, the sea gnawing at the land. It was all so strange, year after year, the slow disappearance of one contour to be replaced by another, it was hard to notice that anything had happened until something substantial, like [a] house, fell down on to the strand. (Tóibín, *Heather* 32)

The vision is tragic—something "small" and yet "substantial" has been singled out by fate. The sea here is personified, like some figure out of Dante's *Inferno*, not only successfully "gnawing at" the land but dismantling a house, a symbol of human culture, until, in a particularly insidious way, it precipitates catastrophe.

As he continues his walk along the shore, the visual image of erosion gives way to the noise of small stones, clattering then retreating, and he finds the sound "oddly comforting," even "intimate" (Tóibín, *Heather* 33). The irony of his comfortable response escapes him. The pebbles are all that's left of the stone-studded mud boulders that have rolled down the cliff, regurgitated from the gullet of the land-gnawing sea. Although his first-class education likely introduced him to it, Eamon does not remember that this sound was immortalized a hundred years earlier along an English coastline at Dover Beach, where Victorian poet Matthew Arnold imagined the Greek tragic dramatist Sophocles, walking along the Aegean hearing "... the grating roar / Of pebbles which the waves draw back, and fling, / At their return, up the high strand...." For Sophocles, this sound is identified with "the turbid ebb and flow / Of human misery." For Arnold, it represents the ebbing of a bygone "Sea of Faith," leaving only human love and faithfulness as potential defenses against existential terrors. These pebbles are persistent, timeless reminders of multiple levels of erosive power, but Eamon, in his myopia, lives only in the shallow moment:

> Some mud boulders had rolled down from the cliff and were standing at the bottom; it would be only a short time before the sea would roll up and dissolve them. As he looked up he saw that all the time fine grains of sand were being blown down the cliff face. (Tóibín, *Heather* 34)

This scene of dissolution is prelude to exposing the relentlessly recurring erosions in Eamon's life. There are the losses of his boyhood: the very early loss of his mother; the deaths of his grandfather and uncle, and his grandmother's permanent withdrawal from Eamon's need for comfort, to nurse her own grief; the embarrassment and devastation caused by his father's stroke, difficult recovery, and death. Still more significant, although unacknowledged, are the losses of the older Eamon, specifically, the long estrangement from his family—his son Donal, who is politically active for liberal causes, his daughter Niamh, an unwed mother, and his infant grandson Michael, who screams whenever he looks at him. But by far the most devastating erosive disruption that Eamon encounters comes in the form of another stroke that afflicts his wife Carmel, his only connection to a personal world. Carmel has been the tempering figure in his life, serving as go-between and enabler in Eamon's relationships, especially with their own children.

To a degree, Eamon recognizes the serious impact of Carmel's illness on his life, but he has no idea of the disruption that awaits him. Secure in blind privilege, he takes Carmel for granted just as he does the cliffs and the sea, simply assuming she will always be there to serve his needs. And it is again in proximity to the sea at Cush that insight occurs. From the point of Carmel's stroke to the end of the novel, the sea is the primary force that Eamon relates to. In late autumn, Carmel attempts a slow recuperation in the house at Cush where the stroke occurred. Eamon, on leave from court duties, ventures out for his usual walk along the sea. Again he hears the small stones, this time, as winter approaches, finding their sound "harder, ... more brittle and hollow" (Tóibín, *Heather* 148) than before. The cliffs have been battered by storm, huge mud boulders have tumbled down, and the outer sheds of another neighbor's place have fallen, or are hanging off the cliff (Tóibín, *Heather* 149). As he heads up the gap toward home in pouring rain with the sea at his back, he sees Carmel in distress, limping toward him. The effects of her stroke have worsened and she has soiled herself. In a moving scene in which water seems to rise to something sacramental, he walks her home and lovingly bathes her while she weeps. She does not live long after, and with this loss Eamon experiences a cataclysmic personal erosion that mirrors the natural one affecting the cliffs at Cush. While this sequence of events might represent a recognition comparable to Katherine Proctor's, for Eamon it is only the beginning. Even as he tends Carmel over the weeks of her dying he cannot loosen the strictures of his past, cannot open up, as she herself tells him:

> "I feel I don't know you at all," she said. Her speech was slurred, even more than usual, but he had no difficulty understanding what she said.

"You've always been so distant, so far away from everybody. It is so hard to know you, you let me see so little of you. I watch you sometimes and wonder if you will ever let any of us know you."

"I'm trying to help you all day," he said.

"You don't love me." She put her arms around him. "You don't love any of us.

... Eamon are you listening to me? ... " (Tóibín, *Heather* 152–53)

This is not the first time Carmel has tried to broach Eamon's emotional distance. Throughout, however, his ingrained values and self-sufficient *hubris* prevent him from the possibility of new perspectives that include the needs of others in more than a superficial way. Here, he promises to consider what she's said, but goes off alone to stare into the night sea.

Carmel's death in the winter is the understated turning point of the novel, the primary erosion that at last seizes Eamon's attention and precipitates his change. The first evidence of this occurs as the extended family drives to the cemetery. Carmel's sisters begin to chant the rosary, an established ritual that the earlier Eamon would have endured without question. Now, sensing that this loss concerns more than just himself, he directs the women to pray silently, because he does not want his children, who have distanced themselves from such prescribed customs, to be disturbed. His reward is immediate: at the graveside his children huddle close to him, and "he felt a bond with [them] for the first time in his life" (Tóibín, *Heather* 183).

After the funeral, unable to discard old ways, Eamon regresses, throwing himself into work in Dublin. But further epiphanies have merely been deferred until he takes his usual summer holiday at Cush. There he comes to see that Carmel's illness and death are the "something substantial" (Tóibín, *Heather* 32) of his personal erosion, forcing him to confront that the contours of his life are forever changed, and that he must abandon the patterns that have cobbled him. Even though his summerhouse is still not on the edge of the eroding cliff, he cannot bring himself to enter it, but is compelled by abject misery to lose himself to the elements in a forced march along the shore, the sea his only companion. Each day, from sunrise until after dark, he trudges up and down the coast until his feet bleed, his legs and neck throb in pain, and he is entirely spent. He pauses only briefly to eat and to swim, willing himself not to rest, saving up for what sleep he can steal late at night, in his car. In this he resembles Shakespeare's King Lear, in a storm on the heath, his *hubris* finally chastened, becoming pregnant to pity for those creatures he took too little care of (3.4.8–41). Except that for Eamon there is no storm, there is only the steady, relentless presence of the sea. He is finally forced inside by the arrival of his daughter, who, unable to reach him, is concerned for her father's mental health. This time, he clumsily tries to address her needs, even offering to care for his grandson, an action requiring him to forgo the empowered male role he has lived in so comfortably, for so long. As he plays with Michael, a difficult child with whom he has had no positive interactions, he patiently begins to subordinate his own ego and to listen for what the toddler needs.

The final episode in the novel, as Eamon tends his grandson, recalls the climactic scene from John Millington Synge's Irish masterpiece, "Riders to the Sea" (1904). In this play Maurya, an old woman from the Aran Islands off Ireland's west coast, has lost all the men in her family to incidents at sea. As she blesses the remains of her youngest sons, she empties over them the portion of holy water cherished in every Catholic household as a protection against evil, then turns the cup upside down, declaring that she will no longer have reason to replenish the supply, for there's nothing more the sea can do to her. Having fought heroically against her mighty opponent in an attempt to keep her men from the sea, she now submits, in tragic recognition of her place as a mortal in the universe (Synge 97). There is poignant irony here in Maurya's prior naive faith that a "sup" of holy water might overcome the power of the vast sea. In her subsequent withdrawal from life, she is like Eamon's grandmother who, after the deaths of her men, recoils, prohibiting anyone from touching her ever again. Such tragic resignation could be Eamon's choice as well, given his affinity for solitude and emotional restraint, but it is not. His erosive experiences are, finally, positive, moving beyond tragedy, as they wear down the barricades of fear and success that have trapped him for sixty years. Erosion, unlike more dramatic natural phenomena (blazing heather, for instance), is gradual, stealthy, but—when actively noticed—is something that can be prepared for or managed, the regenerative possibilities of its natural cycles acknowledged and encouraged. Beyond its power for destruction, erosion offers a compensatory cleansing, imaged in the pebbles that the waves return to shore, and the resilience implicit in the ever-changing seascape. As an aspect of nature, erosion accomplishes this as a matter of course, without premeditation or plan. By contrast, the erosion caused by human activity is, at best, inadvertent; at worst, it is a function of myopic greed and ambition. As multiple critics have argued, Colm Tóibín writes his novels with the conscious intention to bring greater honesty to history and memory, and greater freedom to the culture rooted in these stories. A part of this history, perhaps as little obvious to Tóibín as it is to Eamon Redmond, is recognizing the ways in which the willful blindness contributing to personal disintegration is mirrored in the accelerated erosion of the Cush shoreline.

As he begins to listen authentically, and to genuinely respond to others, Eamon too becomes a site for renewal, and his grandson Michael, even while he bears the name of Eamon's intractable father, betokens hope for the future. With a grandfather willing at last to listen and adapt, this new Michael Redmond will be better able to fly by the constrictive patriarchal nets that would entrap his soul, as they had his grandfather's for so long. The action of the sea and its eroding forces do not here result in the death-in-life they held for Maurya or for Eamon's grandmother. While the change that occurs in Eamon is subtle, as is typical of Tóibín's writing, it is nonetheless clear. It bodes for a future mindful of human proportion and perspective where presumption, arrogance, and domination are checked, and where relationships—including those with the natural world—may be nurtured.

In the final scene of the novel, unlike his father who brusquely introduced him to the sea, Eamon is at last patient and responsive, subduing his own ego, listening closely for what his grandson might accept or enjoy. He honors Carmel by repeating what she did with their own children: he quietly, patiently provides young Michael with a basin of water and cups, and stands back to watch, as the child learns by himself to delight in water play. Then, listening deeply for the toddler's preferences and needs, he picks him up and tenderly introduces him to the open sea, wading in gradually, only as far as the child is comfortable. As a quasi-baptism, this action is life-affirming: while there is no cup of holy water here, there is quite literally the hope of regeneration, as Eamon breaks with patterns of blindness and control, to both manifest and model for his grandson the potential for humans to endure, to adapt, to learn.

Although images of water pervade his novels, Tóibín is not explicitly addressing Irish or global policies of pollution or conservation in his work. However, his water imagery works powerfully to expose and erode the blinding *hubris*, inattention, and entrenched authority of the protagonist, who serves as a stand-in for his species. In ancient tragedy, catastrophic experience and suffering are necessary to effect wisdom and to reverse the momentum of destructive human action and neglect. Through Eamon Redmond's experience with the sea, Tóibín offers cathartic instruction about the place of humans in the universe, a place of humility, awareness, and authentic responsiveness to others, including the natural world, increasingly threatened by oblivious, inept, and self-serving human activity. As in the full arc of Greek tragedy evident in Sophocles' last play, when the erring and blinded Oedipus is at last purified and redeemed at Colonus, here too there is hope.

Works Cited

Arnold, Matthew. "Dover Beach." *Poetry Foundation*, Poetry Foundation, www.poetryfoundation.org/poems-and-poets/poems/detail/43588. Accessed 26 March 2017.

Brooklyn. Directed by John Crowley, Fox Searchlight Pictures, 2015.

Carter, Bill. "Resources and management of Irish Coastal Waters and Adjacent Coasts." *Ireland: Contemporary Perspectives on a Land and Its People*, edited by R. W. G. Carter and A. J. Parker, Routledge, 1989, pp. 393–418.

Coleridge, Samuel Taylor. "The Rime of the Ancient Mariner." *The Oxford Book of English Verse*, edited by Sir Arthur Thomas Quiller-Couch, Clarendon, 1919. Bartleby.com, 1999, www.bartleby.com/101/. Accessed 27 March 2017.

Corcoran, Neil. *After Yeats and Joyce: Reading Modern Irish Literature*. Oxford UP, 1997.

Fitzgerald-Hoyt, Mary. "Inventing Enniscorthy: Colm Tóibín's *The Heather Blazing*." *Nua: Studies in Contemporary Irish Writing*, vol. 2, no.1–2, 1998–99, pp. 113-23.

Frawley, Oona. "'The Difficult Work of Remembering': Tóibín and Cultural Memory." *Reading Colm Tóibín*, edited by Paul Delaney, Liffey, 2008, pp. 69–82.

Harte, Liam. "'The Endless Mutation of the Shore': Colm Tóibín's Marine Imaginary." *Critique*, vol. 51, no. 4, 2010, pp. 333–49.

Shakespeare, William. *The Tragedy of King Lear*. Edited by Barbara Mowatt and

Paul Werstine. *Folger Shakespeare Library*, 2010. folgerdigitaltexts.org/html/ Lr.html#line-4.6.0. Accessed 12 January 2017.

Synge, John Millington. "Riders to the Sea." *The Complete Plays of John M. Synge.* Vintage, 1960, pp. 81–97.

Tóibín, Colm. "Afterword." *The Heather Blazing*, pp. 243–48.

———. *Brooklyn.* 2009. Scribner, 2015.

———. *The Heather Blazing.* Pan, 1992 / Scribner, 2012.

———. *House of Names.* Scribner, 2017.

———. Interview by Jenny McCartney, *The Spectator*, 24 Oct. 2015, www.spectator. co.uk/2015/10/colm-Tóibín-on-priests-loss-and-the-half-said-thing/. Accessed 15 January 2017.

———. "No One Ever Asked Us to Go Home" *Irish Times*, 9 Aug. 2011, www.irishtimes.com/culture/books/no-one-ever-asked-us-to-go-home-1.593165. Accessed 20 November 2016.

———. *The South.* Serpent's Tail, 1990 / Picador, 1992.

"Tóibín, Colm." *The Continuum Encyclopedia of British Literature*, 2003.

PART 2

Water Cultures

Nations, Borders, and Water Wars

A Clash of Water Cultures
in John Nichols's
The Milagro Beanfield War

SUSAN J. TYBURSKI

> If I am not for myself, who will be for me?
> Yet if I am for myself only, what am I?
> —Hillel

THIS QUOTATION by the Jewish sage and scholar Hillel the Elder, which appears as a frontispiece for John Nichols's *The Milagro Beanfield War*, encapsulates the tension between individualist and collectivist cultures at the heart of this novel. Originally published in 1974, Nichols's novel builds an engagingly subversive story around a struggling Hispanic farmer and handyman in northern New Mexico named Joe Mondragón who illegally clears and diverts water from a "long unused" irrigation ditch into a beanfield formerly owned by his deceased parents (25). This simple act of defiance serves as the catalyst for his neighbors to come together and, covertly but effectively, take action to preserve their land and their way of life against threatened appropriation by Anglo land developers and government officials. In the course of this narrative, Nichols explores northern New Mexico's acequia culture, and contrasts its communal approach to water management with the edicts of a capitalist legal system encouraging and rewarding individual initiative and profit. This contraposition reveals the benefits of the acequia system, which nurtures communities rooted in cooperation and mutual thriving, and promotes sustainable stewardship and equitable distribution of precious natural resources.

Acequias are community irrigation ditches that rely on the natural force of gravity to deliver mountain snowmelt to water users' fields and pastures (Hicks and Peña 391–92). Communities organized around acequias consider water to be a communal resource; its use is based on a fair and balanced consideration of every community water user's needs. In addition to water, acequia communities often hold pasture and forest land in common (Davidson and Guarino 225–26; Hicks and Peña 392).

Acequia culture is rooted in respect for the environment and its rich resources. It developed as an amalgam of the traditional water management and distribution practices of medieval farmers, as well as the practices of indigenous peoples who established pueblos throughout what is now Mexico and the southwestern United States (Worster 75). Reliance on "'la sabiduría del agua' (the inherent knowledge of water) and the 'juicio de la tierra' (the wisdom of the earth)" formed the basis of the environmental ethics practiced in acequia culture. Key principles include adherence to best watering practices, such as ensuring deep root penetration, watering during the cooler parts of the day, and waiting "until the plants 'piden agua' (ask for water), which is when the leaves start to wilt" (Arellano). These customary norms were followed by the acequia communities in the southwestern United States when these lands were part of a Mexican province and, subsequently, the territory of New Mexico, prior to becoming the states of Colorado and New Mexico (Hicks and Peña 399).

The acequia system is rooted in the "concept of *equidad*," which emphasizes the equitable distribution of resources (Arellano). Under this system, water use is distributed fairly according to the amount of water available, and the needs and past practices of the users (Hicks and Peña 392). Local residents may hold rights (*derechos*) to divert and use the water from the irrigation ditches; however, the water itself is not "owned" by any individual. A "*mayordomo*," also known as a "ditch rider" or "ditch boss," manages this communal resource, with the cooperative assistance of the water users or "*parciantes*" (Mendez). The *mayordomo* is democratically elected, and is entrusted with the responsibility of fairly distributing the available water among the *parciantes* according to the customary norms of equitable distribution (Arellano).

A key traditional practice of the acequia system is "shared scarcity": "a common commitment that water is to be shared in times of scarcity" (Hicks and Peña 389). During droughts, water users self-regulate their own use to allow all to share in the available water. Rather than each user taking as much water as possible to maximize his or her personal profit, members of an acequia system consider their neighbors' needs as well as their own. The "commitment to the customary principle of shared scarcity [is] an essential element in assuring long term community survival by offering protection to vulnerable members of the community" (Hicks and Peña 390). This commitment "promotes" not only the survival, but the "common flourishing," of the acequia community as a whole (Hicks and Peña 399).

Another significant acequia practice is spring ditch cleaning, in which all *parciantes* are expected to participate. This practice is often intertwined with Hispanic Catholic religious traditions, so that the ditch cleaning includes a request for a successful harvest from Saint Isidro, patron saint of farmers (Worster 75). As a new resident of New Mexico, John Nichols participated in spring ditch cleaning after accepting an invitation from a local *mayordomo*:

> I had never worked so hard in my life. It wasn't a very long or difficult ditch, but there were about forty of us who worked hard all day long cleaning up that artery, plugging the *perrito* holes, burning the grass, chopping out *jaras*, and cursing the *viejitos* who just leaned on their shovels and every few minutes shouted *"Vuelta!"* (which translates as "forward," but means that the last guy in the line along the ditch comes to the front) . . . that was the first time I met all my neighbors together, and I had a blast, complaining, bitching about the work, listening to filthy jokes, and to all the *chisme* and *mitote* of the neighborhood and Taos. I picked up a lot of history, too. Stories galore. And plenty of laughter. ("'*Sin agua, no hay vida*': Acequia Culture" 203).

Nichols's description of spring ditch cleaning illustrates the communal heart of acequia culture. Everyone contributes to the cleaning work, according to their abilities, and the work is equitably distributed as the line of workers is rotated. In the process of doing this hard

manual labor, stories, jokes, and local history are shared; the workers become bonded to each other and to their acequia community. As
Nichols explains, "water and the local organizations that dispense it are
the blood that keeps our communities alive" ("'*Sin agua, no hay vida*':
Acequia Culture" 211). In addition to the life-giving nourishment water
provides to the community members, their animals, and their crops,
communal management of this precious resource, with its requirement
that all share equitably in the work and the rewards of their water distribution system, binds and strengthens the community as a whole.

In contrast to the communal acequia system of water distribution,
water law in the western United States is based on a system of "prior
appropriation," in which "prior beneficial use establishes a prior right
to water." When water is scarce, "senior" holders of water rights have
priority to fill their established needs before their juniors, or those who
established their water rights later in time (Hicks and Peña 400). This
system of "first come, first served" is based on competition, rewarding
those who acquire their water rights first rather than on cooperation
like the acequia system that ensures the survival and "mutual flourishing" of the community as a whole (Hicks and Peña 399). The rights of
the individual water user take precedence, individual initiative is encouraged, and water becomes a commodity to be traded or sold for individual profit. Distribution of this precious resource is not organically
and democratically determined by the needs of the community as a
whole, as in acequia culture, but is imposed through abstract formulas
by legal institutions and actors unconnected to the lives of the affected
water users and their natural environment. Rather than promoting cooperation and "mutual flourishing," the system of "prior appropriation"
creates rifts between competing water users and disregards the effects
of water distribution on the surrounding community.

Collectivist and individualist approaches to water management
reflect two distinct water cultures arising from divergent human relationships with the natural world. Environmental historian Donald
Worster compares a natural water system, in which water is interwo-
ven into the ecological fabric of its surroundings and follows "its own
integrity and order," with a modern "hydraulic" system arising from
"a sharply alienating, intensely managerial relationship with nature"

(5). Worster explains that a modern concrete, fenced irrigation canal, "unlike a river, is not an ecosystem. It is simplified, abstracted Water, rigidly separated from the earth and firmly directed to raise food, fill pipes, and make money" (5). Such an artificial construct does not inspire loyalty to "a rooted community," but is a sterile "techno-economic order imposed for the purpose of mastering a difficult environment" for "maximum yield, maximum profit" (6–7).

Worster suggests that one's day–to-day relationship with the water where one lives engenders one's values (11). Working with the natural flow of water in an acequia develops not only a respect for, but an appreciation of, the natural world. As Nichols has described, working alongside others to maintain a common irrigation ditch develops a feeling of camaraderie, loyalty to a community, careful stewardship of a shared natural resource, and respectful understanding of the rhythms of nature ("'Sin agua, no hay vida': Acequia Culture" 203). In contrast, treating water as an abstract commodity to be bought and sold for individual profit develops a self-centered cupidity, disregarding the needs of others or of the larger ecological order. According to Worster, the technological appropriation of water divorced from an appreciation of its natural setting creates a coercive, monolithic, and hierarchical system, ruled by a power elite based on the ownership of capital and expertise (7). Removing water from its natural environment and converting it to a commodity within a free market system not only severs its essential role within an ecosystem, but threatens to destroy the cultural traditions and values of the surrounding communities that have been nourished by that water.

This clash of water cultures forms the core of The Milagro Beanfield War, which explores the specter of large-scale development pursued by a predatory Anglo named Ladd Devine III. Nichols describes the ruthless acquisition of land by the Devine Company, which initially began buying up grazing lands from local sheepherders and acquired controlling interests in a number of local businesses. Along the way, Devine acquired water rights that outranked those held by the residents of Milagro (Milagro 22–23). In this environmental morality tale, water becomes a central metaphor. As Milagro's water is slowly and inexorably appropriated by Devine for personal profit, Nichols shows us how the life is slowly drained from the community. Families are no longer able to earn a living, young people leave, and older people remain to eke out an existence in poverty.

Devine ultimately pursues the construction of a dam in the Milagro Valley, obtaining state and federal support for the creation of a conservancy district to fund and manage the dam and the resulting water distribution. The conservancy district and dam constitute "the essential cornerstone of a Devine development endeavor known as the Miracle Valley Recreation Area" (23). In renaming the valley, the Anglo developers plan not only the appropriation of the surrounding landscape and its water, but the elimination of the traditional Spanish name "Milagro" and replacement with the English "Miracle." The effects of this proposed appropriation, accompanied by the creation of the water conservancy district and creation of the dam, golf course, and subdivisions sought by Devine, would have a devastating impact on the Milagro community. Their land values would increase, and the resulting taxes and "conservancy assessments" on their land would create financial obligations impossible for the residents to meet. As a result, they would be forced to sell or forfeit their land, allowing Devine to acquire it for additional development (44). The community members would scatter, and their traditional way of life, rooted in the land and the water, would disappear.

Nichols contrasts the commodification and attempted appropriation of the Milagro Valley water by developer Devine, aided by state government regulation, with the spontaneous liberation of water by Mondragón that rejuvenates his community. Mondragón's initial diversion of water from an unused acequia creates an immediate connection with the natural environment. After freeing the water to irrigate his field, Mondragón stops to enjoy the peace and natural beauty of his surroundings. Milagro is depicted as a seamless part of this landscape. The smoke from his neighbors' cooking fires intermingles and their adobe houses blend into the scenery, creating a visible connection with each other and with their land (25). Mondragón's liberation of water from the regulated system reminds him, and later his neighbors, of what is most important: their love of the land and their community. The free-flowing water becomes not only an essential source of physical sustenance, but of spiritual nourishment, for Mondragón and the other residents of Milagro. Like the spring ditch cleaning in which Nichols participated after moving to New Mexico, fighting for this water brings the Milagro community together. In this way, Nichols demonstrates how water is the communal lifeblood of the acequia community.

Nichols portrays the tension between individualistic and collectivistic cultures not only through the water rights dispute that develops over Mondragón's illegal diversion of water, but through the contrast of the Milagro residents with Devine and his cronies. Nichols's novel opens with the saga of Amarante Córdova, an ancient resident of Milagro whose story reads like an instructive fable. Throughout his long life, Córdova has suffered an endless array of physical ailments, many of which would have felled a younger, healthier individual. As he ages, he continues to live in his crumbling adobe home, in the only room that still has an intact roof. To the amazement of his neighbors, Córdova lives through each new calamity, surviving many of his children; his shuffling figure becomes the stuff of legend throughout Milagro (13–18). His stubborn endurance and love of life in the face of seemingly overwhelming health problems mirrors the town's almost mystical persistence in the face of seemingly insurmountable political and economic challenges.

Córdova uses each new medical emergency to convince his thirteen children, many of which have left Milagro, to return home one last time for Christmas. He revels in these family reunions, which celebrate shared history and serve to rejuvenate him (14–18). Córdova also becomes one of the early supporters of Mondragón and his illegally irrigated beanfield (18–19). During a community meeting called to discuss the water dispute between Mondragón, Devine, and the state government, the ninety-three-year-old Córdova urges his neighbors to fight for Mondragón and for Milagro (145). His audience at the community meeting consists mostly of aging men like himself. Nichols describes them as forces of nature: "Their faces seemed so old, so dark, calling forth overworked clichés about the earth and the sky and the wind. Old, wrinkled, simple, profound" (147). These ancient souls, inextricably linked to their land, their water and their traditional lifestyles, represent the stubborn core of Milagro.

In contrast, Devine and the Anglo government representatives are mystified, and ultimately foiled, by the Milagro community's persistent support of Mondragón and his illegally irrigated beanfield. Toward the end of the novel, an Anglo federal agent, Kyril Montana, is tasked with finding Mondragón, who has gone into hiding following a series of misadventures. Even though Montana would have preferred to work alone, a group of local men, ostensibly loyal to Devine, have been assembled to assist him in searching the nearby mountains for Mondragón. During a rest break, Montana suddenly realizes he is the only one who really wants to find Mondragón, and the others are only there "to keep up some appearances":

> Whereupon Kyril Montana experienced a rare sensation. These men were all Chicanos, and he was a white man, the person theoretically in charge of this search. That's all, it was nothing more than that, but it gave him a start all the same, made him uncomfortable for a minute . . . .up here, high in the wilderness behind Milagro with this lax, motley crew, he experienced a momentary and an almost terrifying race-consciousness, and felt like a foreigner, a real stranger and intruder in their territory. (364)

Montana's revelation underscores the intrinsic differences between his individualistic, predatory approach to the manhunt, and the laconic attitude shared by the other men as they relax and enjoy the natural beauty of the landscape, focusing on what really matters—their relationship to one another, and to the land.

While Montana is searching the nearby mountains for Mondragón, a number of older male residents gather at Mondragón's home, where his wife and children are waiting. When local lawyer Charley Bloom stops by the home to see if he can help Mondragón, he discovers a group of "ten old men, all wearing cowboy hats and faded jeans and work boots or western-style boots, each with a rifle butt held against the floor between his knees," quietly and unobtrusively guarding the family as they watch television with Mondragón's children (366). Like Agent Montana, Bloom is a white man surrounded by the ancient Chicano residents of Milagro, and becomes disoriented: "The guns, the quietude, the serenity of those old geezers, and the idiotic TV program, the enthralled children without a care in the world—it had upset him, he couldn't get his bearings straight" (166). When Bloom tries to persuade Mondragón's wife, Nancy, to tell him where her husband is, Nancy responds:

> Charley, this isn't putting you down, but for many years everybody around has been letting things get settled by the Mr. Devines and . . . people like that. On their terms. Maybe now it's time to decide something for ourselves. On our terms. And in our own sweet time (368).

Bloom is unable to persuade Mondragón's wife and her protectors that his approach—allowing him to try to use the law to assist Mondragón—is the proper one. Instead, the assembled group understands that their power lies in their quiet, stubborn unity; like the local men assisting Montana in his search, they are willing to wait until things work themselves out. As Nancy joins the group in her home watching television, she explains:

> So we're waiting . . . We're waiting for them to make their moves and for them to finish making their moves and for them to go away. If we have to wait a year for them to leave, we'll wait a year. Who's in a hurry? Not us. (369)

Like the landscape on which they live, the old souls of Milagro are determined to endure and outlast the capitalist forces, embodied in the Devine enterprise. Because Devine and his cronies do not share the Milagro community's endurance, rooted in their traditional collectivist values, they will abandon a project that no longer promises a quick, easy profit.

In fighting to preserve what they hold in common, the residents of Milagro transcend their individual differences and desires, and work together toward a "mutual flourishing" that embodies the heart of acequia culture. Nichols's descriptions of Milagro and its residents illustrate the essential connections between water, identity, and culture, rooted in a specific place. Recognizing and respecting these connections gives rise to a "politics of diversity" that provides a creative, constructive alternative to the homogeneous capitalist system dominating the American West. As ecofeminist scholar Vandana Shiva explains: "A politics of diversity that combines the ecological and the cultural does not leave the politics of everyday life to the market and to corporations" (Shiva viii). The anarchic group of characters that inhabit Milagro exemplify such a "politics of diversity," as they come together in a shared appreciation of their water, their land, and their "cultural integrity" (*Milagro* 422).

The quotation by Hillel that opens Nichols's novel anticipates and encapsulates the clash of individualist and collectivist cultures at the center of *The Milagro Beanfield War*. Mondragón's rebellious diversion of water to irrigate his beanfield threatens Devine's development plans by sparking a series of spontaneous protest actions by other Milagro residents. Therefore, even though Mondragón's diversion of water, as a unilateral act, would appear to violate the norms of the communal acequia system, neither the *mayordomo* nor the other Milagro residents take action to dispute his use. Instead, the community of Milagro slowly rallies around Mondragón and his right to irrigate his beanfield in defiance of the state government and Ladd Devine. And that is the *milagro*, or miracle, at the heart of this story: the conversion of an individual act of anarchism into a victory for the collectivistic values of the community.

Nichols's portrayal of the conflict between the Milagro acequia community and the encroaching forces of capitalism arose from personal experience. His interest in political and social issues began when, as a young man, he traveled to Guatemala in 1964, and came face-to-face with the terrible poverty suffered by the indigenous population (Nichols, *American Child* 42–51). Nichols describes this experience as "the Eden apple, the Pandora's box, the world knocking at my door" (46), prompting him to educate himself about political systems and the exploitation of the poor (46–47). Nichols then spent several years in New York City, writing politically charged essays as well as fiction and, with his wife, supporting different causes, including protests against the Vietnam War (*American Child* 51–73). In 1969, Nichols left the east coast with his wife and son, and moved to Taos, New Mexico, where he was sympathetic to the struggles of the indigenous population, "a largely Spanish-speaking (and Indian) group descended from communal traditions antagonistic to more blatant private property and free enterprise shenanigans" (*American Child* 79). This clash of cultures came to a head during a decades-long water management dispute that arose in the Taos valley.

Soon after moving to Taos, Nichols became a vocal supporter of a campaign by the Tres Ríos Association, a group of local residents and water users, to stop the formation of a proposed conservancy district that would manage the construction of a dam in the Taos valley and the resulting distribution of water. Like the fictional residents of Milagro, the proposed conservancy district and dam threatened the traditional acequia cultural practices of small local farmers, who would be subjected to new water regulations, and heavily taxed for the use of water stored by the dam and managed by the district. In this way, small farmers were in danger of losing their land and their way of life when they were unable to pay the increased taxes that would fund the dam. The tensions Nichols observed between the traditional collectivist practices of his adopted community and the competitive profiteering celebrated by American capitalism became the inspiration for *The Milagro Beanfield War* ("Afterword" 450–51).

In exploring this clash of water cultures, *The Milagro Beanfield War* illustrates the role literature can play in educating readers about issues of environmental justice. In 1988, a film version of the novel, directed and partially produced by Robert Redford, was released, making this environmental morality tale even more widespread. In 1989, the film received the first award issued in the "Democracy" category of the Political Film Society, which recognizes "outstanding achievement in raising political consciousness" (Political Film Society). Like Nichols's novel, the film celebrates the collective force of resistance that emerges organically from the increasingly frustrated townspeople of Milagro as they face threats to the land and water in which their community is grounded. The townspeople's quiet, steady rebellion contrasts with, and subverts, the hegemonic control state government authorities and developer Devine desire to impose over the land and water of the Milagro community. In the end, this stubborn, communal resistance wears down the Anglos, who abandon their plans for the conservancy district, the dam, and the development projects, and as Nancy Mondragón predicted, leave town. The film ends with a festive community celebration in the illegally irrigated beanfield, providing a compelling visual depiction of the triumph of collectivist culture over the individualist forces of capitalism.

In addition to serving as the basis for an influential film, Nichols's novel has been "used in high school and college sociology, literature and Chicano studies classes" ("Afterword" 455). A simple Google search reveals posted lesson plans and syllabi incorporating both the novel and the film into explorations of water management systems and southwestern history. In educating the public about environmental issues and raising political consciousness, *The Milagro Beanfield War* has had an impact on water rights disputes in the American Southwest. For example, after years of court battles and public agitation, Nichols and the Tres Ríos Association scored a major victory when the New Mexico Supreme Court ultimately "threw out" the challenged Taos conservancy district ("Afterword" 455). The clash of water cultures depicted in *The Milagro Beanfield War* informs conflicts over water rights that continue throughout the western United States.

In the last several decades, New Mexico and Colorado have recognized the historical and cultural importance of acequias, and ta en steps to improve legal frameworks for the resolution of such water management conflicts. In New Mexico, acequias are recognized as political subdivisions of the state. Federal and state funds are available to preserve, repair, and improve local acequias (New Mexico Office of the State Engineer). In 1987, an Acequia Commission was established to advise government officials concerning issues that arise involving acequias, and to facilitate dialogue between local communities and state and federal governments when conflicts arise (New Mexico Acequia Commission).

In April 2009, the Colorado legislature brought acequias into the existing body of water law by enacting the Acequia Recognition Law, Colorado Revised Statutes Sec. 7-42-101.5 (amended 2013). This statute allows acequia communities to incorporate under Colorado law; the resulting "acequia ditch corporations" may then pass bylaws that set forth their customary communal practices, affording them protection in the dominant legal system. While the acequia corporations may not prohibit the sale or transfer of water use rights outside of the acequia community, they do hold a "right of first refusal." This right allows the acequia corporation to buy water rights for their fair market value before they are otherwise sold or transferred, and thus keep those water rights collectively held by the community (Peña lecture).

The emerging laws in Colorado and New Mexico represent an important compromise between the free market values enshrined in western American water law and the ethics of environmental and social cooperation at the heart of the acequia system, providing a productive path forward for future clashes between these significant water cultures. The construction and maintenance of acequias requires a respectful stewardship of nature, carefully harnessing the natural forces of water and gravity, and distributing it equitably to ensure the survival of the community as a whole. Recognizing and including this collectivist system in our laws is crucial to protect and encourage a responsible, cooperative approach to water management. By providing acequia communities with the official recognition and protection of the law, we legitimize their communal approach to water management and encourage the rest of us to develop a more responsible relationship with our natural resources.

Nichols's novel, as well as the subsequent film on which it is based, demonstrate the essential interconnection between environmental and social justice issues, and the constructive alternatives offered by acequia culture to the corporate commodification and appropriation of water. The role of literature and film in educating us about environmental issues, and alternative approaches to managing water and other natural resources, will continue to be instrumental in helping us navigate future challenges posed by increasing water scarcity in the wake of climate change. As Nichols comments in the 1993 "Afterword" of the paperback edition of *The Milagro Beanfield War*: "Naturally, I hope this book will continue to inspire people and make them laugh. And if in the process it should also encourage them to overthrow the capitalist system, well, why not?" (456).

Works Cited

Arellano, Estevan. "Acequias: The Way of the Water." *New Mexico History.org*, http:// newmexicohistory.org/people/acequias-the-way-of-the-water. Accessed 16 January 2017.

Davidson, Will, and Julia Guarino. "The Hallett Decrees and Acequia Water Rights

Administration on Rio Culebra in Colorado." *Colo. Nat. Resources, Energy & Envtl. L. Rev.*, vol. 26, no. 2, 2015, pp. 219–76.

Hicks, Gregory A., and Devon G. Peña. "Community *Acequias* in Colorado's Rio Culebra Watershed: A Customary Commons in the Domain of Prior Appropriation." *University of Colorado Law Review*, vol. 74, no. 2, 2003.

Mendez, Rafael. "Sharing the Scarcity in Southern Colorado." *University of Denver Water Law Review*, 4 March 2014, http://duwaterlawreview.com/sharing-the-scarcity-in-southern-colorado/. Accessed 16 January 2017.

New Mexico Acequia Commission. "About the Commission." http://www.nmacequiacommission.state.nm.us/. Accessed 22 January 2017.

New Mexico Office of the State Engineer. "Acequias." http://www.ose.state.nm.us/Acequias/isc_acequias.php. Accessed 22 January 2017.

New Mexico Office of the State Engineer. "Acequia Construction Programs." http://www.ose.state.nm.us/Acequias/isc_acequiasConstruction.php. Accessed 22 January 2017.

Nichols, John. *An American Child Supreme: The Education of a Liberation Ecologist.* Milkweed Editions, 2001.

———. *The Milagro Beanfield War.* Henry Holt and Company, 1994.

———. "'*Sin agua, no hay vida*': Acequia Culture." *Taos: A Topical History*, edited by Corina A. Santistevan and Julia Moore. Museum of New Mexico Press, 2013, pp. 201–11.

Peña, Devon G. "Colorado's 2009 Acequia Recognition Law: Punching a Hole in Prior's Hegemony." Lecture to the Water Center, 2 March 2010, University of Washington.

Political Film Society. "Previous Awards." http://polfilms.com/previous.html. Accessed 24 January 2017.

Shiva, Vandana. "Subversive Kin: A Politics of Diversity." *Chicano Culture, Ecology, Politics: Subversive Kin*, edited by Devon G. Peña. U of Arizona P, 1998, pp. vii–ix.

Worster, Donald. *Rivers of Empire: Water, Aridity, and the Growth of the American West.* Oxford UP, 1985.

Watershed Ethics and Dam Politics

Mapping Biopolitics, Race, and Resistance in *Sleep Dealer* and *Watershed*

TRACEY DANIELS-LERBERG

> He supposed that even in Hell, people got an occasional sip
> of water, if only so they could appreciate the full horror of
> unrequited thirst when it set in again.
>
> —Stephen King, *Full Dark, No Stars*

"THERE ARE MANY forms of thirst" that haunt the human imagination (Langewiesche 5). And in America none seem so parched as those who exist along the racial, cultural, and economic "borderlands," to borrow Gloria Anzaldúa's freighted, but especially generative term, where they seem to reside perpetually out of view, evaporating from our collective consciousness. This project undertakes a biopolitical and material feminist reading of Percival Everett's novel *Watershed* (2003) and Alex Rivera's film *Sleep Dealer* (2008). The novel and film take up the contested places of the American West, where the very dearth of resources makes them ever more precious and where there is little opportunity for what Alice Walker calls a "revolution to love what is plentiful" (237). *Watershed* and *Sleep Dealer* unambiguously demonstrate the corporeal "precarity" of marginalized and racialized subjects, but also the vulnerability of those vested with pseudo-authority who are not realized in contradistinction to these racialized others. In deemphasizing the hegemonic cartographic aesthetic that stresses boundaries over affiliations, "barricades" overflows and seepages, *Sleep Dealer* and *Watershed*

FIGURE 7.1. Members of the San Carlos Indian Agency constructing an irrigation ditch in Arizona, 1886.

adopt a biopolitical position that refuses to embrace authoritative controls or replicate asymmetrical relations of power. Instead, they work to make visible the hidden sociopolitical and economic apparatuses that turn people and resources into commodities; these texts expose what Michel Foucault identifies as the "techniques of governmentality," that turn water resources into tools of control along predictable and well-worn cultural tributaries. These artistic renderings of experiences in the American West reveal that it was and is a ripe "ground for both economic and cultural exploitation," that has been "defined, maintained and altered through the impact of unequal power relations" that includes the natural world, as feminist geographer Linda McDowell states (McDowell 5). The book and film represent powerful descriptions of the problem of uneven distribution and access to dwindling and diverted water flows, tenaciously reject narratives of embodied detachment, and implicate all of us in the fight to ensure that the "future is not a thing of the past" as Mr. Cruz warns in *Sleep Dealer*.

The American West is a particularly generative site for the interrogation of colonial and neocolonial forms of bio-power because even today, "language that can easily express [. . . the] ideas of inclusion and continuity" (Berleant 5) remain elusive in this place even as there has been an increasing awareness of the "need to root . . . ethics to place" (Proctor 295). And, many science scholars remain uncomfortable with the kinds of discursive and material "collisions and convergences" that feminist scholars argue might ultimately produce a more balanced relationship between humans and the environment (Alaimo, "Trans-Corporeal" 237). The American West is marked by regimes of surplus and forced scarcity, where state-sanctioned hoarding of resources by the government itself or by the elite often dictates networks and flows, and authorizes new forms of control that validate the needs of the privileged at the expense of those who may need access to resources the most. The problem of water's history and the continued manipulation of water resources emerge as the single-most significant crisis in Everett's novel and Rodriguez's not-so-futuristic film.

The fictive location in *Watershed* serves to interrogate what Thomas Lemke identifies as the "authoritarian mechanisms" of governmentality that serve to repress the needs and desires of particular bodies (40). In the US, racialized others are most at risk of subjection to these powers, and their ability to articulate their concerns are often ignored. Givanna Di Chiro, drawing on historical records, highlights "a historical pattern of disproportionately targeting racial minority communities for toxic waste contamination" (304); furthermore, those who are most at risk of "pollution, resource exploitation, and land-use" (306) disputes are often the least likely to have access to the power that might transform or evade the environmental conditions that affect their communities.

It is no accident that Percival Everett's *Watershed* is set in the "Plata" Indian Reservation, which highlights the ongoing plight of Native Americans on reservation lands, and the historical and current US policies that dictate their existence. The "Plata" of Everett's fictional novel is only a thinly disguised version of the Colorado Plateau, a historically significant temporal and geographic location in the development of the American West. *Watershed* operates on several levels of significance, encompassing the political, scientific, economic, historic, and colloquial. A watershed often marks an important moment, a turning point, a time of significant change, or a disruption in the status quo. Such can be true for an individual, a group of individuals, or an entire society. A watershed of this type can be seen as positive by some, disruptive or dangerous by others. In the case of Everett's novel, each of these meanings is at play. Everett explores the persistence of the myth, too often constructed around race, gender, sexuality, and economic status in the novel, which explores a contemporary water dispute between the Plata Indians and their white neighbors as it is revealed through an African American hydrologist. That these three racial groups are brought into intimate contact in the narrative is also of no small consequence to the novel, nor to the development of the North American West. Historian Gerald Nash, in tracing the history of the "social mingling" of these three racial groups, argues that their interactions shaped "the course of American history for generations" (8). The novel initially appears to highlight a western landscape and people who have recovered from the historical traumas of the past. But the tensions that have been simmering below the surface erupt into violent confrontation, and demonstrate the "enduring significance of repression and violence" that are exerted by those in authority (Lemke 40). *Watershed* reveals that many of the contemporary problems that exist at the crossroads of race and place, including a disregard for people, the land, and animals, may be better hidden and less explicitly rendered than they were in the past, but they are no less insidious. Indeed, the novel demonstrates what Foucault identifies as "the administration of bodies and the calculated management of life" that may be deliberately opaque and thus even more dangerous for particular bodies (44).

Early in the novel, Robert Hawks, the black hydrologist who is charged with surveying the Plata, is confronted by a group of townsmen who demand that he tell them who has the right to the water. The white men are upset because their water flows are drying up and they believe the Indians are responsible, claiming that "them injuns" are "just fuckin' greedy" (30). The irony of course is that the Plata Indians have had water and other resources extracted from their lands for nearly two centuries in order to satisfy the wants of those living off the reservation. The men live off the reservation both in terms of their geographic location outside of the boundaries of the reservation, and therefore are not bound by or subject to the legal or moral codes of the reservation, but also in the sense that their survival depends on the siphoning off of resources from tribal lands. But the white men, who have comfortably embraced their "naturally" sanctioned rights, suspect the hydrologist is on the side of "them injuns" because he is black. Hawks does not fare much better with the Native Americans, who are suspicious of his government affiliations. The Plata people recognize that their mountain and their people are sick and dying, and they correctly suspect that the US government is responsible. They believe Hawks, a man of science who is imbued with a form of pseudo-authority, is just another government agent sent to cover up the sickness. Members of the tribe excavate past betrayals to interrogate Hawks:

> "You know about the Buffalo soldiers?" Kills Enemy, a Plata native, asks. "They were colored soldiers who fought against us. The white men sent them to do their dirty work. You know about them?"
>
> "Yes, sir," Hawks responds. "I know a little."
>
> "Are you a Buffalo soldier?" Kills Enemy wants to know. (35)

Kills Enemy retains a historical distrust of African Americans. The Buffalo Soldiers, despite having few rights as citizens themselves, fought alongside US troops during the Indian Wars. In the novel, the implication is clear: Hawks stands in for the state and has aligned himself with white privilege even if his race betrays such an affiliation. And he is indeed there to observe, record, and report his findings without regard for the historical context of the place. Hawks does not recognize the significance of Plata's sociopolitical history, nor his own historically marginalized status—he has been fully incorporated into the state regimes and simply wants to escape the implications of his history, and the problems of the present. Hawks wants nothing to do with the political implications of his work. His response to both the whites and the natives is that he does not "get involved in political stuff" that has underwritten the past (56). Yet, he has never been free of the political undertow. His physician grandfather and radical father were often at odds over the value of and need for the civil rights movement in improving the status of African Americans in the US. As he recalls his politically charged history, he remembers the eldest Hawks warning his father not to bring a minister to the house because the man stood for that "Christian bullshit that encouraged "black people" to "run around after some white man's invention" (112). Later, Hawks was sent away from his father's home for his own safety while "Dr. King" visited (120). His father, then, was a pivotal figure in the support of the civil rights movement, but Hawks has distanced himself from this past. He does recognize the significance of this history and simply wants to escape it. He is the all too familiar independent man of western myth, and he declares that his "blood is [his] own" in a misbegotten effort to eschew his lineage and his own historical marginalization (3). Lemke argues that such "rationalizations" are not merely hypocritical, but instead demonstrate a "specific articulation of autonomous subjectivation and disciplinary subjection, freedom and domination" that remain "messy and contradictory" (41). Hawks cannot escape the messy and contradictory world from which he has come, nor the one that he has entered. The problems of his history, Native history, American history have not been erased and they cannot simply be forgotten. Rather than being eradicated, the cultural entanglements of the past have simply migrated into the present along cultural streams that leak into all aspects of the lived experiences of those still banished to the margins. Furthermore, race and environment in the American West cannot be seen as completely independent categories. *Watershed*, despite its main character's desire to resist the entanglements of environmental racism, examines the policies that have marred Native lands and have had serious material consequences for those living upon the land, both humans and other animals. The "unequal protection from environmental hazards" has often been drawn along race and class boundaries (Tarter 225). Although Jim Tarter is most concerned with the implications for human life, Giovanna Di Chiro observes that environmental justice requires the integration of the "histories and relationships of people and their natural environments" since humans are not the only living organism affected by pollutants (317).

Yet Hawks attempts to resist the entanglement of race and the environment, and instead continues to believe he operates in a neutral position, declaring that he "seldom involved [himself] in the use of [his] findings or any kind of agenda promotion" (152). He cloaks himself in the detachment of a scientific enterprise that demands neutrality that he is more than happy to hide behind. And besides, he argues, "Terrace formation and sediment evaluation were simple, observable things and meant only what they meant" (152). Hawks, like John Wesley Powell, the nineteenth-century explorer and geologist credited with mapping the Colorado Plateau, is a man of science and reason, and he does not want to be sidetracked by the problems of the people involved—those who call it home and see it in terms other than merely scientific. Hawks believes in the standard scientific tenet that its findings, measured in specific selected data points, are neutral. Hawks believes that the place exists independently of the people. The study of place does not necessary include the people who live in a certain location, according to Hawks myopic view. In his scientific estimation, facts and figures are intrinsically impartial. The myth of scientific neutrality is deeply embedded in the notions of rationality and progress that informed the development of the American West, but science is "never neutral," nor is it ever "value free" (Arditi, et al. 28). And as noted feminist science studies scholar Donna Haraway argues, "scientific knowledge, like all other kinds, remains constitutively historical and non-innocent" (*Haraway Reader* 4). Haraway recognizes the tangled "web" that all scientific knowledge emerges from; the web includes sociopolitical and economic factors as well as scientific inquiry, and as such emerges out of these forces rather than develops independently from them as Hawks insists.

Hawks is charged with taking measurements and providing detailed cartographic and topographic notes about the geologic features of the Plata. His "formal" reports follow the language and form of those produced by Powell. Many of the fragments—descriptions set off by italicized text that both contribute to and also interrupt the main narrative—in Everett's novel take the form of hydrology diaries:

> *During the field study, 23–27 September, examinations of the geology, hydrology, and soil-erosion processes were made of the Plata Mountain watershed. Observations of the Plata and Silly Man Creeks were made from Rural Route 13 above the confluence of the Silly Man and Red Creeks, from the mining road numbered A-28 traversing north-south along Silly Man Ridge and from various locations along the two main creeks.* (Everett 18)

In the brief excerpt, Hawks's language is strikingly similar to that of the Powell reports:

> On August 19, 1889, the river was discharging at Willow Creek, 202 second feet, and on October 15, at Three Forks, 333 second feet. There is no permanent gauging station on the Jefferson itself, the

work being confined to measurements of Red Rock Creek at the town of Red Rock on the Utah and Northern Railroad. At this point the bed is of gravel, the banks about 4 feet high and the channel very tortuous. This locality was selected from the fact of its being one of the places on the river which were not dry during the summer in 1888 and 1889. This creek is the headwaters of the Missouri, or, in other words is the stream which is farthest removed from the mouth of the river, as the water flows. It rises in a loop in the Continental Divide, about 15 miles west of the National Park and it continues nearly due west for 60 miles before turning northerly, passing on its way through the open and elevated Red Rock Valley. (Powell 40–41)

Hawks's observations draw on the same distilled, often purely descriptive, language of Powell's reports. There are no meaningful interactions with the location, the people, or the other life forms that depend on the Plata to sustain their lives. The reports are meant to provide purely descriptive language of observations made at a particular time in a particular location. The place is abstracted to the point of emptying all meaning. The rationalist and instrumentalist language of observation creates an ocular understanding of the place, but such language fails to reveal the cultural and symbolic web of the relationships, interactions, and conflicts that have also shaped and defined the place.

Other fragments in *Watershed* even adopt the formal identification of documents Powell later submitted to the US Geological Survey (USGS) that included recommendations and even court proceedings:

Observed also were expansive structural relations in the region, including the Silly Man Ridge monocline, a fault running north-south, several east-west faults, and a portion of Plata Mountain. Another fault, which is suggested by the topographical features of the west face of Plata Mountain, may have some impact on surface drainage. The major north-south fault and the east-west structural facets in Plata Canyon have impacted the Plata Mountain watershed itself, evidenced in the field, and confirming Fran Rocker's work on the geology of Plata Mountain watershed (USGS Paper 45679-T [1981]). (Everett 21)

In these moments, Hawks adopts the scientific language and report identification features that closely match those of the actual geographic surveys done in the American West during the late-1860s and 1870s—a time that marked a "turning point" in western expansion, according to the director of the US Geological Survey, Clarence King (7). In his 1880 report King exalted the work of Powell and declared that the geological sciences had "ceased to be dragged in the dust of rapid exploration" and instead took a "commanding position in the professional work of the country" (7). Although Hawks works to distance himself from the environment he observes, his scientific objectivity is not exalted in the text. Instead the text demonstrates that Hawks has internalized the logic of paternalism and embraces his role in subordinating both nature and other marginalized subjects to the demands of the privileged. He is a part of the "very techniques for achieving the subjection of bodies and the control of [certain] populations" that are the hallmarks of bio-power (Foucault 45). Hawks, for instance, describes himself as a hired gun, thereby recognizing both his position of power and also the violence associated with such power. From the distance of formalized language, knowledge, and institutional power, all things can be seen in aseptic terms, but ultimately Hawks, as a black man who remains outside the bounds of privilege, cannot ignore the implications on the people and place. Feminist science scholar Londa Schiebinger argues that there is a historical practice of using science and pseudo-science to "justify social inequalities" by marking bodies differently and then mapping knowledge over those differences in an effort to support social ideologies and practices of domination (27). Scientific evidence is frequently employed as a tool to reify standards of difference, rather than to eliminate them. Schiebinger demonstrates the way in which science can be implicated in insidious acts of defining, identifying, marking, and categorizing to create hierarchies of control that tend to withstand, at least initially, discursive strategies of resistance by marginalized identities. As Haraway argues, the "rational classifying activity" associated with scientifically supported notions of race "masked a wrenching and denied history" (*Haraway Reader* 253). The main narrative in *Watershed* reveals that Hawks himself has been subjected to these regimes throughout his life, has belonged to a "population at risk" that his education and profession cannot protect him from. And while Hawks has embraced a kind of identity politics that Wendy Brown identifies as a revolt against "exclusion," he cannot quite mask or deny his own racial history or his own racial victimization (65). Just as water itself can move across county, state, and even national boundaries, making it difficult to define rights or even to determine starting and stopping points, institutionalized and government sanctioned racism is diffused in a way that tracing its history becomes nearly impossible. The novel highlights the complicated entanglements that have underwritten violent histories and racial hatred in the American West, and more importantly, that bleed out across porous geographic and temporal boundaries. Like water, it weeps and seeps, drips and drizzles. And sometimes it pours.

The conspiracy of denial that emerges in *Watershed* interrogates the ways that science and pseudo-science have been used to obfuscate and deny the material implications for questionable environmental practices that target communities of color. Reports often claim that the evidence does not prove a connection between particular activities and increased number of health problems, or that not enough evidence exists to determine a connection. As Tobin Siebers argues, "Victims are denied the means to demonstrate that they have been wronged," thus those outside of traditional routes of power "are doubly victimized as they have both suffered injustice and [have] been deprived of the means to argue their case" (294). Although Siebers is interested in how power and privilege have been used to suppress the disabled, this has been true for the Native American community whose reservation lands have been resource rich even as those living on them have suffered "pervasive poverty" (Brook 106). Much of the uranium mining in the US in the twentieth century was conducted on lands "supposedly reserved for the exclusive use and occupancy" of native peoples (Moore-Nall 15). The most significant mining occurred in areas of the greatest concentration of Native people living in the Four Corners area of the Colorado Plateau. In addition to extracting resources from below the surface, the government contractors also exploited the labor of reservation residents who were "extraordinarily vulnerable" and had been chronically unemployed" (Brook 132–34). The ongoing material repercussions for Native Americans and reservation lands have been tremendous. But "Native Americans, like all other victimized ethnic groups, are not passive populations in the face of destruction from imperialism and paternalism" (Brook 106). Many tribes, financially motivated and having few other opportunities for economic improvement, have accepted the risk. Vocal Native American representatives have expressed repeated complaints over the long-term effects of "environ mental spoliation" on reservation lands at the hands of the US government and businesses contracted by them (Brook 105).

Hawks only begins to reconsider his position when he "discovers" what he describes as an "improvisational" dam, a neutered term for an unauthorized and illegal dam, up on the Plata Mountain and realizes the effort that had been put into diverting what he suspects is contaminated water away from the town and onto the reservation, thereby selectively poisoning the Plata Indians and protecting the white residents below. Hawks, who had refused to "believe" that the US government "had been illegally storing anthrax" and other "biochemical agents" on the Plata Reservation, who had "done so much to remove all things political" from his life abandons his stronghold on detached objectivity (140, 152). Hawks finally bridges the gap, connecting his vulnerability and exploitation to that of his African American ancestors and even to the vulnerability and exploitation of the Plata people. He is finally mobilized. He tells one of the Native American rebels that "apparently they don't give a shit about Indians" in describing what the government has done to the reservation's water supply (189). And he realizes they don't give a shit about him either. The revelation leads Hawks to reflect on his own vulnerable position. He remembers the Tuskegee experiments on African American men, and is amazed by his own failure to believe: "[T]he scariest part of all, that in spite of knowledge of past transgressions, I still resisted belief in a new one" (140). This is Hawks watershed moment as he declares that he had believed that "[his] country was somehow [him]. . . . But it wasn't [his] country" (140). He joins the Plata Indian fight, carrying supplies to those holding an FBI agent hostage, while they demand answers about why their people and their land are dying. Hawks becomes "a little angrier and more determined" to expose the truth (189). His valance of scientific and professional detachment dissolves.

As a scientist, Hawks's discovery is the key to getting the word out to the public. As he escapes the compound on a mission to deliver the evidence, he realizes he has ultimately sacrificed his life to a cause he never intended to join. Forced to crawl through the poisoned water in order to make his way down the mountain, he wonders "how long it would be before the symptoms of anthrax" would ravage his body as it had already done to so many of the Plata Indians and their lands (198). Hawks gazes back at the mountain as he drives away from the town for the last time, and it still "looked so peaceful, so clean, so inert," and yet it has become a deadly site. As Stacy Alaimo argues, the novel ultimately "corrodes the boundaries between science, activism, and even one's own corporeal integrity" (*Bodily* 65). As Hawks sheds his well-maintained ignorance, the readers shed theirs. The text forces readers to reconsider the landscape: what appears beautiful might also hide something quite deadly, and science alone may not provide the answers. The reader "knows" that industrial pollution targets primarily minority and low-income communities, often drawing on the support of science—not by accident, but by design, as Di Chiro argues. Just as it works to unearth the hidden calamity, the text also pushes readers to question how much their privilege will protect them from environmental catastrophe. Hawks recognizes that his privilege is tenuous, so too is the reader's in the face of environmental disaster. The text engages us in an important aspect of environmental justice, which "explicitly undertakes a critique" of a variety of practices and the tendency to privilege "Western scientific notions of objective truth and control of nature, and the hierarchal separation between nature and human culture" (Di Chiro 310). Objective dispassion therefore becomes an untenable position. Disobedience becomes the only appropriate, ethical response, which promises not only to save others, but ourselves as well even if this requires sacrifice and disorder.

Unlike Hawks, *Sleep Dealer's* Rudy Ramirez is not a man of science, but he too operates under the guise of distance. He is a man of action and a man of violence. He has trained his entire adult life to protect the American way of life from those who would threaten it. Rudy is literally a hired gun, but he is separated from the "dry, dusty, disconnected" places where he and his fellow fighters administer justice on behalf of the private Del Rio Water Inc., which has dozens of Rudy's safeguarding their water storage. While *Watershed* examines the local water supply that is being purposefully poisoned, *Sleep Dealer* imagines the sweeping transnational corporatization of the government and the misappropriation of natural and human resources. *Sleep Dealer* focuses on the slow removal and consolidation of resources away from the most vulnerable populations and, just as in *Watershed*, those least able to strike back because they are denied access to legal recourse as well. The massive multinational conglomerate is interested only in potential profits. People are a means to this end, but are otherwise insignificant to the corporation. Rivera's film builds on the fears Powell expressed upon his subsequent trips into the American West. Powell identified widespread misuse and wasting of natural water sources to be an increasingly urgent problem. "The matter thus left to itself is becoming a striking instance of the survival of the man highest up the stream, irrespective of his rights or the best use of the water" (Powell 75). In the future of Rivera's world, Del Rio Water Inc. is the "man highest up the stream" and corporate interests supersede individual "rights." Needs matter very little, and as in *Watershed*, the film highlights the "unjust and intolerable social practices at the environmental level" that are explicitly drawn along class and racial boundaries (Tarter 224).

The film opens with a young Mexican man, Memo Cruz, drifting in and out of a watery dream about his past as he works at a virtual labor "factory" in Tijuana, Mexico. His boss tells him, and others like him, that he is participating in "the American Dream." Neither the boss nor any of the factory workers have ever been across the highly fortified US-Mexico border, which has been permanently closed; thereby forever settling the "immigration issue." Node workers, who are literally plugged into networks by "Coyoteks," transport their virtual labors to many large cities. The technological interface creates an aseptic border that is never penetrated; thereby giving "the United States what they've always wanted . . . all the work without all the workers" (*Sleep Dealer*).

Memo's bodily plight, like his Native American counterparts in *Watershed*, can be traced to the water, and forces the viewer to remain focused on the often-invisible contact zone "between human corporeality and more-than-human nature" (Alaimo, "Trans-Corporeal" 238).

Humans do not live outside their interaction with the natural world, and the plight of the natural world is not neutral in terms of human outcomes. The Cruz family had lived and successfully worked their Santa Ana cornfield for generations before Del Rio Water Inc. built a dam that choked off their water supply and killed the land, forcing the thriving farmers into corporatized submission. The film highlights the ways that the "transformations of nature seem to lead [so] naturally to vestments of power, to overt and vicious exploitation of the other" (Poulsen 2). In one of his watery flashbacks, Memo recalls his final argument with his father, who steadfastly refused to surrender his land to corporate greed. His father, like the Plata elders, remembers a lush past, a land of health and plenty, and he will not abandon his fields. Memo does not understand his father's attachment to the now useless land in Santa Ana. He wants his father to give up, to give in, and to move on. Memo fails to recognize that the land has been a vital part of his history, and has an intimate connection to his future. "We had a future," Mr. Cruz reminds his son. Their future, he tells him was stolen when "they dammed up the river." But Memo does not remember a world without the dam. He has lived his entire life in its shadow and under its control. The dam itself has a history in the US that has been associated with the protection of the privileged. The US government subverted treaties with Native Americans through hydrology projects that diverted water from Native American communities in order to deliver electricity to white urban centers. In *Sleep Dealer* the dam is a highly fortified militarized no-man's zone "patrolled" by heavily armed militia who watch from the other side of the border, ostensibly to protect the water and the profits of Del Rio Water. In order to gain access to water, Santa Ana residents must march across their own parched earth and stand before an electronic gate as a security camera "searches" them. They are warned in Spanish and English not to "make any sudden moves!" before being ordered to insert $85 for 35 liters of water.

Lest the viewer feel safe that the film is about those people on the other side of the border, she soon learns that all water supplies are at stake in *Sleep Dealer*. A multinational conglomerate Del Rio Water Inc. has amassed a fortune gathering up water resources in at least twelve massive projects around the world. The film never makes clear whether Del Rio Water Inc. operates completely independently as a commercial enterprise, or whether it has accumulated its holdings with the assistance of government authorities. The obscuring of these two sources of authority is consciously constructed and the viewer never sees those responsible for building the dams where the world's water supplies are being hoarded. The nebulous conglomeration is anonymous and disinterested, and it leaves those on the cultural and economic borderlands in a perpetual state of subservience. The hazy fault lines between private industry and the governments charged with protecting its citizens emerges as an especially insidious problem in a globalized world economy and often makes it difficult for victims to identify the culprits or hold them responsible. The film contemplates the water's "vulnerabilities," which have now reached a potentially "global" scale. In addition to natural disasters, susceptibilities include the "loss of water-dependent ecosystems and biodiversity," but also "the insecurity and even violence that arise from perceived injustices over contested waters, can all reach across borders" (Sadoff, Kemper, and Grey 1). Insecurity and violence erupts in *Sleep Dealer* as the injustice of hoarding resources leads to further abuse of the most vulnerable. There are no formal channels that allow individuals to express their complaints; nor any person who might provide assistance. What is made clear is that Del Rio Water Inc. is not interested in wasting a single drop of the water it controls. People around the world are welcome to it, so long as they can afford the rates, which often increase without warning. Also made clear is that protecting those supplies from a growing and dangerous "Aqua-Terrorist Insurgency," falls to American pilots. The faceless jet fighters are glorified as "high tech heroes" using "cutting edge technology" to "blow the hell outta the bad guys" on *Drones*, a reality TV show with a live studio audience. The heroes remain safely on the "right" side of the border, using drones to police those on the "wrong" side.

On his first mission, Ramirez targets the Cruz home after Memo is caught using "unauthorized technology." Memo, dreaming of a different future, and unable to cross the border, jumps onto satellite transmissions to listen to what is happening in other worlds; worlds that call to him from across the borders that he is not allowed to breach with his material, bodily self. But his dreaming is captured by those with better technology, and he is identified as a potential terrorist threat, his family home a safe house for terrorist activities. Ramirez is sent to eradicate the threat. He strikes the home in spectacular fashion and the studio audience erupts with applause. Memo's father, who is the only person at home at the time of the precision airstrike launched from nearly five hundred miles away, is wounded but survives the initial assault. The elder Cruz crawls from the rubble of his small home, turning his bloodied face up to the unmanned weapon. A disembodied female voice breaks into the live television broadcast and in bemused excitement declares that "this is unusual." She reminds *Drones* viewers that an "agent" rarely comes "face-to-face" with one of his targets. Rudy hesitates, but ultimately obeys his military training, maintaining a psychological distance that dehumanizes the bloodied man before him. He is a professional and as such does his job, firing a final shot and killing Memo's father and thus becoming a national hero.

But Rudy is changed by his first kill. It is his watershed moment. The carefully constructed boundaries employed to keep Ramirez from empathetic identification with Del Rio Water's victims is shattered. Like Hawks, Rudy closes the distance between himself and the victimized other, traveling back into Mexico "at his own risk" in order to find Memo, who has finally escaped Santa Ana in shame. Forced to leave his home to support his family following his father's death, Memo heads to Tijuana, where he becomes a node worker. The laborers of Memo's world no longer need coyotes to transport them covertly over the border. They rely on node pushers, the coyoteks, who can get them plugged into the system so that their labor can be swiftly exported, even as their scarred bodies remain firmly in place, and out of sight. In the film, technology does not fulfill the promise of global access or global equality. Just as the naturalized exploitation of water and land resources is merely enhanced by increasing global technologies that are controlled by the powerful, so too is the naturalized exploitation of humans.

And just as manifest destiny focused on the potential that new lands offered those emigrating across the American West in the nineteenth century, those who champion the promise of technology can overlook the way that these emerging technologies are sometimes used to replicate rather than mitigate contemporary constructions of power. Feminist scholars have warned that despite the promise, "virtual reality technologies are implicated in the production of a certain set of cultural narratives that reproduce dominant relations of power" rather than offering new modes of escape for the oppressed (Balsamo 123). Anne Balsamo argues that "a better approach for evaluating the meaning of these new technologies and, more importantly, the use of such technologies" is needed and suggests that technological shifts be examined based on the "broader social and cultural forces" that give rise to their implementation (123). Balsamo's call rejects the oversimplification of technological advances. And it refuses overly idealized attitudes and forces us to consider the broader implications: to see the people in the technology and to recognize that technological advances do not happen outside human interactions. As Manuel Castells argues, identity "takes place in a context marked by power relationships" and these do not cease to exist in a networked society (7). In many ways, technological advances simply duplicate, overlay, and may even exacerbate relations of power that already exist rather than wresting power from the privileged. Only after Rudy and Memo meet do the two young men realize that they are not very different—they recognize that they have both been "devalued" or "stigmatized by the logic of domination" (Castells 8). They become friends, forming what Castells defines as "project" identities and together they destroy the Santa Ana Del Rio dam, restoring water to the people living there in a temporary victory (8). Memo and Rudy have little to celebrate as they recognize that it is only a matter of time before the dam is repaired and the supply cut off once again. And while neither man can ever "go home," the running water opens both men to the possibility of a new future. Memo and Rudy attempt to "redefine their position, and by doing so, seek the transformation of the "overall social," political, and economic structure that led to their subjection (Castells 8). For the first time, Memo believes that if he can connect, not to the machinery but to the people, they can all have a future worth fighting for.

    Watershed and *Sleep Dealer* illustrate the concerns over the demand and distribution of water resources that Powell acknowledged in his many reports. While land in the American West has been a site of conflict, especially as Native American tribes were forced onto smaller and smaller parcels to satisfy the needs of Euroamericans, "no issue [has] ever triggered more savage interstate conflict than the question of water rights. And no state was uninvolved" (Lamm and McCarthy 191). But if resistance is a condition of possibility for emancipatory practice, as Andrew Robinson argues *Watershed* and *Sleep Dealer*, provide models for the creative impulse that gives rise to it. They remind us that many of the traditionally segregated categories that define our relationships and interactions are the product of politically motivated desires aimed at perpetually marking and high-lighting difference, maintaining boundaries. And while "transforming the world will take much more than bringing people to an awareness of their differences or to a consciousness of environmental crisis," *Sleep Dealer* and *Watershed* illustrate that it is possible to shake off the techniques of control—that it is critical not only to human survival, but to the survival of the planet (Adamson 83). And yet, both texts also demonstrate that such moves can only occur through radical affiliations among those who are sorted through regimes of control. As Hawks's father states, "[T]hings are changing. They're changing slowly, but they're changing. It's happening," and we can all become a part of that change, but only if we, like Hawks and Rudy, risk our own privileged positions and shake off the protective vestments of neutrality (Everett 112). This mobilization could be "the living power of the people" that Hannah Arendt imagined might change the world (41).

Watershed and *Sleep Dealer* demonstrate that the "landscape is not only the complex system of environmental elements such as air, water, soil etc.," which it certainly is, but it is also a "mental institution" that has been constructed by those in power (Drexlar 9). The way that human technologies become "part of the everyday landscape, making its drastic alterations ... seem ordinary" and inevitable (Scott 1). The stories also highlight the long-lasting and broad-sweeping implications of America's early constructions of the "mental institution" of landscapes and race to our national identity and highlight the intra-dependence among traditionally segregated categories that remain permeable and leaky, bleeding and crossing into one another despite strong political efforts to establish, or more precisely, to manufacture distinct boundaries that are tremendously difficult to undo even if the imaginative field provides fertile ground for our reconsiderations.

Works Cited

Adamson, Joni. *American Indian Literature.* U of Arizona P, 2001.

Alaimo, Stacy. *Bodily Natures: Science, Environment, and the Material Self.* U of Indiana P, 2010.

———. "Trans-Corporeal Feminisms and the Ethical Space of Nature." *Material Feminisms*, edited by Stacy Alaimo and Susan Hekman, U of Indiana P, 2008, pp. 237–64.

Anzaldúa, Gloria. *Borderlands/La Frontera: The New Mestiza.* 3rd ed. Aunt Lute Books, 2007.

Arendt, Hannah. *On Violence.* Harcourt, Brace & World, 1970.

Arditi, Rita, Pat Brennan, and Steve Cavrak, editors. *Science and Liberation.* Black Rose Books, 1980.

Balsamo, Anne. *Technologies of the Gendered Body.* Duke UP, 1999.

Berleant, Arnold. *The Aesthetics of Environment.* Temple UP, 1992.

Brook, Daniel. "Environmental Genocide: Native Americans and Toxic Waste." *American Journal of Economics and Sociology*, vol. 57, no. 1, 1998, pp. 105–13.

Brown, Wendy. *States of Injury: Power and Freedom in Late Modernity.* Princeton UP, 1995.

Castells, Manuel. *The Power of Identity: The Information Age—Economy, Society, Culture.* John Wiley & Sons, 1997.

Di Chiro, Giovanna. "Nature as Community: The Convergence of Environment and Social Justice." *Uncommon Ground*, edited by William Cronon, W. W. Norton, 1996, pp. 298–320.

Drexler. Dorá. "Mythological Landscape and Landscape of Myth: Circulating Visions of Pre-Christian Athos." *Symbolic Landscapes*, edited by Gary Backhaus and John Murungi, Springer, 2009, pp. 109–31.

Everett, Percival. *Watershed.* Beacon Press, 2003.

Foucault, Michel. "Right of Death and Power over Life." *Biopolitics: A Reader*, edited by Timothy Campbell and Adam Sitze, Duke UP, 2013, pp. 41–60.

Haraway, Donna. *The Haraway Reader.* Routledge, 2004.

Irrigation Ditch in Arizona, 1886. 111-SC-83712. Photographs of American Military Activities, ca. 1918–ca. 1981. National Archive, Washington, D.C. *National Archive* Web. https://www.archives.gov/research/american-west, 4 April 2017.

King, Clarence. *Annual Report of the United States Geological Survey.* Government Printing Office, 1880.

King, Stephen. "Fair Extension." *Full Dark, No Stars.* Gallery Books, 2011, pp. 247–80.

Langewiesche, William. *Sahara Unveiled: A Journey Across the Desert.* Vintage Books, 1997.

Lemke, Thomas. "Foucault, Politics, and Failure: A Critical Review of Studies of Governmentality." *Foucault, Biopolitics, and Governmentality*, edited by Jacob Nilsson and Sven-Olov Wallenstein, Södertörn University, 2013, pp. 35–52.

McDowell, Linda. *Gender Identity and Place: Understanding Feminist Geographies.* U of Minnesota P, 1999.

Moore-Nall, Anita. "The Legacy of Uranium Development on or Near Indian Reservations and Health Implications Rekindling Public Awareness." *Geosciences*, vol. 5, no. 1, 2015, pp. 15–29.

Nash, Gerald. *Creating the West: Historical Interpretations, 1890–1990*. U of New Mexico P, 1991.

Poulsen, Richard C. *The Landscape of the Mind: Cultural Transformations of the American West*. Peter Lang, 1992.

Powell, John Wesley. *Eleventh Annual Report of the Director of the United States Geological Survey, Part 2—Irrigation: 1889–1890*. Government Printing Office, 1891.

Proctor, James. "Whose Nature? The Contested Moral Terrain of Ancient Forests." *Uncommon Ground*, edited by William Cronon, W. W. Norton, 1996, pp. 269–97.

Sadoff, Claudia, Karin Kemper, and David Grey. "Calming Global Waters: Managing a Finite Resource in a Growing World." *Global Issues for Global Citizen : An Introduction to Key Development Challenges*. Edited by Vinay Kumar Bhargava, World Bank, 2006, pp. 265-284.

Schiebinger, Londa. "Skeletons in the Closet: The First Illustrations of Female Skeletons in Eighteenth Century Anatomy ." *Feminism and the Body*, edited by Londa Schiebinger, Oxford, 2000, pp. 25–57.

Siebers, Tobin. "Disability Experience on Trial." *Material Feminisms*, edited by Stacy Alaimo and Susan Hekman, Indiana UP, 2008, pp. 291–307.

Sleep Dealer. Directed by Alex Rivera, Maya Entertainment, 2008.

Tarter, Jim. "Some Live More Downstream than Others: Cancer, Gender, and Environmental Justice." *The Environmental Justice Reader: Politics, Poetics and Pedagogy*, edited by Joni Adamson et al., U of Arizona P, 2002, pp. 211–28.

Walker, Alice. "We Alone." *Saving Place: An Ecocomposition Reader*, edited by Sydney Dobrin, McGraw-Hill, 2004, p. 237.

Thomas King Tells a Different Story

Dams, Rivers, and Indigenous Literary Hydromythology

Rebecca Lynne Fullan

IN CHEROKEE WRITER Thomas King's 1993 novel *Green Grass, Running Water*, Clifford Sifton, a representative of the Canadian hydroelectric company Duplessis, tells Eli Stands Alone, "[Dams] don't have personalities, and they don't have politics. They store water, and they create electricity. That's it" (119). Duplessis has built a dam containing a river that otherwise would flow through Blackfoot land. Eli Stands-Alone has opposed the operation of this dam for a decade, through a series of legal interventions, and primarily through his refusal to leave his mother's house, which would be flooded and destroyed if the dam were to operate. *Green Grass, Running Water* chronicles the Blackfoot community to which Eli belongs, as well as the river and the dam that are part of that landscape. In this novel, water is the foundation of the world and of all possible stories. Water begins the novel: "So. In the beginning there was nothing. Just the water" (1), connects otherwise disparate pieces of the narrative, and ends the book as well. While the river behind the dam is unable to act without constraint throughout much of the book, other rivers demonstrate themselves *as* selves, actors, personalities, and political players, and water in other forms flows toward and through the dammed river, until it is able to break free. Rivers take action and participate in the world around them, and the behavior of rivers and of others in relation to them throughout the novel reveals conflicting settler and Indigenous hydromythologies.

Hydromythology refers to the way core cultural beliefs about and understandings of water create stories, relationships, and actions.[1] A dam, as a way of relating to and controlling a river, is a possible outcome of relating to water as, paradoxically, a disturbing force to be controlled and a nonbeing/resource to be exploited. Hydromythology is a story-map that leads to meaningful actions, and shapes the relationships between people and water in the cultural context from which it emerges and to which it contributes, and the story-map overlays the physical and spiritual relationships that arise to and out of specific places. To put it another way, how human beings talk about, deal with, imagine, and relate to water is directly and powerfully creative, and this matters very much, as people without water cannot be people at all. In his nonfiction book *The Truth about Stories: A Native Narrative*, Thomas King repeatedly asserts that "the truth about stories is that that's all we are" (154). He also insists that stories make and change the foundations of all human behavior, relating this directly to how values are made real in the world: "Want a different ethic? Tell a different story" (164). In the conjunction of place, story, ethic, narrative, and behavior, hydromyths inspire dangerous, powerful, violent, kind, and humorous actions. The foundational stories of what (and who) water is inspire consequential human behaviors, including building and resisting dams. Geographers Soren C. Larsen and Jay T. Johnson explore Indigenous-led movements in which Indigenous people preserve and remain in life-giving relationship with four places, against the manipulations of the settler states of United States, Canada, and New Zealand. The frameworks of thought Larsen and Johnson offer are useful for understanding the hydromythologies present in *Green Grass, Running Water*. Specifically, Larsen and Johnson assert that place has agency, that this agency is recognized and interacted with by many Indigenous peoples worldwide, and that place exercises agency in calling and compelling all beings to interrelate and coexist. ". . . [P]laces are both the progenitors and custodians of . . . relationships, guiding human and nonhuman beings along the knotted paths of responsibility" (4). *Green Grass, Running Water* demonstrates a call of place through the active agency of river and water, and the people in the novel are variously able and unable to answer this call according to the hydromyths that inform and imagine the world through them.

When the river finally breaks free and the dam falls, Eli drowns, and his house is destroyed. The rise, stagnation, and fall of the dam are paralleled by the flow, imprisonment, and eventual freedom of the river. This double narrative reveals converging and conflicting hydromythologies that inform the book and its characters. There is a hydromythology of Indigenous people, including Eli's Blackfoot nation, that understand water as living and relational, personalized and agential. There is also a hydromythology of settlers, expressed through concepts of instrumentalized development and depersonalization of water and land that animate Canadian law. This essay traces the narrative revelation of both these hydromythologies in King's novel. I follow the river, the dam, Eli, and Clifford through *Green Grass, Running Water* and identify some results of the hydromythologies by which they live. These results reveal the danger of a hydromythology that is unresponsive to the real behaviors of water and rivers, but also expansive possibilities for collective political action arising out of a hydromythology that attends to the autonomy of rivers. In the end, readers of and characters in this book must both choose how to orient themselves in relation to the hydromythologies the book illuminates.

The rivers in the novel exemplify how multilayered collective action can arise out of hydromythology. The rivers also help unite the seemingly disparate mythic and realistic narratives and characters present throughout the book. While water is ubiquitous in the story, the most significant river is imprisoned behind a dam for most of the novel. Other rivers demonstrate what undammed rivers can be and do. These rivers are playful, excited, and mischievous. They like to flow, carry others along, and mix things up. They are clearly in relationship with other beings. In one of the more mythic sections of the novel, "that River" convinces Thought Woman that she should get in it, then convinces her to come into its middle: "Hee hee, says that River . . . it keeps going faster . . . it goes right off the edge of the world . . . Oooops, says that River . . . Thought Woman floats right out of that River and into the sky" (255–56). This is one version of the many creation stories in the text, most of which have one of four mythic Women (also called the Old Indians) falling out of the sky and beginning the world as human beings know it. In addition to being a character in this story, Thought Woman is a creator/mother to the human race who descends from Sky World to Water World (which becomes the Earth), and also takes on the name Robinson Crusoe after a case of mistaken identity. In this version of the story, the play of that River is silly, but its agency in this playfulness contributes to the creation of the earth. Even (perhaps especially) in its games, water is powerfully creative.

We also see a personalized, talking river in another part of the story about the four Women, who are all misrecognized and given the names of famous white literary or cultural characters. In this episode, they escape from prison in Fort Marion. They walk west and find Big Muddy River who greets them:[2]

> "Ho, ho, ho, ho," says that Big Muddy River. "I suppose you want to get to the other side."
> "That would be nice," says the Lone Ranger. "We are trying to fix the world." . . .
> "Okay," says that Big Muddy River. "Hang on."
> So along come this earthquake. "Rumble, rumble, rumble, rumble," says that Earthquake . . .
> . . . [W]hen all the bouncing is done, [they] are on the other side of the river.
> "Boy," says the Lone Ranger. "That was pretty good."
> "Yes," says that Big Muddy River. "But it's pretty tiring. Good thing I don't have to do that every day." (458–59)

This Big Muddy River is not as hyperactive and mischievous as the River who interacts with Thought Woman; instead, it is genuinely welcoming, enjoying the dance of the Earthquake as they collaborate to help the Old Indians. Here, too, we see what seems to be temporally the first (though, narratively, it is almost the last) mention of the fact that the Old Indians are traveling to "fix the world." This playful, helpful earthquake enters the story directly after the narration of the earthquake that destroys the dam. Coyote, who is listening to and participating in the story, is overwhelmed by the narrative proliferation of earthquakes: "'[Y]ou never know when something like this is going to happen again,' I says. 'Wow!' says Coyote, 'Wow!'" (458). This exchange reveals a plurality of beings, of events, and of meaning that cannot be reduced to narrative expectations about what is possible or makes sense, in fiction or outside of it. This irreducible plurality produces Coyote's wonder, and also reveals one of the foundational contributions of an Indigenous hydromythology in which water is a relational agent among many others. A world with such a proliferation of actors, whose undeniable personhoods are so different from each other, is a wonderful world and a livable world, but it is not a world that can be understood or predicted through the consciousness of any one kind of being, including human beings. Such a world will, then, always be experienced (at least by humans) as somewhat chaotic, while also always being created through willed action and inescapable relationality among disparate beings. It is the relationality itself that makes sense of life in many Indigenous communities, as Sylvia Moore details in her study of various implementations of Mi'kmaw education: "Perhaps today the wind has something to teach me, but if I seek knowledge as something to be gained, I doubt I will understand. Can I learn without a goal of gaining knowledge that can be parceled in my head?" (102–03). The rivers in *Green Grass, Running Water* help answer such questions, as they offer learning that is relational whether or not it is easily categorized by human beings.

In each of the interactions with rivers in the novel, it is impossible not to perceive the rivers as autonomous beings who make choices that are sometimes helpful and sometimes dangerous to others around them. It is also very difficult to understand the rivers in isolation from the others around them. In this combination of personalized rivers that act and play and kill, a network of relationships among various beings, and the wonder of converging events that defy narrative expectations, readers experience the hydromythology that informs Eli's decade-long practice of resistance. Since water is autonomous, it ought to be given freedom to act. Since water is difficult to control, and even dangerous, a functional response from human beings is not to try to force it to our will, but to interact, play, and relate. Sometimes this relationship will give particular human beings exactly what we or they need, and sometimes it will be catastrophic and destructive to particular human beings. Always, the river and the other beings interacting with the river exist as specific, changing, active individuals entirely entwined in relationality with other beings, while remaining rooted in a consistent experience of what water is and can be. This kind of hydromyth gives rise to the stubborn, rooted, welcoming Eli Stands Alone whom we see throughout the novel, and to the forms of political resistance that he chooses, as well.

Within a worldview and hydromythology based on the interaction of many human and nonhuman beings, all of whom have autonomy that should be respected, taking right actions requires ever-shifting discernment. The rivers in the text act according to their own natures, but also with flexibility based on their personalities and the ways that other beings are engaged with them at the moment. The other characters in the book also must reassess their behaviors and desires based on their interactions with rivers and other beings, including humans. Toward the end of the novel, the Old Indians assert that they "fixed up part of the world." At the same time, one of them concedes that "part of it got messed up too" (466–67). It is unclear which parts got fixed and which parts got messed up, though there are hints in their reactions to various events. Most especially, it is impossible to say for sure if the fall of the dam is a fixing or a messing—it seems, in its causes and effects, to be both. This ambivalence makes sense as part of a mythology and ethic in which many autonomous beings interrelate constantly: How would fixing ever mean just one thing? It cannot, because the interplay of relationships continues, constantly changing whatever has been fixed up or messed up. How could resolution or finality be found? The narration of the novel itself ends not with resolution, but with the beginning of another story (469). The irresolution and lack of fixity in the text, combined with the strong continued intentions of many characters, human and nonhuman, to help improve the worlds they are part of, reveal a larger mythic structure to which the hydromyths that inspire Eli's resistance belong. Such a polyvocal mythic world looks like nonsense when perceived through settler hydromythology, in the shadow of the dam, but makes creative, powerful sense outside and beyond it.

What does it mean to be in the shadow of the dam? More precisely, what is the settler hydromythology that is revealed through dams and faith in them as impersonal, apolitical, and more powerful than the rivers they contain? The settler hydromythology present in *Green Grass, Running Water* conceives of water as dangerous and powerful and simultaneously assumes that it lacks any agency that is worthy of respect.

A dam is a physical manifestation of such a hydromyth. Ongoing political and legal struggles between settler states and Indigenous nations and peoples exist around rivers and dams outside of the novel as well as within it, and inform the story that the book tells. Telling stories about dams and rivers in twentieth-century Native American fiction connects the literal with the metaphorical, and emphasizes the damage done on both levels by stopping the natural movement of water (Donaldson 74). Hydromythologies give rise to damming projects, and also shape Indigenous resistance to these projects. *Green Grass, Running Water* is part of a tradition of North American Indigenous fiction about damming projects, the trajectory of which Donaldson traces.[3] The literary work of these novels can give readers access to think within and beyond the hydromythologies that drive decisions about how to interact with actual rivers and dams, and *Green Grass, Running Water*'s fictional damming project has echoes of a specific contemporaneous damming project in which settler and Indigenous hydromythologies clashed.

Through language and the duration of the struggle against Duplessis, *Green Grass, Running Water* connects itself to a real-world conflict over rivers and damming. From 1986 to 1994, the Crees of Quebec fought against the Great Whale River hydroelectric project, which intended to change the course of every river leading to the James and Hudson Bays, mostly through dams. The Grand Council of Crees of Northern Quebec provides a summary of the struggle against the Great Whale project. Their summary describes the way this project damaged the previously mutually beneficial relationship between Cree people and the water involved ("Cree Legal Struggle"). The legal and political battle against the Great Whale project led to mandates that Hydro-Quebec produce an environmental assessment of the project, which they failed to do. In 1994, the project was canceled. The timing of this real-world damming project parallels that of the fictional Grand Baleen project in *Green Grass, Running Water* (Cox 231). King published his novel in the midst of this conflict; the final victory for these Cree nations came two years after the novel's publication. The standoff between Eli and Duplessis, then, has particular weight when placed in relation to this real-life struggle.

King makes a connection between his fictional damming project and the Great Whale project through the name he chooses for the former. The dam in the book is called the "Grand Baleen dam." Baleen is the substance inside the mouths of some whales that allows them to filter the sea creatures they eat from salt water. The name shift from "Great Whale" in real life to "Grand Baleen" in the novel preserves the oceanic mislabeling of the real-life project: these are rivers being dammed and no whales are involved. Calling a project that involves damming rivers the "Great Whale" project implies that the act of damming these rivers is powerful, like a whale, but also highlights that something unnatural and disconnected is happening, since whales do not actually swim in these rivers. This disconnection arises from a lack of observation and deliberate ignorance of the specificity of places that is very useful to a settler cosmology in which all places are in some way interchangeable, rewritable in the image of other places that have been appropriately used and controlled. A great whale is also recognized within settler hydromythology as a powerful being, while the rivers being dammed are not, perhaps alluding to some anxiety even among those planning to build the Great Whale project dams about the question of where power lies in this project and whose autonomy may or may not exist or require respect.[4] When Thomas King transforms the real-world project "Great Whale" to "Grand Baleen," as he names his fictional dam, it makes the pomposity of the former name sound funny. Instead of a whole whale, we are now given just the image of one body part of the whale; baleen is interesting and useful, but it is not usually referred to as "grand" all on its own. Additionally, since whales use baleen to eat, this name makes explicit the fictional project's consumption and dissection of a river and the Native communities that depend on that river. The implication is, then, that the Great Whale project, along with other real-world damming projects, is also a project of consumption, which makes sense when considering how the Grand Council of Crees contextualized their opposition to the Great Whale project. The Grand Council of Crees quotes Robert Bourassa, a political architect of the damming project that eventually became the Great Whale project, describing his relationship to Northern Quebec as that of a "conqueror," and describing the man as having no relationship with Cree people at all ("Cree Legal Struggle"). Bourassa's behavior connects him to the hydromythology of King's fictional company, Duplessis, and its representative, Clifford Sifton. In this settler hydromythology, dams are conceived of as natural, neutral, and indestructible precisely because rivers are perceived as problematically out of control, lacking agency when it comes to having respectful relationships with them, but perhaps having agency when figured as dangers that must be constrained.

Clifford Sifton, the character who manages the Grand Baleen project, enthusiastically subscribes to and thus demonstrates the details of the settler hydromythology that enables that project. As in much of King's other fiction, nearly every white character in this novel has a name belonging to some historical, literary, or mythic figure, and Clifford Sifton is no exception. Both as a character in the book and as a historical allusion, he remains a purveyor of settler colonial mythologies. He is named after a historical Canadian politician who was active in "settling" the West (Cox 230). The historical Clifford Sifton lived from 1861–1929, and "aggressively" promoted settler immigration to the Canadian West. Obviously, he was ideologically wed to Canadian settler colonialism. He was also a proponent of railway expansion, which connects him directly with the novel's dam-loving Clifford Sifton, in terms of how each conceives of land and water as resources to be used, controlled, and overcome (Hall). Both Cliffords, then, act to violently dispossess Native people. None of this historical information is mentioned in the novel, but knowing about Clifford's nominal predecessor clarifies the character's position as a representative of broader North American settler colonial ideologies and the mythologies, hydro and otherwise, that flow through and from those foundations. Settler hydromyth creates a world in which Indigenous dispossession and destructive transformation of waterways become explicable, digestible, and even intensely desirable for those whose worlds are overlaid by these story-maps.

The novel's Clifford Sifton loves dams in a concrete way: he wants them to be solid objects detached from politics, persons, and relationships. Clifford believes in dams as almost magically indestructible objects. A dam controls a river and is therefore more stable and reliable than the river. While Eli thinks about the possible damage to the dam, Clifford thinks (and talks) about the beauty of the dam. In one conversation, Clifford and Eli seem to be discussing the same topics, but their hydromythological foundations are so different that their threads of conversation barely meet. Clifford waxes poetic about the dam's beauty, while Eli refuses to look at it. Instead, Eli questions the dam's physical integrity (148). Eli's understanding of the dam is accurate to the ways it and the river actually behave, while Clifford's is fantastical and fanciful. Clifford's belief in the dam is so strong that he is unconcerned about the weather and the physical state of the dam. Clifford expects eloquence from Eli that will herald (and even create) Eli's capitulation, in a long and loved settler tradition of Native people eloquently describing their own defeats. In the absence of this behavior, Clifford cannot figure out what is going on, saying, "'It's hard work walking down here every day, and it would help if sometime you would tell me why'" (149). Eli does not offer direct explanations, but his "no" can be interpreted in his discussion of the dam's ugliness, the cracks in the dam and the upcoming storm (148–49). Perhaps he says no because he wants to protect his mother's house. Perhaps he says no because the dam is ugly like a toilet (148). Perhaps he says no because he knows water is ubiquitous and powerful and will persist beyond the attempts of the dam to control it. All of these reasons are present in Eli's behavior, even though he does not offer them specifically to Clifford. Clifford, however, is unable to perceive the whys in this behavior because his dam-loving hydromythology is so consuming.

While the men talk, the clouds are taking action. These clouds contain the rain that will, soon, work to free the river from the dam: "The clouds to the northwest were filling up the sky. They had been organizing and gathering all day. Eli turned his face into the wind. Rain" (149). The clouds and the rain, in relation to the river, are the actors in this moment, more than the human beings. Of course, once the rain comes and helps to swell the river to a point where, through the power of the earthquake, it can break through the dam, that rain will also become part of the river. The collectivity of beings here is, quite literally, fluid: as the water gathers to take action and join the flow of the river, Eli notices the gathering of the clouds. He helps to enable the rain's eventual action by resisting and refusing the dam's function, as he has done every day for a decade. That is, if the dam were functioning as intended by its makers, the rainwater would not be able to do its work, in its own time, to destroy the dam. Eli's stubborn, slow persistence acts in partnership with the rain's sudden (but heralded) storm. Eli's hydro-mythology allows him to perceive the gathering clouds as connected to the river and its imprisonment behind the dam, while Clifford's hydromythology imagines the water in the clouds as fundamentally separate from the river behind the dam.

His belief in the dam as natural and impersonal makes Clifford perceive its fall as entirely shocking. The description of his experience as the dam falls is chaotic and disturbing, implying a fundamental, senseless destruction: ". . . beneath the power and motion there was a more ominous sound of things giving way, of things falling apart" (454). Clifford, standing in for Duplessis and a settler hydromythology, has only been able to conceive of the dam as unchangeable once it comes to exist, he experiences the dam's breakage as an apocalyptic undoing. It can only be conceived of as the world's end, in some way, because what else would cause the dam to fail and fall? This moment is the last we see of Clifford. We do not know if he is hurt, survives, loses his job, or anything else that happens to him. Narratively, it's as though he cannot exist without the dam and Duplessis; they are so fundamental to his understanding that he has nothing, apart from them, to say or do in this story.

Eli's experience of the dam breaking is quite different from Clifford's. He starts the morning thinking about his relatives at the Sun Dance, and ends up entertaining the Old Indians. Despite the breach of the dam proving fatal to Eli, the description is much less horrifying and disturbing from his perspective than it seems in Clifford's experience. Just before the dam breaks, Eli is turned away from it. He perceives the dam's effects, unsuited to the landscape, but gives his attention to the sun instead. In the context of the ongoing Sun Dance, the sun connects his thoughts to many of his family members (448). When the Old Indians arrive, Eli welcomes them, and, eventually, their conversation turns to the dam.

They understand the river and the dam through their shared hydromythology, and this carries them through to the moment when the dam breaks:

"It's going to be a good day," said the Lone Ranger. "I can feel it."
"You bet," said Eli . . . But . . . the land began to dance. . . .

[Eli] felt the wind explode at his back, and he heard the sound
of thunder rolling down the valley. Above him, the sun continued in a clear sky. (449–50)

This moment seems far less catastrophic than what Clifford witnesses. The explosion of the wind and the sound of thunder are under-
standable either as the moment just *before* the dam breaks, or as the
moment *of* the dam breaking. This ambiguity is possible because Eli is,
literally and figuratively, turned *away* from the dam. Clifford's experience of chaos and destruction, on the other hand, happens through his
fixed orientation *toward* the dam. This is not to say that Eli does not
care if he drowns, but that his story unfolds in less catastrophic terms,
even in the process of his death. There is no direct narration of Eli's
death, and the description above is the last in the book from his perspective. While the day contains Eli's death, his experience of the day
in the narration is marked not by horror, but by the rising and the continuance of the sun. The land dancing in another playful earthquake,
the wind exploding, the thunder rolling—all of these actions are part
of what frees the river, all done by autonomous yet connected beings,
and Eli participates in these relationships, even as he dies. Eli is not
the center of this action, so his death is not centered either. This makes
Eli's death neither meaningless nor unimportant; instead, it changes
the frame of reference for what is happening to be about the river and
the actions the water is taking, actions in which Eli has participated. It
is disturbing and sad that his death is a part of these relationships and
actions, but it occurs as a direct result of settler manipulative overlay of
the land and water, not as a malicious action on the part of the water.
Eli's death is significant, but it is neither a center nor an end of the story
as a whole, not even of Eli's own story.

Eli's story is centered, instead, around his decisions and relationships,
and these are the ground of his political resistance as well, a resistance
that can look like individual passivity, but is in fact a form of community-based action. After his mother's death, Eli comes back to see her house
before it is demolished, and has his first encounter with Clifford Sifton,
whom he immediately mistrusts. When Clifford says construction on the
dam will begin soon, Eli replies, "'Maybe it will, and maybe it will have to

wait'" (125–26). Eli's statement hardly sounds like an immovable declaration of resistance, yet it begins the resistance in which Eli will remain for the rest of his life. When Eli tries to describe to his nephew, Lionel, why he came back, he tells a piece of his life story, explains that this piece was *not* the reason, and then narrates another experience, in a cycle of story and disavowal. When Lionel asks why he returned, Eli says, "'Can't just tell you that straight out. Wouldn't make any sense. Wouldn't be much of a story'" (400). Sense making and storytelling, for Eli, require complexity and ambiguity that the receiver(s) of the story must interpret. Eli's refusal of "why" as a question that can or should be answered in a straightforward manner is a consistent part of Eli's behavior, and a significant part of his resistance to the dam.

As Eli refuses to allow the dam to be operated, Clifford, with less patience than Lionel, struggles to understand Eli's motivations and to interpret the story Eli is telling through his resistance. Clifford compares Eli to Melville's Bartleby the Scrivener, unyieldingly passive, and suggests this will lead to his death. Eli replies, "'We all die'" (155–56). Clifford's framing of Eli's potential death suggests a tragic, dramatic, traceable cause-and-effect connection between Eli's forms of resistance and his demise. Eli's framing, on the other hand, suggests that his death is one iteration of a universal experience of living beings, not necessarily a crisis, a failure, or something that can be explained in a clear, causal sequence of events. Some critics seem to agree with Clifford's judgment of Eli: Donaldson is troubled that Eli perceives the dam's fragility and yet "does nothing, except stubbornly refuse to move out of his house" (89). James Cox suggests that Eli literally "Stands Alone" and sees himself not as a community activist but as an isolated actor against Duplessis and the dam (231). Cox's claim is part of a worthwhile reading of King's work as a whole in its suspicion of traditional forms of human community activism, but in this aspect, both critics may be taken in by the same deceptive appearances of passivity that annoy Clifford. Eli's resistance is in fact a much more active and community-based project than it appears to be on the surface. Through an understanding of Eli's hydromythology, in which the river is a being with agency, and his overall orientation toward a world that is full of various kinds of agential beings, we can also perceive the community within which Eli takes action. Eli notices the river, the weather, and the dam. He sees that the land and water are acting, and what looks like his inaction (staying in the house) helps the actions of these other beings to result, finally, in the river's freedom. Eli stays put not out of isolated passivity, but because he is part of a complicated collective of living, dead, human, and nonhuman beings.

Eli would not be on the land if it were not Blackfoot land, nor in the cabin except that it was his mother's, and he would not have known to return if his sister, Norma, had not told him about Duplessis's plan to destroy the house. When Eli makes the decision to stay in his mother's house, he does so in the context of remembering his mother building the cabin, and remembering himself and his sisters helping her (122). On the day of Eli's death, when he watches the sun rise, his appreciation of its beauty occurs in the context of a whole list of family members he hopes are seeing the sun, as they congregate at the annual Sun Dance (448). Some of these people are prominent characters in the novel, and some never appear; it is Eli's context that matters here, because these are Eli's people, with and through whom he is making his seemingly solitary stand.

All of this evocation of relationships and memories is not what we usually recognize as collective action of living humans for a political goal. Despite this, Eli's behavior is also not isolated just because it is done, physically, by one human person, nor passive because he does not explain his actions, just like his resistance is not necessarily unsuccessful because he dies in the course of it. Eli's resistance is a form of collective action in which the collective consists of dead people, living people, mythical beings like the Old Indians, and the sun and water themselves. In this communal context, change occurs, but how exactly that change is victory or defeat is not something at all simple to unravel. Victory and defeat may not even be useful terms for assessing the changes, since so many beings are involved and no one thing can be good or bad for all of them. Eli's resistance to the dam is a form of collective action engaged in by collectives that do not make sense in settler terms, and that include all those who are present in the terms available to this Blackfoot community. Understanding these other collectives makes it impossible to see Eli Stands Alone as truly a lone figure, and strengthens the sense of his resistance as political, communal, and not limited by the boundaries of his life.

The continuance of Eli's resistance beyond his death is made apparent because unlike Clifford, he does not disappear after the fall of the dam. He is dead, but he is also present in his family's conversations and actions. Eli's sister Norma tells their nephew Lionel: "'Eli's fine. He came home'" (461). We have seen Eli's orientation (away from the dam, toward the sun, toward his people, with the flow of the river) throughout the book. This orientation is why Norma says he *is* fine, although he has died. His orientation helps explain the persistence of his presence after his death, even while Clifford, probably alive, is inaccessible without the dam. As Larsen and Johnson put it, on the paths of place-based and relational responsibility, ". . . you are nourished in relationship with others; lacking these relationships, you are unconnected, unidentifiable, vulnerable, near inexistent" (4). This perfectly describes Eli (on the paths of responsibility, even as he is carried out of life by the water), and Clifford (inaccessible to the narration without his dam). In the aftermath of Eli's death, relationships with him continue as Norma establishes that she and other family members are going to rebuild the cabin. Even as various relatives find Norma's plan to rebuild bizarre, they help her start to enact it (464). Eli is dead, and their mother is dead, but these actions do not take place without them. The cabin is full of meaning before it is rebuilt because these people lived in it, and Eli's not-at-all alone, deeply relational resistance in it has contributed to the meaning that remains in its (and his) physical absence. All of these relationships, too, are facilitated and inflected by the actions of water and the river—including the actions that kill Eli. In a nonfictional context, Larsen and Johnson describe a lake taking action to reveal the bodies of ancestors as a "sacred reversal" that both reveals disruption of and repairs relationships between the water and the Cheslatta/Carrier Nation, and their description of the experience and results of this disruption reverberates through the scene of unexpected, communal rebuilding at the end of *Green Grass, Running Water*: ". . . water actually had fulfilled its responsibilities. Water took the form of a crisis that brought the people home, which in turn began the painful process of linking the circles of life and death back together" (65). Once a body of water is understood, through fiction, through experience, and/or through hydromyth, to be a relational being, interpretation of any experience with that water is transformed, and perhaps transformative, as we see for Eli, Norma, and their family.

At the end of the novel, the dam is destroyed, the river is free, and the narrative is beginning again, water once again described as being "everywhere" (469). The last description of the dam and the river encapsulates the hydromythologies that have been explored, tested, and revealed throughout King's novel: "[The dam] had a long, ugly crack running all the way down the face . . . Water was running out of the crack and down the face, the river slowly coming back to life" (461). Neither the dam, with its "face," nor the river, are impersonal here. This is a scene of destruction, certainly, and the power of the river has broken both the dam and Eli's life. The river, though, is "running" through and by means of this destruction, and the final words about it are words of rebirth and continuance.

According to the settler hydromythology lived out by Clifford, we are witnessing a senseless, violent end. According to an Indigenous hydromythology demonstrated by the river's life, and by the collective action in which beings including the river, the clouds, dead people, mythic figures, and living people all participate, we are witnessing a restorative beginning. *Green Grass, Running Water* makes it clear that both interpretations are available, depending on the hydromyths that make various orientations and perceptions possible. Like Eli, we as readers must orient ourselves and our attention to determine which story we experience, and, outside of the novel, the orientations provided by hydromythologies and other foundational stories, will determine in what communities we know ourselves to be acting and which other beings we acknowledge or ignore. In *The Truth about Stories*, Thomas King lists choices each person has about what to do with a story after hearing it, but insists, ". . . don't say in the years to come that you would have lived your life differently if only you had heard this story. You've heard it now" (29). Being unaware that significant interpretive choices exist is no longer an option, once the story has been told. There are choices to be made about which hydromythology we are oriented toward, but *Green Grass, Running Water* makes it impossible not at least to know that such a choice exists. Attending to this novel, readers have heard of a world in which rivers, and water, are not forces to be controlled, but beings to be respected, and, attending both to the novel and the world around it, we have reason to suspect this may, in fact, be the world in which we live.

Notes

1. Melissa K. Nelson, in her discussion of Anishinaabeg hydromythology, describes water stories, or hydromyths as "moral landscapes that help us navigate social complexity and ecological unpredictability" (215). She also describes "the opportunity to have visceral, hands-on, embodied experiences of a reality not made by human thought" as critical to the development of these moral landscapes (216).

2. The prison at Fort Marion is an inevitable destination for all four Old Indians in the text. It is also a real, historical prison in which Native American warriors were kept in the mid-to-late 1800s. Big Muddy River is a real river in Illinois.

3. Donaldson specifically focuses on *Runner in the Sun* and *Wind from an Enemy Sky* by D'Arcy McNickle, *Wolfsong* and *Nightland* by Louis Owens, and *Solar Storms* by Linda Hogan, in addition to *Green Grass, Running Water*. It may be of particular interest to readers of this essay that Hogan's *Solar Storms* also draws from the real-life Great Whale project.

4. In an allusion that creates a loop connecting the real Great Whale project, the fictional Grand Baleen project, and the favored whale of settler colonial literary imagination, Moby Dick, King includes a segment in which Changing Woman ends up on the *Pequod* and takes first Queeqqueg and later Ishmael's name, eventually swimming off with Moby Jane, who is a Black lesbian whale misrecognized by Captain Ahab as the "Great White Whale" of *Moby Dick* (220–21, 248–49). These projects, like the whaling project of the *Pequod* here and in the original *Moby Dick*, spring from a (mis)understanding of who is a relatable being and how those relationships should and should not be enacted.

Works Cited

Cox, James. "One Good Protest: Thomas King, Indian Policy, and American Indian Activism." *Thomas King: Works and Impact*, edited by Eva Gruber, Camden House, 2012, pp. 224–37.

"Cree Legal Struggle Against the Great Whale Project." *Grand Council of the Crees*, www.gcc.ca/archive/article.php?id=37. Accessed 4 June 2017.

Donaldson, John K. "As Long as the Waters Shall Run: The 'Obstructed Water' Metaphor in American Indian Fiction." *American Studies International*, vol. 40, no. 2, 2002, pp. 73–93.

Hall, David J. "Sir Clifford Sifton." *The Canadian Encyclopedia*. Historica Canada, 22 January 2008, www.thecanadianencyclopedia.ca/en/article/sir-clifford-sifton/. Accessed 4 June 2017.

King, Thomas. *Green Grass, Running Water*. Bantam Books, 1993.

———. *The Truth About Stories: A Native Narrative*. U of Minnesota P, 2005.

Larsen, Soren C., and Jay T. Johnson. *Being Together in Place: Indigenous Coexistence in a More Than Human World*. U of Minnesota P, 2017.

Moore, Sylvia. *Trickster Chases the Tale of Education*. McGill-Queen's UP, 2017.

Nelson, Melissa K. "The Hydromythology of the Anishinaabeg: Will Mishipizhu Survive Climate Change, or Is He Creating It?" *Centering Anishinaabeg Studies: Understanding the World Through Story*, edited by Jill Doerfler et al., Michigan State UP / U of Manitoba P, 2013, pp. 213–33.

Shifting Tides

A Literary Exploration of the Colorado River Delta

PAUL FORMISANO

FOR MANY PEOPLE familiar with the Colorado River, images of soaring Rocky Mountain peaks or the sublime depths of the Grand Canyon come to mind. Thus, it is not surprising then that the majority of the textual and visual representations about the river and watershed tend to focus on these celebrated landscapes. Yet such representations offer a limited perspective to the wide spectrum of voices, participants, and landforms that have and continue to define the watershed. Nowhere is this oversight clearer than in considerations of the river's delta. Charles Bergman explains in *Red Delta* (2002), perhaps the most comprehensive of the recent examinations of the region, that "[t]he delta has always challenged westerners. . . . It's the hottest place in North America. . . . It gets only a couple of inches of rain per year. The delta was, ironically, one of the first places in North America that Spaniards explored. But it has remained one of the least known" (17). In the case of the Colorado, the delta has largely remained an enigma to the millions of people who rely on Colorado River water every day (172). Spanning an area one hundred miles long and eighty miles wide, the delta stretches southeast from California's San Gorgonio Pass just northwest of Palm Springs through vast deserts to the river's terminus in the Gulf of California in Mexico (Fradkin 333). However, massive irrigation projects have made these deserts bloom, turning the region into the ultimate realization of the Garden myth as it boasts some of the most fertile and productive agricultural areas in the US and Mexico.[1] While these efforts to reclaim the desert have made many areas in the upper delta very profitable, they have also substantially altered the river and its impact on the lower delta. With decades of dam building cutting off the river's annual flooding and even its exit to the sea, the lower delta's once lush and vibrant ecosystem is largely a desiccated expanse of sand flats and stunted vegetation.

Over a century's worth of laws, policies, and attitudes about water and its users have largely caused the river's demise in this region. Engineering the river to meet an exploding population and its many needs within the basin's seven US states, the US federal government has operated on an idea of ownership that has drastically compromised the river's integrity and the livelihoods of those in Mexico who depend on the Colorado.[2] Yet these problems are not just a result of xenophobic laws and shortsighted regulations. Bergman astutely observes that the challenges hampering the river, particularly within the delta, are issues of imagination and language:

> I have come to believe that this question of language—of what words we use for the delta, what metaphors we apply—is fundamental. . . .
>
> We have made the delta into an "other," an alien place, not seeing all the while that it was already home to people and creatures. Through our metaphors, we may have imposed ourselves upon the physical landscape, but we have not yet learned to live there. (279–80)

As Bergman correctly observes, a crisis of representation has mired the Colorado River Delta region, evident in the many accounts of this place that extend from its "discovery" in 1539 to well into the twentieth century. Along the way, however, alternative narratives have emerged to more accurately represent the historical and social conditions that have shaped this place. Thus, like the delta's famous tidal bore (or surge) that once roared upriver from the Gulf of California capsizing boats, the story of the delta is one of flux, of competing perspectives focused upon assessing its impossibilities and possibilities.

The purpose of this chapter, then, is to examine the origins of this crisis and to trace the delta's story through a range of documents spanning exploration narratives, boosterism, memoir, fiction, management plans, and film. To chart this course, I address a number of representative texts beginning with European contact and moving through later accounts of the delta's exploration, transformation to an agricultural paradise, and eventually to its restoration. The purpose here is not to be exhaustive but to identify key texts that have significantly impacted how the region has been imagined and how such representations—in some cases—have translated into direct manipulations of the Colorado River and the delta ecosystem. A particularly useful approach for examining the delta's shifting representations derives from historian Patricia Limerick's categorization of encounters with North America's deserts. She demonstrates how a host of scientists, explorers, and writers captured these arid regions through a range of perspectives which include "attitudes toward nature as a biological reality in human life—vulnerability to hunger, thirst, injury, disease, and death; . . . as an economic resource—a container of treasures awaiting extraction or development; and as an aesthetic spectacle" (6). While her attention focuses on nineteenth- and twentieth-century texts, Limerick's framework nonetheless aptly illuminates earlier accounts of the delta by the Spanish explorers and missionaries, as well as providing an excellent foundation for considering more recent documents indicative of agricultural boosters, nature writers, and journalists. However, Limerick's orientation neglects more recent responses to the Mexican Delta. As the final portion of this chapter demonstrates, the recent cooperative alliance between governments, environmental organizations, local inhabitants, and indigenous groups promotes a new vision of restoration and redemption, thereby adding another chapter to the Colorado River Delta's developing story.

Among the many indigenous peoples who have lived in and continue to inhabit the delta, the Cucapá (or Kwapa as they know themselves) are perhaps the most widely acknowledged in the literature of the region.[3] Known as the "River People" ("Welcome"), the Cucapá are central figures in the exploration accounts of the Spanish and later visitors to the region. Not until recently, however, has their role in the delta's destiny been more widely respected and valued. Without a written language and subject to colonization, their voice has been largely neglected until recently when their intimate connection with and knowledge of the delta and river have gained widespread attention. But before addressing their involvement in the delta today, we must return to the delta's first written accounts which come from the Spanish in the sixteenth century and which set the precedent for the many narratives that follow in subsequent centuries.

Among the first Spanish explorers to enter the delta and the first to provide a written account of the Colorado's terminus into the Gulf of California was Francisco de Ulloa, who arrived at the river's mouth in 1539. Working under the leadership of Hernán Cortés, Ulloa sailed north up the Gulf of California to locate Cíbola, the fabled Seven Cities of Gold. While he found no riches, he learned that California was not an island but a part of the continent and that a mighty river stretched to the north (Starr 22; Fradkin 325). A year later, Hernando de Alarcón arrived at the site of Ulloa's discovery at the command of Antonio de Mendoza, the viceroy of New Spain, to explore upriver in order to unlock the New World's mysteries and secure its wealth.[4] Navigating "those shoals . . . so perilous and fearful that it was a thing to be considered whether with our skiffs we could enter among them," Alarcón and his men eventually "came to the very head of the bay, where we found a very mighty river, which ran with so great a fury of a stream that we could hardly sail against it. In this way I determined as well as I could to go up this river" (Elsasser 11). Following the knowledge these men provided of the delta and the subsequent maps and accounts of the native inhabitants living here, Spanish priests such as Eusebio Francisco Kino traveled throughout the region in the seventeenth and eighteenth centuries seeking converts, establishing missions, and further adding to the understanding of this place. Notwithstanding the difficult geography, Kino saw the potential of harnessing the area's human and ecological resources to spread Spain's influence and his faith throughout the Western Hemisphere.

Toward the end of the eighteenth century, another Spaniard traversed the delta, leaving a detailed account of his travels through what was then known as *La Frontera,* or the frontier—the northern part of today's Baja California. José Joaquín Arrillaga, acting governor of Alta and Baja California, traversed the delta four different times in 1796 and, similar to his predecessors, his preoccupation with establishing trade routes, locating resources, and engaging the indigenous peoples to further Spain's foothold in the New World fills his record.[5] During his fourth expedition, Arrillaga approached the Colorado River from the west as he had done in his previous journeys, noting the sparse vegetation, the varied topography, and the little settlements scattered throughout the region. Arrillaga's rather matter-of-fact account of his surroundings offers the reader a sense of the delta's unique ecosystem characterized by the constant mixing of fresh and salt water, the native plant species dependent on the erratic flows, and the significant human presence that had adapted over millennia to these conditions. While such knowledge proved useful to the crown and its attempts to colonize the region, the difficulty in converting the native peoples and establishing significant outposts ensured that the river and surrounding desert would largely be left as they had been before European arrival.

With the dawn of the nineteenth century, the delta would once again capture the interest of those seeking to understand this remote and largely undeveloped region. With Spain's waning influence in the New World and Mexico's fledgling government struggling to police its northern borders, visitors from the United States entered the region determined to see what this new frontier might yield. Yet for many of these explorers, trappers, and settlers, the delta proved to be a considerable foe, as it had been for earlier groups. Consider the account of James O. Pattie, a beaver trapper and trader, who, in 1828, traveled with his father and fellow trappers down the Colorado River and into the delta where they found themselves hemmed in by the river's tidal bore and a group of hostile Indians.[6] His journal offers us one of the most vivid explanations of the tide's incredible power and the danger it presented to those attempting to make it to the gulf. Alerted to the sound of rushing water toward their camp, "We all sprang to our canoes, which the rush of the water had almost capsized, . . . In twenty minutes the place where we lay asleep, and even our fire place was three feet under water, and our blankets were all afloat" (151). Similar to many of his predecessors, Pattie entered the delta with dreams of economic success but found that the environmental conditions and often hostile human presence demanded a high price from those willing to test their luck.

Following the closing of the Mexican American War in 1848, just two decades after Pattie's memorable visit to the delta, Colorado

Delta literature entered a phase reflective of what historian William Goetzman identifies as the "Great Reconnaissance," a period in which the United States, acting under Manifest Destiny, attempted to civilize and understand the American West (305). During the 1850s, the Topographical Bureau charged the Corps of topographical engineers, the outfit primarily responsible for opening up the American West to development and settlement, with cataloging "the plants, animals, Indians, and geological formations of the country traversed" (303). Lieutenant Joseph C. Ives's expedition up the Colorado with the Topographical Engineers in 1857–1858 is indicative of the various responses to nature and science at this time. Accompanied by a host of scientists, Ives attempted to navigate the river by his steamboat, *The Explorer*, in hopes of establishing a workable trade route to the settlements in New Mexico and Utah (*Report* 5). Advancing up the Colorado from its mouth as Alarcón had done three centuries earlier, he reached only as far as Black Canyon on the western end of the Grand Canyon where he left his ship to proceed on land. Commentary on the climate, extensive waterfowl, ubiquitous shoals, dangerous tides, as well as the nascent shipping economy at the river's mouth and the Cucapás presence fill the first chapter of his *Report upon the Colorado River of the West* (1861), leaving the impression that the delta was an otherwise worthless place.

The difficulties described by Pattie's and Ives's expeditions continue to reinforce the delta's perceived impossibilities evident in the Spanish accounts. However, as the nineteenth century wound to a close, dramatic transformations to the delta's physical and imaginative landscape would reject the impossibilities of the past to celebrate the delta's potential as an irrigated Eden and economic boon. Chief among those promoting the delta's possibilities was William E. Smythe, best known for his lengthy tract *The Conquest of Arid America* (1900). Smythe begins the work stating, "The economic greatness of the United States is the fruit of a policy of peaceful conquest over the resources of a virgin continent" (3). This premise dictated the policies of the United States government over the next half century, and had drastic implications for the Colorado River, the land it seasonally flooded, and the human and nonhuman environment it supported.

The same year that Smythe published *Conquest*, he ran an article in *Sunset* magazine, the promotional tool of California's Southern Pacific Railroad, entitled "An International Wedding: The Tale of a Trip on the Borders of Two Republics." Therein, Smythe paints the river and delta through descriptions dripping with romanticism as he suggests that "the most famous of all the waste places in America" will soon become "as densely populous as the lands of the Nile, as rich in industry as the Kingdom of Holland" (286). As he travels upon the river between the California and Arizona banks of the northern part of the delta, he "s[ees] the dark, deep water flowing uselessly to the ocean" (286). Writing during a time when conservation meant the wise use of nature's resources for the greatest good, Smythe champions an all-out assault on the Colorado to exploit its life-giving waters to redeem "an empire that has waited for centuries to feel the thrill of its living touch" (288). His descriptions of the delta mark an important departure from earlier accounts preoccupied with survival as Smythe promotes the idea that this place was none other than a western Shangri-La wherein "[t]he soft, sweet atmosphere, the rich, level soil, the graceful mesquite trees, the abundance of pure spring water, the warm river, . . . seemed to soothe the sense and fill us with inspiration. We felt as if we might be content to live here forever" (292). The idealism with which he portrays the delta is hard to ignore.

This unabashed California booster uses such overtly bucolic scenes to champion his irrigation crusade. As if there was any doubt to the potential he saw in this region, Smythe muses:

> the mighty delta of a mighty river—is rich in the potentialities of production beyond any land in our country which has ever known the plow. . . . Without the right and the ability to use this water nothing is possible; with it, everything is possible. . . . in no part of the wide world is there a place where Nature has provided so perfectly for a stupendous achievement by means of irrigation as in that place where the Colorado River flows uselessly past the international desert which Nature intended for its bride. Some time [*sic*] the wedding of the waters to the soil will be celebrated, and the child of that union will be a new civilization. (293–94).

The legacy of Smythe's lofty rhetoric helped shape the attitudes and policies toward arid America in the coming decades. In 1902, Congress passed the Reclamation Act which opened the American West to large-scale federal assistance to redeem the nation's supposed waste places. The implications of this act not only facilitated the ongoing cultivation of the delta into one of the world's great agricultural regions, but they also enabled policies and practices that would, in the decades to come, alter the delta in ways that those on both sides of the border could hardly imagine at the time. Central to these transformations is the underlying assumption that the United States should exert its control over nature to make such agricultural and economic transformations possible. Yet such control comes with a price as Donald Worster reminds us: "[T]he domination of nature in the water empire must lead to the domination of some people by others" (*Under Western Skies* 31). The realization of Smythe's vision not only brought the Colorado River and the delta under the control of powerful political and economic forces, indigenous groups and Mexican citizens also came under the reign of the United States' control and manipulation of water.

Up to this point in the delta's literary record, the first-person exploration/travel narrative dominates readers' understanding of the area. However, in 1911, Harold Bell Wright published a novel representing one of the best articulations of the shift from the delta's impossibilities of sustaining communities and economies to its potential as a latter-day Eden. *The Winning of Barbara Worth* is a shameless tribute to the reclamation era as it centers on Jefferson Worth and his efforts to irrigate the King's Basin, the fictional representation of California's present-day Imperial Valley, and to tame the outlaw river toward the novel's end.[7] In the opening pages, Worth and his caravan travel across the desert where they find an orphaned child (Barbara) whose mother died of thirst trekking west toward the California coast. Although Worth gestures to take the girl and raise her as his own, Barbara exclaims, "Barba wants drink" and embraces the civil engineer instead (44). The girl's request and choice of the engineer, a man known throughout the novel as "the Seer," gives the reader a not-so-subtle nod that the land-as-female acquiesces to the advancement of technology, progress, and, ultimately, Western reclamation. Early in the novel, one of the Seer's employees explains that "[t]hey call him the Seer because av his talk av the great things that will be doin' in this country av no rain at all. I've heard him say mesilf that hundreds av thousands av acres av these big deserts will be turned into farms, an' all that be what he calls 'Reclamation'" (24). We also find out that King's Basin is also known as La Palma de la Mano de Dios—the hollow of God's hand—a title suggesting that the land is under a divine mandate for redemption from its forlorn state. Because the novel hit the literary market during a period when massive flooding repeatedly destroyed crops and the delta's fledgling towns, and when reclamation doctrine dominated the nation's collective psyche, it is no wonder that *The Winning of Barbara Worth* was not only a bestselling novel but later, in 1926, a major motion picture starring Ronald Coleman, Vilma Banky, and Gary Cooper.

The drive to reclaim the nation's deserts evident in Smythe's promotional literature and Wright's fiction culminated in a host of Congressional actions, including the 1922 Colorado River Compact and the 1928 Boulder Canyon Project Act that eventually led to the Colorado River and its delta's ultimate demise. In line with Smythe's prophetic statement that who controlled the river controlled the region's development, the Compact divided the Colorado River's waters between the seven basin states with little consideration of Mexico. Not until 1944 and 1973 would the US be legally required to deliver to Mexico water of a specified quantity and quality.[8] The Boulder Canyon Project Act paved the way for the first massive dam on the river to control the seasonal floods that devastated the communities and fields along the lower Colorado. Although Hoover Dam became the envy of the engineering world and a symbol of America's ingenuity and resolve during a time of great economic difficulty, the dam put an end to the annual flooding crucial to the delta's vibrant ecosystem and initiated an era of extensive reclamation efforts that would forever alter the delta on both sides of the US-Mexico border.

Four years after Hoover's completion, Godfrey Sykes aptly summarized the delta's prior considerations in *The Colorado Delta* (1937) that primarily "afford us fleeting glimpses of an unattractive land, traversed by a great river which was difficult of access, surrounded by inhospitable deserts of unknown extent, and guarded from a sea approach by great and violent tides" (171). Based on his expedition to the region in 1890, Sykes's narrative significantly contributes to the understanding of the delta at this time by providing both an excellent discussion of the delta's unique value and a prophetic observation that its importance will likely disappear as a result of the dam's construction. Not only does he describe how the delta's fertile soil is the remains of the Grand Canyon deposited by the Colorado through eons of erosion, he hypothesizes that "[c]urtailment of the surface water supply and its restriction to the cultivated areas and a narrow channel zone will eventually result in the reversion to the condition of the surrounding deserts of much of the region which is at present occupied by luxuriant vegetation" (1, 175). What emerges in this last reference challenges what centuries of earlier accounts had suggested: that the delta is a wasteland. As Sykes notes the extent of plant growth in this desert region, he also recognizes that the desert will likely reclaim these oases when the river's regular flows no longer reach the sea.

Sykes's conclusions came at a time of monumental attitude shifts regarding nature. While conservation represented one perspective on nature, a growing wilderness ethic emerged in the early twentieth century to advocate for nature's inherent rights and the human need for undeveloped places. These latter sentiments urged writers venturing to the delta to view it not as a resource for exploitation and profit but as an aesthetic wonder of beauty whose worth lies in its ability to enrich the soul. John C. Van Dyke, one of the nation's foremost art critics, traveled to the lower Colorado River and the surrounding desert to remediate his health. From his time there he penned *The Desert* (1901), an important volume celebrating the beauty of this underappreciated ecosystem. This perspective represents a significant departure from previous assessments of the delta focused primarily on survival or resource development. Noting the plans to reclaim the delta and the projected economic and agricultural boon this will provide the nation, Van Dyke nonetheless petitions the reader to consider the delta's aesthetic value, which "is just as important a factor in the scheme of human happiness as the corporeal sense of eating and drinking" (60). Critical of the "practical men" (60) who seek to transform the delta for profit, Van Dyke argues that "The deserts should never be reclaimed . . . and should be preserved forever" (59).

In subsequent years, Aldo Leopold, whom many consider as the father of modern ecology, echoes Van Dyke's preservationist stance to express perhaps one of the most celebrated and well-known descriptions of the delta often invoked today. The chapter "Green Lagoons" from the environmental classic, *A Sand County Almanac*, chronicles his 1922 trip to the delta with his brother to hunt birds and is a tribute to a bygone era, one that speaks to the "luxuriant vegetation" Sykes notes in his study. Leopold describes the incredible wealth of wildlife that he sees along his journey, listing the egrets, cormorants, avocets, willets, mallards, widgeons, teal, bobcat, raccoons, coyotes, and deer, saving his most reverential descriptions for "el tigre," the elusive jaguar whose presence was felt more than seen as its "personality pervaded the wilderness" (151). He also explains that the free-flowing river had transformed one of the most inhospitable places on the continent into a verdant oasis. "On the map the delta was bisected by the river," he writes, "but in fact the river was nowhere and everywhere, for he could not decide which of a hundred green lagoons offered the most pleasant and least speedy path to the Gulf" (150). Upon these waters Leopold floats through what he calls a "milk-and-honey wilderness" (155) that abounds in the possibilities wild places offer: a tonic from the rat race of the city, a place in which to lose oneself, an opportunity to commune with nature outside human interference. Although Leopold's chapter overflows with nostalgic delight so typical in wilderness narratives, his work becomes an elegy for a lost place whose possibilities as a modern-day paradise succumb to the passage of time and the agricultural potential inherent in the delta's rich soils. Thus, this chapter's representation of the delta embraces on one hand the possibilities of wilderness and on the other the impossibilities of finding wildness in a region now dominated by the advent of industrial agriculture. Toward the end of his chapter Leopold explains, "All this was far away and long ago. I am told the green lagoons now raise cantaloupes ... Man always kills the thing he loves, and so we the pioneers have killed our wilderness" (157). This lament starkly contrasts with the celebratory rhetoric of Smythe's and Wright's agricultural visions of the delta as it appeals to wild nature unfettered by human intervention.

Leopold's penchant for a wild, unaltered delta reflects the sentiments of many authors in the twentieth century who similarly express a desire to experience a free-flowing river and healthy delta ecosystem. Ellsworth Kolb's *Through the Grand Canyon from Wyoming to Mexico* (1914) offers a fascinating account of their source-to-sea voyage, while Mary Remsen North's *Down the Colorado* (1930) chronicles the journey from the Boulder Dam site to Yuma, Arizona, and across the delta's southeastern desert through the eyes of an 11-year-old Girl Scout. Frank Waters, a prolific author of the American West, gives his own source-to-sea survey of the river in *The Colorado* (1944). In the post-war years, the delta's literature begins to shift to more closely reflect Leopold's lament as the environmental impacts of the Bureau of Reclamation's dam-building spree during this era become key touchstones for a burgeoning environmental ethos across the nation. Thus, in works such as Philip Fradkin's *A River No More* (1968), Colin Fletcher's *River* (1997), and most recently, Jonathan Waterman's *Running Dry* (2010), we see the authors mourn the delta's demise as they lead the reader through their first-person accounts of traveling downriver from the beauty of the headwaters, through the majesty of the Canyonlands, to the delta where the river no longer reaches the sea. Yet, as Waterman's account and a number of twenty-first-century texts suggest, the delta's possibilities have emerged once again, this time to the tune of restoration.

As writers, scientists, environmentalists, and delta lovers have longed for the return of the delta's former splendor, works across a variety of genres have imagined how such restoration would occur. One of the more extreme possibilities surfaces in Gary Hansen's novel *Wet Desert* (2007). Building on Edward Abbey's classic *The Monkey Wrench Gang* (1975) wherein a merry band of eco-marauders fantasize about blowing up Glen Canyon Dam to free the Colorado, *Wet Desert* describes an ecoterrorist's destruction of the dam and the protagonist's attempt to catch him and save the dams and communities downriver. In the novel's conclusion, Grant Stevens, the engineer-hero, attempts to apprehend the culprit as the Colorado floods the delta to join the sea once again.

A more plausible approach to restoring the delta and river comes from Bergman's *Red Delta*, a book whose beautiful photographs and accompanying prose offer the most comprehensive view of the delta at the start of the new millennium as it traces the history of the delta's demise while also addressing efforts of restoring this region that many had all but felt was lost. Bergman's attention to the local Mexican and indigenous connections to the delta constitutes one of the more important aspects of the book and reflects a greater concern for these stakeholders and their role in restoring the river. Whereas groups like the Cucapá have occupied minor roles in the narratives of earlier visitors,[9] documents representing partnerships between the Sonoran Institute, Pronatura Noroeste, and the Asociación Ecológica de Usuarios del Río Hardy y Colorado (AEURHYC), for example, witness the growing chorus advocating for their place at the decision table.[10] Since the delta's transformation represents a significant environmental justice concern as the river's absence has severely impacted the Cucapá's traditional fishing practices, groups such as those above are working with the tribe to advocate for their rights. The Sonoran Institute, for example, has produced a two-page document entitled "Land of the Kwapa" that maps the Cucapá's homeland and offers an overview of the tribe's connection to the delta. Among various infographics and photographs of the Cucapá past and present, a statement from tribal elder Colin Soto clearly states his people's dependence on a free-flowing river. Soto remarks, "The Kwapa people are the river. Our whole life was based on the river. . . . When you take the river, the trees and the wood away, I have no identity. I have nowhere to go. If the river stops flowing, we will no longer exist."

Recently, the Cucapá's intimate connection to the Colorado has become an important asset among restoration efforts evident in AEURHYC's *Plan Estratégico* or Strategic Plan for 2004–2006 which outlines the organization's efforts "to conserve and restore the ecosystems of the Delta and the Colorado River and promote the wise use of its resources for the realization and continuation of activities that will allow for the economic, social, and cultural development of the local communities" (7).[11] Collaboration among various stakeholders, including the Cucapá people, is integral to AEURHYC's mission with decisions meant to be "based on the opinions of everyone" (4). As Germán Muñoz López, a founding member of the group, explains in the plan's preface, "There are few of us left who have seen the Colorado River in its splendor before its flow almost completely stopped. Most of us, now members of the Association, had our first encounter with the Colorado River during the 1950s, while others like members of the Cucapá tribe have been here for hundreds of years" (2). Lopez's recognition of the long-standing human presence in the area starkly contrasts with the wasteland, uninhabited wilderness trope that resounds through earlier delta narratives. By foregrounding both his community's reliance on the river as well as the Cucapá's, Lopez speaks to the delta's potential and the role these groups will have in molding that vision.

Along with written works, film and digital media have emerged as powerful means to promote restoration. Alexandra Cousteau's short film, *Death of a River: The Colorado River Delta* (2010), depicts the barren, parched sands that once supported rich ecosystems while giving voice to some of the locals working to restore the delta. The *Raise the River Coalition* website also houses images, video, and testimonials of the restoration efforts of a group of government and nonprofit organizations. The coalition's short film, *Renewal: A Reborn Colorado River Once Again Finds Her Path to the Sea* (2014), articulates one of the most effective portrayals of these activities. Created after the signing of the Minute 319, a binational agreement between the US and Mexico which grants a minimum flow to be released from Mexico's Morelos Dam as an experiment to regenerate the delta's flora and fauna, this film witnesses the impact that even a small percentage of the Colorado's flow can have on all of the delta's many communities.

Narrated by Robert Redford, *Renewal* opens with stunning shots of the delta and Redford's reassurance that "when allowed, nature has immense power to restore its own balance, to find its own rhythm, in the world as it should be." Sound bites from key personnel from organizations such as the Environmental Defense Fund, the Nature Conservancy, and Pronatura Noroeste join time-lapse images showing the river's inundation of the previously parched riverbed; various close-ups of the flora and fauna attest to the positive response of the river's return. These shots offer the viewer a powerful reminder of the ecological possibilities that a little water can have while also emphasizing the impact the river's presence has on the human communities. Redford notes that perhaps the greatest finding so far to the river's release has been the human response. The segment capturing the celebration that erupts at San Luis Rio Colorado, a town on the Mexico-Arizona border, speaks to the intimate ties this community has with the river. In this footage, a time-lapse sequence captures the slow progression of the river filling the sand-laden riverbed as crowds of locals make their way to play in the water. Then, multiple shots of children playing in the water and families gathering to enjoy this precious resource couple with sound bites from locals who praise the river's return as a "blessing." Amid these scenes of celebration among those living along the river's banks and those who have worked to create Minute 319, the film concludes with Redford inviting viewers to "restore life to the delta, help us continue the positive change on the way." This resounding message of hope offers a welcome tonic to the despair marking many of the delta's narratives in the post-dam era.

In his introduction to *Red Delta*, Bergman addresses the growing optimism that characterizes the responses to the delta today. He admits, "That people have slowly come to care about the Mexican delta of the Colorado River is one of the most remarkable environmental stories on the continent" (14). Indeed, this growing awareness of the delta's inherent value has been a long time coming when we consider that for centuries the delta was cast off as a desert wasteland that inspired fear and disregard from those entering the region from more well-watered and temperate climes. Of course, the Kwapa have cared for the viability and integrity of the delta long before it was valued for its incredible agricultural potential or wilderness appeal. They have intimately known for generations what others are now coming to more clearly understand: *"agua es vida"* (water is life). Only time will tell, though one thing is for sure: subsequent chapters to the delta's literary history will have to contend with ongoing drought, ever-increasing demands for the Colorado's water among a broader range of interests, and a growing sense of the delta's ecological importance to humans and nonhumans alike.[12] Finding a balance between these realities ensures further drama for the region and its readers.

Notes

1. These include the Imperial, Coachella, Palo Verde, Mexicali, and Wellton-Mohawk Valleys throughout southeastern California, northern Baja California and Sonora, and southwestern Arizona, respectively.
2. Portions of Arizona, California, Colorado, Nevada, New Mexico, Utah, and Wyoming make up the Colorado River Basin. The Mexican states of Baja California and Sonora also make up part of the watershed.
3. The Cucapá is a tribe residing on both sides of the US-Mexico border. In the US, the tribe is referred to as Cocopah.
4. As Albert B. Elsasser explains, Alarcón's record of his 1540 voyage up the Colorado River has not been located. However, a summary of his exploits contained in a letter to Mendoza provides us with a glimpse of the geography and people he encountered (8).
5. Father Crisóstomo Gómez, president of the Dominicans in Baja California, petitioned then Governor José Antonio Roméu to establish missions in the delta. His request arrived after Roméu's passing, and Arrillaga, as lieutenant governor, stepped into to fulfill Gómez's wishes. See John. W. Robinson's introduction to Arrillaga's journal for more on the Governor's involvement in La Frontera's settlement and a brief history of other Spanish entries into the region.
6. Pattie recalls that his group found the Cucapá Indians friendly.
7. In 1904, the Colorado River broke through a rudimentary irrigation diversion where it followed a historic river channel, thereby filling the remains of an ancient lake bed known as the Salton Sink. This flood, which ended in 1907, created the Salton Sea, which today provides important bird habitat along the Pacific Flyway and collects the agricultural runoff of countless acres. George James's *The Wonders of the Colorado Desert* (1906), George Kennan's *The Salton Sea* (1917), and William deBuys' *Salt Dreams* (1999) represent a few of the works dedicated to this lake.
8. The 1944 Act granted Mexico 1.5 million acre feet of water while Minute 242 dictated the level of salts flowing south of the border.
9. See Anita Alvarez de Williams's *Travelers Among the Cucapá* for more on Cucapá representations in delta literature.
10. Pronatura is Mexico's largest environmental organization. AEURHYC is the Ecological Association of Colorado and Hardy River Users.
11. Spanish translations are mine.
12. Minute 319 expired in 2017. In September of that year, Mexico and the United States signed Minute 323 to oversee restoration efforts, water quality and quantity issues and drought mitigation plans through 2026. See Minute 323, pp. 15-18 for specifics about delta restoration efforts.

Works Cited

Abbey, Edward. *The Monkey Wrench Gang*. Lippincott Williams and Wilkins, 1975.

Arrillaga, José Joaquín. José Joaquín Arrillaga: Diary of His Surveys of the Frontier,

1796. Translated by Fory Tiscareno, edited by John W. Robinson, Dawson's Book Shop, 1969.

Asociación Ecológica de Usuarios del Río Hardy-Colorado, (AEURHYC). "Plan Estratégico." *Colorado River Delta/Delta del Rio Colorado Research Coordination Network.* U of Arizona P, 2004. www.geo.arizona.edu/rcncrd/documents/Plano_Estrategico.pdf.

Bergman, Charles. *Red Desert: Fighting for Life at the End of the Colorado River.* Fulcrum, 2002.

Death of a River: The Colorado River Delta. Executive producer Alexandra Cousteau, 2010, www.alexandracousteau.com/videos/.

deBuys, William. *Salt Dreams: Land and Water in Low-Down California.* U of New Mexico P, 1999.

Elsasser, Albert B., editor. Alarcón, Hernando. "Explorations of Hernando Alarcón in the Lower Colorado River Region, 1540." Translated by Richard Hakluyt, *Journal of California and Great Basin Anthropology,* vol. 1, no. 1, 1979, pp. 8–37.

Fletcher, Colin. *River: One Man's Journey Down the Colorado, Source to Sea.* Knopf, 1997.

Fradkin, Philip L. *A River No More: The Colorado River and the West.* 1968. U of California P, 1995.

Goetzman, William H. *Exploration and Empire: The Explorer and the Scientist in the Winning of the American West.* Texas State Historical Association, 1993.

Hansen, Gary. *Wet Desert.* Hole Shot Press, 2007.

International Boundary and Water Commission United States and Mexico. "Minute Number 323." International Boundary and Water Commission United States and Mexico, 2017. https://www.ibwc.gov/Files/Minutes/Min323.pdf.

Ives, Joseph C. *Report upon the Colorado River of the West.* Government Printing Office, 1861. *Google Books.*

James, George. *The Wonders of the Colorado Desert.* Little, Brown, 1906.

Kennan, George. *The Salton Sea: An Account of Harriman's Fight with the Colorado River.* Macmillan, 1917.

Kino, Eusebio Francisco, S.J. *Plan for the Development of Pimería Alta, Arizona &Upper California, a report to the Mexican Viceroy.* Translated by Ernest J. Burrus, Arizona Pioneers' Historical Society, 1961.

Kolb, Ellsworth L. *Through the Grand Canyon from Wyoming to Mexico.* 1914. Macmillan, 1952.

Leopold, Aldo. *A Sand County Almanac: With Essays on Conservation from Round River.* Ballantine, 1970.

Limerick, Patricia Nelson. *Desert Passages: Encounters with the American Deserts.* U of New Mexico P, 1985.

Murrieta-Saldivar, Joaquin, and Mark Lellouch. "Colorado River Delta: Land of the Kwapa," *The Sonoran Institute.* 2009. https://sonoraninstitute.org/files/pdf/colorado-river-delta-land-of-the-kwapa-english-08062009.pdf.

North, Mary Remsen. *Down the Colorado By a Lone Girl Scout, Mary Remsen North.* Putnam's Sons, 1930.

Pattie, James O. *The Personal Narrative of James O. Pattie, of Kentucky.* Edited by Timothy Flint, E. B. Flint, 1833. *Google Books.*

Renewal: A Reborn Colorado River Once Again Finds Her Path to the Sea. Produced by Andrew Quinn and Owen Bissell, 2014, *Sonoran Institute*, sonoraninstitute. org/card/ colorado-river-delta/.

Smythe, William E. "An International Wedding: The Tale of a Trip on the Borders of Two Republics." *Sunset,* vol. 4, November 1900, pp. 286–300. *Google Books.*

———. *The Conquest of Arid America.* 1899. U of Washington P, 1970.

Starr, Kevin. *California: A History.* Modern Library, 2005.

Sykes, Godfrey. *The Colorado Delta.* Lord Baltimore P, 1937.

Tiscareno, Fory, translator, *José Joaquín Arrillaga: Diary of His Surveys of the Frontier, 1796.* Edited by John W. Robinson. Dawson's Book Shop, 1969.

Van Dyke, John C. *The Desert: Further Studies in Natural Appearances.* 1901. Johns Hopkins UP, 1999.

Ward, Evan R. *Border Oasis: Water and the Political Ecology of the Colorado River Delta, 1940-1975.* U of Arizona P, 2003.

Waterman, Jonathan. *Running Dry: A Journey from Source to Sea Down the Colorado River.* National Geographic, 2010.

Waters, Frank. *The Colorado.* Swallow P, 1946.

Williams, Anita Alvarez de. *Travelers Among the Cucapá.* Dawson's Book Shop, 1975.

"Welcome to Cocopah Indian Tribe." *Cocopah Indian Tribe,* 2017. www.cocopah.com/.

Worster, Donald. *Under Western Skies: Nature and History in the American West.* Oxford UP, 1992.

Poetry and Revolution
on the Brink of Ecological Disaster

Ernesto Cardenal and the
Interoceanic Canal in Nicaragua

JEREMY G. LAROCHELLE

Acabar con el Lago de Nicaragua sería el crimen más grande
de la historia de nuestro país, y Ortega pasaría a ser una figura
más abominable que William Walker.

[Destroying Lake Nicaragua would be the worst crime in
the history of our country, and Ortega would become a more
abominable figure than William Walker.]

—Ernesto Cardenal

AT THE AGE OF ninety-two, the celebrated Nicaraguan poet, priest, and liberation theologian, Ernesto Cardenal, speaks out vehemently against the construction of an interoceanic canal in Nicaragua, approved by President Daniel Ortega, his former "compañero" during the Sandinista revolution, calling it the "monstruosidad del canal" and vowing to dedicate what remains of his life to prevent the project from coming to fruition. The canal would have grave ecological effects on Lake Nicaragua, the location of the island of Solentiname, now a national monument, where in the 1970s Cardenal established poetry and art workshops with *campesinos* who went on to take up arms to overthrow the Somoza dictatorship. In an article in *La prensa*, Cardenal stated that, "Con este canal el lago de Nicaragua, que para nosotros es una gran bendición de Dios, se convertirá en una maldición" (With this canal, Lake Nicaragua, which for us is a great blessing from God, will become a curse).[1] What is equally concerning is the fact that Ortega has signed into law, *Ley 840, Ley especial para el Desarrollo de Infraestructura y Transporte Nicaragüense,* which concedes sovereignty to billionaire Wang Jing for the next 116 years. Although as of late 2017, construction of the canal is currently on hold (recent newspaper articles ironically depict the current "canal," a dirt path populated by horses and cows), protests continue in full force across the country.

In light of the social and environmental crisis that will likely ensue in Nicaragua if Ley 840 is not repealed and if an interoceanic canal is completed, I feel compelled to return to the poetry of revolution by Cardenal, and the period of optimism that was palpable across the country in the years immediately following the Sandinista victory of 1979. Cardenal's poems from this time of optimism, alongside work by the *campesino* poets of Solentiname, serve to illustrate the abominable fall from grace of the Sandinistas as well as the potential for the people to once again rally together against a dictatorship.

The optimism that there would be both social and environmental change for Nicaragua was thwarted by a number of factors including the US-backed contras through the 1980s and corruption from within the revolutionary regime. Whether ultimately successful or not, Cardenal and the *campesino* poets of Solentiname were proof of the power of poetry to facilitate revolution. Now, nearly four decades since the victory in 1979, that revolutionary spirit can be seen across the country as people fill the streets declaring "no quiero el canal." From political cartoons to songs to other creative manifestations against the canal and against Ortega, we see the same spirit of revolution in which the social and environmental are inherently connected. If the canal project comes to fruition, the people of Nicaragua will no longer be able to depend on the lake as a healthy source of fish and drinking water. Islands such as Solentiname will be a forgotten relic in the midst of a contaminated lake. One resident there told Cardenal recently: "Voy a estar comiendo mucho pescado, porque después ya no habrá más pescado que el enlatado por los chinos" (I am going to be eating a lot of fish, because afterwards there won't be any left, only Chinese canned fish) (Cardenal web). In light of these catastrophic changes afoot, which are currently causing large-scale social uprising in the country, I wish to revisit work by Cardenal and the poets of Solentiname that illustrate the importance of the lake for both the humans and nonhumans that live along its shores as a call for action.

Campesina leader, Francisca Ramírez, the face of the anti-canal movement in Nicaragua, embodies this call for action and is fighting all she can to effect change despite threats to her personal safety. On Earth Day, 22 April 2017, Ramírez, along with the *Consejo nacional en defensa de nuestra tierra, lago y soberanía* (CENIDH, National Counsel in defense of our land, lake and sovereignty), led the 87th national protest to demand the repeal of Ley 840 since Ortega signed it into law in 2013. For Ramírez, life in her town, Nueva Guinea, resembles the police state conditions and infringements upon her freedom that existed under the Somoza regime. In a recent interview in March 2017, Ramírez discussed her experience of being put in jail and stated that the commissioner, upon being asked for official papers to enter her home, said: "Él nos dijo que no le interesaba nada, que no estaba para escuchar a nadie y que él podía hacer lo que quisiera en el pueblo. Que nadie podía reclamar nada" (González). (He told us that he didn't care about anything, that he wasn't there to listen to anyone and that he could do whatever he wanted to do in the village. That nobody could file a complaint.)

Although President Ortega stated unequivocally in May of 2007 that by no means would he put Lake Nicaragua, the largest supply of fresh water in Central America, at risk with a megaproject like the Interoceanic Canal—"No habrá oro en el mundo que nos haga ceder en esto" (There will not be enough gold in the world that will make us budge on this)—he signed Ley 840 into law only six years later in 2013. This dangerous and hypocritical change in policy is certainly not lost on Francisca Ramírez, or on lawyer and human rights activist Mónica López Baltodano, the other most prominent leader of the movement against the canal and against Ley 840. López Baltodano is also the president of the Fundación Popol Na, an NGO founded in 1990 and dedicated to bringing about a Nicaragua in which "the economy, democracy, and relationships between people are just and equitable"—many of the same principles that formerly were in line

with Sandinista values (Fundación Popol Na). Popol Na has created
a community manual educating the people about the dangers of 840
and the canal. She also recently published a book entitled *La entrega
de un país: Expediente jurídico de la concesión canalera en Nicaragua*
(The surrender of a country: Legal File of the canal concession in
Nicaragua), which provides insight into the legal implications of the
law and the struggle for sovereignty. In a recent article, she emphasizes
the irresponsible and dangerous nature of Ley 840 in privatizing precious resources even if the canal is never constructed:

> La intención es privatización de los más preciados bienes co-
> munes del país, como el agua, las tierras y los bosques. Es un
> proyecto de despojo de las comunidades. Y va más allá de que
> se construya o no un Canal, pues el esquema jurídico es tan
> tramposo que fue montado para que se mantenga vigente por
> 116 años, incluso si nunca llegan a construir el Canal. (Le Lous)
>
> (The intention is the privatization of the most precious com-
> munal resources of the country, such as water, land, and forests.
> It is a project that will strip communities of these resources. And
> it goes well beyond whether or not the Canal will be constructed,
> as the legal terms are so tricky that it was created so that it will
> remain in effect for 116 years, even if the Canal is never built.)

Baltodano clearly states the intention of the law and the devastating effect
it would have on the communities most dependent on the clean water,
land, and forests of the country. She and Ramírez, together with tens
of thousands of protestors across the country, are speaking out to bring
about the repeal of 840 as well as prevent the construction of the canal.

Despite the protests and grassroots movement against the project, there
are those who support Ortega's decision either because they feel that it is in
their economic interest or out of desperation and the belief that it may provide a possible way out of poverty. In her recently published book on the
canal, Baltodano states that the notion that the construction of the canal
could eradicate poverty in Nicaragua appeals to "an anxious and resigned
citizenry after many collectively shared frustrated expectations" *(seduce y
somete a una ciudadanía ansiosa y sedienta de la realización de muchas ex-
pectativas colectivas frustradas) (Baltodano, La entrega de un país)*. Despite

a history peppered by optimism followed by frustrated expectations, the promotional materials from the firm that proposes to construct the canal, HKND (Hong Kong Nicaragua Canal Development Investment Company), utilize a grandiose rhetoric as they present the hope the project brings. In a promotional video available on YouTube, HKND affirms that the project will bring about *"la felicidad, la paz de la humanidad y el desarrollo mundial"* (happiness, peace for humanity, and world development). It also addresses environmental concerns and proposes that the canal will promote *"armonía ecológica y cultural"* (ecological and cultural harmony). With the exception of *"desarrollo mundial"* (global development), the values highlighted sound eerily similar to the goals of the Sandinista revolution. The video delineating the proposed route for the canal is entirely devoid of people and, although narrated in Spanish with relaxing piano music in the background, includes Chinese characters throughout, labeling locations and features of the proposed canal. The video does address the fact that there are environmental concerns but affirms that the canal project will occur "al servicio de la naturaleza" (in service to nature). The cognitive dissonance of this message is certainly not lost on the estimated 280 communities and approximately 100,000 people who will be expropriated of their land, many of whom depend on el Lago de Nicaragua for their livelihood (Huete-Pérez et al.). The propaganda in the video also plays on Nicaragua's history of unwelcome intervention from the United States and characterizes disapproval from the US as part of *"un gran juego en América Latina"* (a great game in Latin America).

One of the arguments of those who support the project (and who continue to argue against the relevance of environmental issues in Latin America) is precisely that the potential economic benefits outweigh the losses and from this standpoint the thousands of displaced are merely the *"víctimas de modernización"* (victims of modernization), (following Fernando Mires in *El discurso de la naturaleza*, The Discourse of Nature), the social cost of "progress." Mires, however, argues that change is possible only when those most affected, the very victims of the processes of modernization, actively participate:

Ecology is not, nor can it be, a secondary issue in Latin America, above all if one considers that the preservation of nature has to

do with, more than anything, the material and cultural survival
of the majority of the inhabitants of the continent. Nevertheless,
that preservation only will be possible if Ecology moves from the
most specialized laboratories toward the world of political discussions and decisions. How this advance will be possible in each
country cannot be known ahead of time. It is definitely possible to
anticipate that it will only be realized with the active participation
of the very victims of the processes of modernization. (Mires 12)

In the case of the Sandinista Revolution of the 1970s and 1980s in
Nicaragua, these "victims of the processes of modernization," the *campesinos* who took up arms and joined the FSLN *(Frente Sandinista de
Liberación Nacional),* actively fought to repair the ecological and social
destruction caused by the Somoza dynasty, and more specifically, United
States–supported Anastasio Somoza Debyle, the third of the Somoza
family to rule Nicaragua. They also participated, along with Ernesto
Cardenal, in poetry and painting workshops in which they voiced their
vision for a Nicaragua free of the grips of the Somoza regime. These writings, along with Cardenal's poetic work, both before and shortly after the
Sandinista victory of 19 July 1979, provide ample material for analyzing
the environmental, in addition to the social, underpinnings of the revolution. Moreover, Cardenal's particular approach to representing this
inseparability is useful in rethinking the interconnectedness of humans
with the local ecology on which they depend for survival.

In the context of present-day Nicaragua, Mires's emphasis on the
need for active participation by the victims of modernization is ur-
gently relevant in light of the pending canal and Ley 840, as the people
brace themselves to be forcibly removed from their land en masse and
to have that very land, knowingly, be contaminated. The largest freshwater lake in Central America, the very scene where Cardenal and
many of the campesino poets were inspired to fight and give their lives
in many cases for a movement against the bloody Somoza dictatorship,
will now be the site of the largest infrastructure feat of all time. In an interview with *El país* in 2015, Cardenal exclaims: "*¡Tengo que luchar por
Solentiname, por mi lago. Con el canal no quedaría nada!*" (I have to
fight for Solentiname, for my lake. With the canal nothing will be left).

This spirit of urgency to save the lake and the people that Cardenal expressed in 2015 is clearly reminiscent of the call for action against the Somoza dictatorship in the late 1970s.

As the Sandinista revolution was a social revolution with the goal of bringing about safer, healthier living and working conditions for the people and freedom from the political corruption and violence caused by the United States–supported Somoza regime, the environmental factors are often overlooked by critics.[2] One critic who analyzes Cardenal's work from this perspective is Niall Binns in his 2004 book *¿Callejón sin salida? La crisis ecológica en la poesía hispanoamericana* (Dead end: The Ecological Crisis in Spanish American Poetry). Binns argues that Cardenal's hope for a brighter future for Nicaragua, both ecologically and socially, is an idealization and utopian. Adrian Kane in a recent book chapter also discusses "Nueva ecología" in the present-day context and affirms that "Despite its bleak portrayal of the environmental scenario of 1979 as a result of Nicaragua's oppressive past, 'Nueva ecología' presents an optimistic view of the future" (Kane 270). Likewise, Steven White who provides an excellent analysis of poems relating to the indigenous past and ecology, writes that his poetry *"sirve como base para imaginar mejores maneras de habitar la Tierra"* (serves as a foundation to imagine better ways of inhabiting the Earth) (350). In Cardenal's work, and that of some of the *campesino* poets, we see a positive narrative for Nicaragua's future, although, sadly, a narrative that did not come to pass in the long-term. Liberation theology largely informed Cardenal's perspective concerning the rights of the people, both social and environmental, which formed one of the driving forces of the revolution.[3] Looking more closely at the philosophy of liberation theology, we see that it also demands environmental responsibility.

When Cardenal began giving sermons on the island of Solentiname in 1965 in the Lago de Nicaragua, he worked to establish a contemplative community based in discussions of the gospels and the communal allocation of tasks. The people there were met with a philosophy they had not heard before: instead of waiting until one dies to be compensated for one's suffering on Earth, one can seek liberation from the injustices one suffers from while still living.[4] This idealistic philosophy based in a combination of Marxist thought and Catholic theology, asserted that while paradise is not wholly possible to achieve here on Earth, people can work to make their living conditions, including their human interactions and their connection to the natural world, as healthy as possible.[5] In order to do that, however, many found that it was necessary to fight for those ideals. Many *campesinos* from the community in Solentiname, and throughout Nicaragua, enthusiastically joined the FSLN (*Frente Sandinista de Liberación Nacional*)—established in 1961 by Tomás Borge, Carlos Fonseca and President Daniel Ortega himself as a group primarily comprised of students and intellectuals—and took up arms against Somoza (Nieto 132).[6] Some of those who took up arms also participated in poetry and painting workshops that took place on Solentiname, established with the support of Mayra Jiménez in the late 1960s, in which they found their voices and expressed their hopes for the future. These workshops continued throughout Nicaragua up until the late 1980s when, as a consequence of the Contra War, the *Ministry of Culture* was forced to shut down due to extreme budgetary constraints.[7] By 1988 the country was in a state of shambles, as a result of continued armed conflict between the Sandinista army and the United States–supported *Contras*.[8]

Throughout the writings of these poets, we see that social and environmental concerns were viewed as interconnected issues rather than as separate phenomena. The poets wrote extensively of how they envisioned the land: polluted lakes and rivers that had been diverted to the farms of wealthy landowners, or polluted by harmful toxic materials would be restored to health, once again providing the people with an abundance of resources with which they could sustain themselves. The following poem from the workshops, *"Pesca"* (fishing) written by *miliciano y alfabetizador* (militian and literacy teacher), Sergio Vizcaya, clearly articulates the state of the Kayaná River at that time:

The boy fishes
in a deep section of the Kayaná River.
His dark underpants
have foam and slimy clay on them.
When he takes out his fishing net he feels the stench of rotting mud.
On the shore
the pieces of rags

woman's underwear
and the branches he takes out of the water.
The black water
with leaves and *michiguiste* flowers that float
on his arm, foam.
The boy takes silver-backed fish, bream fish, sows
and trash from the river.
(Nicaraguan Peasant Poetry 96)

The boy in the poem fishing on the Kayaná river experiences first-hand the ecological footprint that his fellow humans have brought about in his local river. As he removes garbage along with various types of fish from the river, it is evident that the title *"Pesca"* relates not to sustainable fishing in clean water to feed local families, but to "fishing" out pollutants that block not only the natural flow of water, but also the community's healthy access to the resources of a local waterway.

In Cardenal's collection *Nostalgia del futuro: Pintura y buena noticia en Solentiname* (Nostalgia for the future: Painting and the good news in Solentiname) (1982), the reader has the opportunity to further see the revolution from the perspective of the people, through their words, poetry, and paintings. The paintings, poetry, and recorded dialogue with Cardenal all express a strong sense of the need to bring about justice to the natural world, as a means of establishing justice for the people of Nicaragua. Alejandro, a young painter from Solentiname, says the following about painting, and about the natural world, especially the importance of the lake, which appears in almost every painting:

Everyone puts the lake in their paintings; because the lake serves
a series of functions and for that reason it appears in many paintings, the person lives on the lake, and the painter, then, lives from
the lake; the lake represents more than a road, of course, the lake
is a fountain of life; the people drink from the lake's water, and eat
its fish, they make use of it as a means of communication. People
sit on a rock, or in front of a ranch to see the lake, to observe it.
When the lake appears in the paintings, it does so because none of
the paintings could exist without the lake. (Cardenal 40)

If the canal project indeed comes to fruition, this lake will be severely altered. In an article from 5 June 2015, Keith Schneider in *Circle of Blue*, an online advocacy platform for water resources, outlines the extent of the damage to the lake and watershed and the issues the scientific panel has with the environmental feasibility report submitted by Environmental Resources Management:

> One of the panel's deepest concerns is the safety of Lake Nicaragua, Central America's largest lake and a relatively shallow, clean, and oxygen-rich source of fresh water for thousands of people and a thriving fishery. HKND proposes to cut a 105-kilometer (40-mile) channel across the lake so deep and wide that it would require a wet-excavation project of silt and mud five times larger than constructing the offshore airport in Hong Kong." (Schneider)

Although the study indicates that the damage would be "minimal" from dredging, the panel states unequivocally that it would "dramatically damage the lake's important fisheries, and seriously degrade the lake as a source of drinking water."

In the face of this pending destruction, Cardenal is as dedicated as ever to fight for the future of the lake and for the people of Nicaragua. There is a thread of optimism in his work—which also comes out in his recent interview at ninety years of age—and that can be found the most clearly in "Nueva ecología" from *Vuelos de Victoria* (Flights of Victory) (1984), published five short years after the Sandinista victory of 19 July 1979, and according to Binns, "dyed with the euphoria of the revolution". In the poem, Cardenal makes reference to decisions made by the Somoza dictatorship that had destructive immediate consequences on the local ecology. The speaker affirms that in addition to destroying the lives of the people, Somoza also harmed "lakes, rivers, and mountains", and "diverted the course of rivers toward their large farms":

> The Somocistas also destroyed the lakes, rivers and mountains.
> They diverted the course of the rivers toward their farms.
> The Ochomogo River dried up last summer.
> The Sinecapa River dried up because of the clear-cutting done by

wealthy landowners.
The Río Grande of Matagalpa, dried up during the war,
out by the plains of Sébaco.
They put two dams along the Ochomogo River,
and the capitalist chemical waste
fell into the Ochomogo and the fish swam around like drunks.
The Boaco River with its black waters.
The Moyuá Lagoon had dried up. A Somocista colonel
robbed the lands from the peasants and constructed a fort.
The Moyuá Lagoon that for centuries was beautiful
   in that place.
(but the little fish will come back).
They deforested and put up dams. (31)

Upon diverting the rivers to their plantations, or putting up a dam along the Ochomogo River and depositing "capitalist" chemical waste into the river—causing the fish to "swim around like drunks"—the *Somocistas* end up not only making future earning impossible, but also destroying the resources and the ecosystems that the people depend on for their well-being. In relation to Cardenal's portrayal of rivers in the poem, Adrian Kane affirms: "Indeed, the overall effect of the rivers in 'Ecología' is to portray a country sucked dry by greed and contaminated by a corrupt form of capitalism" (271). The inclusion of "but the little fish will return soon," in parentheses, gently makes the call for ecological recuperation to be part of the agenda of the triumphant revolution. Given the state of Nicaragua in 1984 when *Vuelos de victoria* was published, this hope that ecological concerns will become part of the agenda of the new government can be seen as an even stronger call for help given the mass destruction that was occurring as a result of continued war between the Sandinistas and the US-armed *contras*. Cardenal's hope that Nicaragua's ecology be restored by the Sandinista government would have to wait until the bloodshed and destruction ended. Kane notes, however, that on 24 August 1979, IRENA (Nicaraguan Institute of Natural Resources and the Environment) was created by the newly formed Sandinista government and did, in fact, include a number of environmental programs including pollution control, reforestation, and watershed management, which were part of the Sandinista agenda during the early years: "The environmentalist vision presented in 'Nueva ecología' thus corresponds with the Sandinistas' actions during the early years of the FSLN's rule" (271).

At the end of "Nueva ecología," the speaker in the poem is optimistic that the environment has changed since the revolution and that it suddenly seems more beautiful again; now everything is more peaceful without the reign of the Somoza dictatorship. In the final stanza of the poem, Cardenal calls for the revolution to continue as an ecological revolution:

> But the mountain fish and the fresh-water shark have
>   already breathed.
> Tisma is again full of great Herons
> reflected in its mirrors.
> It has many rooks, armadillo, *güises, zarcetas.*
> The flora has also benefited.
> The *cusucos* are happier under this new government.
> We will recover the forests, rivers and lagoons.
> We will decontaminate Managua Lake.
> Not only humans longed for liberation.
> The whole ecology longed for it. The revolution
> is also of the lakes, rivers, trees, and animals. (31)

Here in the last stanza, we see once again the spirit of hope and optimism that the newly established government could rebuild after the revolution and bring about peace and health for all, humans as well as nonhumans. He states that it was not only humans who felt desperation for liberation from the clutches of the Somoza regime: "toda la ecología gemía" (the whole ecology longed for it). In the poem Cardenal describes the environmental recovery of the mountain fish and fresh-water shark and declares in no uncertain terms: "We will recover the forests, rivers and lagoons. / We will decontaminate Managua Lake." These images of rebirth and an ecstatic local ecology, suddenly healthy and thriving, after being released from the clutches of the oppressive Somoza regime function in sharp contrast to Cardenal's language about Ortega, thirty-two years later: "With this canal, Lake Nicaragua, which for us is a great blessing from God, will become a curse."

Although in his poetry Cardenal represents the empirical reality of ecological and social destruction that contributed to the decision of many to take up arms and join the FSLN, his vision for a brighter future for Nicaragua is evidence of the need for narratives that go beyond that of denunciations of destruction. Narratives such as Cardenal's description of ecological restoration for Nicaragua offer constructive suggestions that have the potential to move people to begin to bring about change. The optimism of the early 1980s seems painfully out of touch with current reality nearly four decades later, with the pending interoceanic canal project looming. Yet, in revisiting these early poems by Cardenal and the poets of Solentiname that he supported, we see how relevant their call to action is to the current situation unfolding in Nicaragua. By articulating a positive narrative rather than a narrative of disenchantment and resignation to the destruction ahead, Cardenal along with tens of thousands of recent protestors shouting, *"no quiero el canal"* (I don't want the canal) and, *"pueblo, unido, jamás será vencido"* (a people, united, will never be divided), continues to maintain some hope that this will not come to pass. Cardenal's message of the need to integrate environmental and social concerns regarding the future of the people of Nicaragua remains poignantly, and painfully, relevant.

Notes

1. Translations mine unless otherwise indicated.
2. A 1969 document, inspired by Carlos Fonseca, one of the founders of the FSLN, set out the goals of the revolution. According to Clara Nieto, one of the goals was also to nationalize the industries such as mining and lumber, in order for them to benefit Nicaragua as a whole, not just the elite and the United States. After taking power by armed force, they would install a revolutionary government "based on an alliance of workers and campesinos and supported by all anti-imperialist forces." It also had the intention of "nationalizing the mining and lumber industries and of reclaiming riches 'usurped' by Yankee monopolies, the properties, factories, sugar refineries, transportation systems, and other possessions 'usurped' by the Somoza family and other 'enemies of the people,' such as politicians, military officers, and other accomplices in the corrupt administration" (Nieto 133). Moreover, "Capitalist agricultural industries, large land holdings, and 'parasitic' tenancy of the land by exploiters would be expropriated" (133).
3. These discussions and sermons have been collected in four volumes entitled *El evangelio en Solentiname*.

4. Critics such as Priscilla Hunter and Edward Elias discuss liberation theology in relation to Cardenal's work, but focus solely on social justice, without referring to the environmental aspects also present. "*La teología 'mística marxista' de Cardenal y su base utópica vistas a través de la alegoría de la niña/humanidad*" by Priscilla Hunter, for example, is a study that illuminates the connection between christianity and Marxist ideology found in Cardenal's work. This study, similar to, "Prophecy of Liberation: The Poetry of Ernesto Cardenal" by Edward Elias, does not mention the environmental factors and their connection to the social injustice discussed in Cardenal's work.

5. Rather than refer to the "utopic" conditions to which the revolution aspires, as Binns does, I argue that the Sandinistas were fighting for "better" conditions. Environmentalism has often been rejected in Latin America for being "utopic"—an unattainable goal. Utopic thought, in contrast to that which we see in Cardenal's poetry, does not accept second best. Aspiring to greatly improve conditions for the people—to be able to establish schools, have better health care, less pollution in local waterways—is not a "utopic" ideal that can never be achieved.

6. Clara Nieto notes that the "armed struggle against Somoza began in 1958," before the establishment of the FSLN, in which "Ramón Raudales, Chale Haslam, and other veterans of Sandino's army once more resorted to armed struggle to combat the dictatorship. Between 1960 and 1962 some twenty anti-Somoza, nationalist, anti-imperialist, and revolutionary organizations emerged, some of them identified with the Cuban Revolution." The FSLN was "the most important of these groups" (132).

7. Karyn Hollis notes the elimination of the funding of the Ministry of Culture, of which Cardenal was put in charge after the revolution, as the decisive moment when the poetry workshops greatly diminished: "A severe blow came in February 1988 when funding for the Ministry of Culture had to be cut. But the movement did not die, and if prosperity ever returns to the country, it seems likely that the poetry workshops will flourish again" (Hollis 2).

8. Nieto describes the state of Nicaragua in the late 1980s as a result of the war: "The war ruined Nicaragua's economy; 50 percent of the national budget went toward defense. The country was staying afloat only by new issues of money that was nothing but paper. Inflation was on the rise, prices were spinning out of control, and industry was collapsing. Children were begging in the streets, hospitals had no anesthetics and pharmacies had no aspirin, stores were empty, and the people's desperation was growing, reported one correspondent" (359). This state was about as far as possible from the hopes that the Sandinistas had for a liberated Nicaragua after their triumph on July 19, 1979.

Works Cited

Baltodano, Mónica López. *La entrega de un país: Expediente jurídico de la concesión canalera en Nicaragua*. Fundación Popol Na, 2017.

Binns, Niall. *¿Callejón sin salida? La crisis ecológica en la poesía hispanoamericana*. Prensas Universitarias de Zaragoza, 2004.

Cardenal, Ernesto. *El evangelio en Solentiname*. Ediciones Sígueme, 1975.

——. "La monstruosidad del Canal." *La Prensa*, 1 November 2014, www.laprensa. com.ni/2014/11/01/columna-del-dia/216594-dla-monstruosidad-del-canal. Accessed May 5 2017.

——. *Nostalgia del futuro: Pintura y buena noticia en Solentiname*. Nueva Nicaragua, 1982.

——. *Vuelos de victoria*. Visor, 1984.

Elias, Edward. "Prophecy of Liberation: The Poetry of Ernesto Cardenal." *Poetic Prophecy in Western Literature*, edited by Raymond-Jean Frontain, Fairleigh Dickinson UP, 1984, pp. 174–85.

Fundación Popol Na. popolna.org. Accessed 5 May 2017.

González, Alejandra. Entrevista: Francisca Ramírez: "A mí no me han quitado los huevos." *La Prensa*. 3 July, 2016. Laprensa.com.ni. Accessed 5 May 2017.

Gonzálaz Harbour, Berna. "Ernesto Cardenal. "El papa Francisco hace la revolución." *El País*. Accessed 5 May 2017.

HKND Group. "HD Nicaragua Canal." *Youtube*, uploaded by George Antonio Lazo Sánchez, 22 November, 2015, https://www.youtube.com/ watch?v=DCBzEOWwx18.

Hollis, Karyn. "Nicaraguan Poetry Workshops: The Democratization of Poetry." *Studies in Latin American Popular Culture*, vol. 11, 1992, pp. 109–22.

Huete-Pérez, Jorge A., et al. "Scientists Raise Alarms about Fast Tracking of Transoceanic Canal Through Nicaragua." *Environmental Science and Technology*, vol. 49, no. 7, 2015, pp. 3989–96.

Hunter, Priscilla. "La teología 'mística marxista' de Cardenal y su base utópica vistas a través de la alegoría de la niña/humanidad." *Selecta: Journal of the Pacific Northwest Council on Foreign Languages*, vol. 6, 1985, pp. 99–105.

Kane, Adrian. "The Nicaragua Canal and the Shifting Currents of Sandinista Environmental Policy." *Ecological Crisis and Cultural Representation in Latin America: Ecocritical Perspectives on Art, Film, and Literature*, edited by Mark Anderson and Zélia Bora, Lexington Books, 2016, pp. 269–75.

Le Lous, Fabrice. "Los tres peligros de la Ley 840, del Canal de Nicaragua." *La Prensa*, 23 April, 2017 <Laprensa.com.ni.>. Accessed 5 May 2017.

Mires, Fernando. *El discurso de la naturaleza: Ecología y política en América Latina*. DEI, 1990.

Nicaraguan Peasant Poetry from Solentiname. Translated by David Gullette, West End Press, 1998.

Nieto, Clara. *Masters of War: Latin America and United States Aggression from the Cuban Revolution through the Clinton Years*. Seven Stories Press, 2003.

"No quiero el canal." *YouTube*, uploaded by NO QUIERO EL CANAL, 26 October 2014, www.youtube.com/watch?v=-1iy_rzeIZo.

Presentación del Proyecto del Gran Canal. "Presentación del Proyecto del Gran Canal Interoceánico de Nicaragua." *YouTube*, uploaded by La Prensa Nicaragua, 21 November 2014, https://www.youtube.com/watch?v=v_S7GizvkkU.

Schneider, Keith. "Nicaragua Canal Environmental Assessment Criticized as Scientifically Weak, Technically Inadequate". *Circle of Blue.* 5 June 2015, www.circleofblue.org/2015/world/nicaragua-canal-environmental-assessment-criticized as-scientifically-weak-technically-inadequate/. Assessed 5 May 2017.

White, Steven. *Arando el aire: La Ecología en la Poesía y la Música de Nicaragua.* 400 Elefantes, 2011.

"Bad for the Glass"

Chinatown's Skewed Rendition
of the California Water Wars

ROBERT NIEMI

TERMED "the Citizen Kane of the Seventies" by film scholar Jonathan Kirshner, Roman Polanski's *Chinatown* (1974) is rightfully regarded as one of the gems of the New American Cinema (Kirshner 178). Polanski's neo-noir masterpiece has also been considered an iconic evocation of the history of Los Angeles—but that is a popular misconception. Though the film certainly engages the history of Los Angeles, it transposes, conflates, simplifies, and distorts elements of that history while suffusing its revisionist narrative with a strong whiff of lurid melodrama that makes for a powerful film but also results in further dehistoricization. *Chinatown* is indisputably a great movie—one of Hollywood's greatest—but as radical filmmaker and critic Thom Andersen notes,

> *Chinatown* isn't a docudrama, it's a fiction. The water project it depicts isn't the construction of the Los Angeles Aqueduct engineered by William Mulholland before the First World War. *Chinatown* is set in 1938 [*sic*], not 1905.[1] The Mulholland-like figure, Hollis Mulwray, isn't the chief architect of the project, but rather its strongest opponent, who must be discredited and murdered. Mulwray is against the Alto Vallejo Dam because it's unsafe, not because it's stealing water from somebody else.

As Andersen notes, William Mulholland (1855–1935) was superintendent and chief engineer of the Los Angeles Water Department from 1902 until his retirement in 1929. In partnership with one-term Los Angeles mayor Frederick Eaton (1855–1934), a civil engineer, power broker, and real estate speculator, Mulholland oversaw the financing and construction of the Los Angeles Aqueduct (completed in 1913): the vital water conveyance that allowed Los Angeles, a desert town, to transform itself into a vast metropolis with a current population of 4 million (the population of greater Los Angeles exceeds 10 million). Indeed, Mulholland and Eaton were the de facto cofounders of modern Los Angeles. Loosely basing *Chinatown*'s main plot on the so-called "California Water Wars" (c.1902–1928)—protracted turmoil surrounding the building of the aqueduct—screenwriter Robert Towne turned William Mulholland into the civic-minded Hollis Mulwray and rendered Fred Eaton as Noah Cross, Mulwray's ruthless nemesis, thus creating a good-versus-evil moral schema that radically simplifies the actual history, which is highly complex, involving labyrinthine business dealings, political machinations, and a series of enormous civil engineering projects at far-flung locations. The real history of the founding of Los Angeles might be adequately represented in a carefully constructed documentary film or mini-series but could only be hinted at in a detective mystery/melodrama. What Towne did instead was to sketch some broad aspects of the history to construct an allegorical critique of oligarchic capitalism.

 Chinatown began in 1971, when producer Robert Evans offered Robert Towne $175,000 to write a screenplay for *The Great Gatsby*.[2] Towne felt he could not improve upon F. Scott Fitzgerald's masterpiece so he asked Evans for $25,000 to write an original screenplay for a Thirties detective story that eventually became *Chinatown*. Evans agreed. Regarding the creative wellsprings that fostered *Chinatown*, Robert Towne cites "a number of moments that contributed to the ultimate birth" of the film (Simon). In the late 1960s and early 1970s, Towne, still a relative unknown, was having trouble getting his script for *The Last Detail* made into a film due to what studio executives considered its excessive use of profanity. Feeling stymied, Towne began to look for new sources of inspiration for another film project. In 1969, he came across an illustrated article entitled "Raymond Chandler's L.A." in a copy of *West Magazine* (the now defunct Sunday magazine of the *Los Angeles Times*). As Towne explains it, what intrigued him were about half a dozen photographs taken in 1969 meant to represent LA in the 1930s:

There was a shot of a Plymouth convertible under one of those old streetlamps outside of Bullocks Wilshire.[3] There was a shot of a beautiful Packard outside of a home in Pasadena. There was another shot of the old railway station downtown.[4] I looked at them, and realized "My God, with a selective eye, you could recreate the L.A. of the '30s." Then owing to a number of other experiences—walking on the Palisades and things like that which brought back a lot via sense memory, I began to realize and reflect upon how much I felt had been lost about the city in the intervening 30-35 years. (Simon)

For Towne, these evocative trace images of an almost vanished world generated a strong desire to try and recreate Depression-era Los Angeles on film while it was still possible. Another factor in the gestation process, which set the political tone of the film, was the blatant corruption that Towne observed in the development of real estate in Deep Canyon near his home in Beverly Hills: greed-driven chicanery that Towne saw as endemic.

Yet another source of inspiration emerged when Towne was in Eugene, Oregon, in 1970, working as an uncredited script doctor on Jack Nicholson's film, *Drive, He Said*. At the University of Oregon's library, Towne discovered a book by the noted investigative journalist Carey McWilliams entitled *Southern California Country: Island on the Land*. A section in chapter 10 of McWilliams's book briefly recounts the California Water Wars that were decisive in the early development of Los Angeles. Towne remembers the material as being "a revelation" to him (though born and raised in San Pedro, an LA suburb, Towne was unaware of the city's fraught history): "And I thought 'Why not do a picture about a crime that's right out in front of everybody. Instead of a jewel-encrusted falcon, make it something as prevalent as water faucets, and make a conspiracy out of that. And after reading about what they were doing, dumping water and starving the farmers out of their land, I realized the visual and dramatic possibilities were enormous. So that was really the beginning of it" (Simon). Intrigued, Towne went on to consult other sources, for example, Morrow Mayo's *Los Angeles*, and even the Department of Water and Power's own accounts (Piper 15).

Still another shaping factor was Robert Towne's friendship with Jack Nicholson. As Towne recalled in a 2009 interview for *CNN*, "We were very close friends, and I think that his kind of insouciance suggested itself for a very cocksure detective who was cynical but with a hidden idealistic streak, who really thought he knew all the answers but in fact had no notion how evil somebody could be" (Leopold).

With all the formative elements in place, Robert Towne put in six months of intensive work to fashion a first draft of his screenplay. Initially coming in at 178 pages in length (equivalent to almost three hours screen time), the convoluted script underwent two more complete revisions to streamline the plot and clarify its overall structure. At 144 pages the shooting script was still unusually long and complex but Towne and director Roman Polanski had managed to excise multiple extraneous scenes and subplots and produce a coherent narrative. Polanski wanted to title the movie *Water and Power* but feared lawsuits from the LA Department of Water and Power, so he went with *Chinatown* instead (Piper 15). Inevitably, in order to establish a 1930s noir setting, the timeframe for the California Water Wars was moved ahead some thirty years. Fred Eaton and William Mulholland first explored the Owens River Valley in 1904 and oversaw the construction of the first Los Angeles Aqueduct between 1908 and 1913. *Chinatown* is set in 1937, long after the most critical and arguably most corrupt period of LA's development. Towne and Polanski developed a script around Eaton and Mulholland but altered their fictive counterparts to create characterizations, backstories, and a rendition of events markedly at odds with history.

The drift away from the historical record can be attributed to two factors: (a) the aforementioned fear of lawsuits and (b) the need to adhere to well-established narrative strictures governing cinematic melodrama in general and the mystery-detective film genre in particular. Both sets of imperatives dictated that history's complexities be reduced to an intense psychodrama involving just a handful of characters. Towne and Polanski did not, however, merely follow genre formulae in rote fashion. *Chinatown* invokes the standard noir narrative paradigm only to subvert it; the tough guy private investigator who is supposed to triumph is ultimately outsmarted and neutralized; the normally evil femme fatale character turns out to be a tragic heroine; the intrigue, usually a private matter, morphs into a hybridized plot that is both intensely personal in nature but also political in its large-scale ramifications, namely, the fate of the entire metropolis is at stake.

LA private eye Jake Gittes (Jack Nicholson) is hired to surveille a supposedly wayward husband, only to discover that the woman who hired him wasn't really the man's wife and that the man in question—LA Water Department chief Hollis Mulwray (Darrell Zwerling)—was actually being targeted for character assassination. After Mulwray is subsequently murdered, Gittes joins forces with Mulwray's real wife, Evelyn (Faye Dunaway), to investigate his murder. Gittes makes some surprising discoveries. He learns that Mulwray was killed by his former business partner, a powerful tycoon named Noah Cross (John Huston), because Mulwray opposed Cross's plan to usurp part of LA's water supply for private gain. Gittes also discovers that Evelyn Mulwray is Noah Cross's daughter and that Cross raped and impregnated her and that she had a daughter named Katherine (Belinda Palmer), now a teenager (who is, of course, also Evelyn's sister). In the film's dénouement in LA's Chinatown neighborhood, Evelyn is shot and killed by police as she tries to flee the scene in order to keep her daughter away from her evil father. Held at gunpoint by Cross's goons and then mistakenly arrested, Jake Gittes is unable to save Evelyn Mulwray, keep Katherine out of Cross's clutches, or prevent Cross from making a highly lucrative land grab by manipulating LA's water supply: a deeply depressing noir ending insisted upon by Roman Polanski over Robert Towne's objections but in keeping with the anticapitalist temperament that prevailed in the 1970s.

Thus, in contradistinction to noir's hyper-masculine-individualist ethos that calls for a brash and resourceful private eye to solve the big case and vanquish his enemies in the process, pitiable Jake Gittes ultimately finds himself outmaneuvered and emasculated by the omnipotent Noah Cross: an incestuous rapist—as if an ordinary rapist were not bad enough—who also figuratively rapes the land and murders anyone who interferes with his schemes. Cross gets away with all of his depredations, public and private, because his vast wealth and power absolves him from the rules of life that govern lesser mortals. A true psychopath, Cross admits that he lacks a conscience. Rationalizing the rape of his own daughter, he tells a bewildered Gittes, "I don't blame myself. You see, Mr. Gittes, most people never have to face the fact that at the right time and right place, they're capable of anything." Untouchable and deeply depraved, Noah Cross epitomizes the cold-blooded rapacity of capitalist imperialism: an iron will to conquer, control, and consume that knows no limits and will brook no opposition—certainly not from a tyro like Jake Gittes.

Noah Cross's water and land boondoggle is very loosely grounded in three key aspects of LA's actual history: (1) the expropriation of water from the Owens River Valley; (2) aqueduct-related land speculation in the San Fernando Valley; and (3) the collapse of the St. Francis Dam in 1928. What follows, in the next three sections, are fairly detailed renditions of these events in order to suggest just how far the film strays from the history it invokes.

As broadly represented by Noah Cross and Hollis Mulwray, their fictive counterparts in *Chinatown*, Eaton and Mulholland were close friends and business partners who eventually had a falling out. In the movie, Cross and Mulwray once co-owned the city's waterworks, but Mulwray insisted that they turn over the water supply to public ownership: a move that Cross adamantly opposed, thus ending their friendship.

The historical reality is quite different and far more nuanced and complicated. Fred Eaton and William Mulholland never "owned" LA's water system per se. From 1868 to 1898 the city of Los Angeles leased the operation of its water supply to the Los Angeles City Water Company (LACWC), a private concern owned by three prominent LA businessmen: John S. Griffen, Solomon Lazard, and Prudent Beaudry. Eaton was appointed LACWC's superintendent in 1874 when he was only nineteen years old. In 1877 Eaton hired Mulholland (just twenty-two) as a zanjero (ditch digger), but the two men became fast friends and Mulholland steadily worked his way up the company ladder. In 1886, after twelve years as superintendent, Eaton left the LACWC to become Los Angeles' surveyor and then city engineer and Mulholland replaced him as LACWC superintendent. In 1897, after a series of disputes over water rates, the Los Angeles City Council tasked Eaton with drawing up plans for a municipal water system. It also gave notice to LACWC that their thirty-year lease would not be renewed when it expired the following year. From 1898 to 1900 Eaton served as the twenty-fourth mayor of Los Angeles, having been elected on the platform of establishing a new municipal water system for the city. In 1899, by a margin of nearly eight to one, city voters approved a $2 million bond measure to purchase LACWC's waterworks (though litigation dragged out the takeover process until 1902). After regaining control of its water system, the city created the Los Angeles Water Department and made Mulholland its superintendent: essentially the same job he had already held with the now defunct LACWC for sixteen years and would hold with its municipal counterpart for another twenty-seven years.

Contrary to the movie's rendition, the falling out between Eaton and Mulholland had nothing to do with opposing views on the ownership of the city's waterworks. In that regard both men would have preferred that LA's water infrastructure stay in private hands, but were savvy enough to yield to the political pressures generated by LA's exponential population growth (from 11,000 in 1880 to 200,000 by 1904). In a larger sense, though, Robert Towne's version of events still contains a grain of truth. What ultimately caused the rift between Eaton and Mulholland was Eaton's avarice. Eaton hoped to sell a land parcel he owned in the Owens River Valley at Long Valley (aka Rickey) Ranch to the Los Angeles Water Department as the site of a storage reservoir for a reputed $1 million. Mulholland thought the sum exorbitant and would not authorize the purchase: a refusal that incensed Eaton and ended their friendship.

Towne's script reflects the Hollywood propensity for creating Manichean melodramas featuring clearly defined heroes and villains by depicting Hollis Mulwray as something of a secular saint and Noah Cross as an amoral monster. Roman Polanski's casting choices for these two key roles mostly reinforces Towne's moral schema. Hollis Mulwray, the Mulholland character in the film, is portrayed by Darrell Zwerling: a thin forty-five-year-old actor whose owlish looks and genteel demeanor nicely conjure Mulwray's basic goodness and vulnerability. Polanski cast distinguished actor-director John Huston in the role of the Fred Eaton figure, Noah Cross. As personified by Huston, Cross presents as a charming, jowly, rather elderly patriarch (Huston was sixty-seven): a figure of impeccable respectability who is, at the same time, a very dangerous maniac. Unlike Hollis Mulwray and Noah Cross, Mulholland and Eaton were not opposite in physiognomy and character, nor were they a generation apart in age. Born just eleven days apart in 1855, both men were ruggedly handsome in appearance, competent civil engineers—both were self-taught—and hard-headed pragmatists very much each other's equals when it came to the hurly-burly of real estate speculation and contentious municipal politics.

Interestingly, Robert Towne did preserve the full personality of William Mulholland by splitting him into two opposing characters, one gentle (Hollis Mulwray) and the other thuggish (Claude Mulvihill, the brawny Water Department security chief played by Roy Jensen) (Brook 137).

Fred Eaton first visited the Owens River Valley, Inyo County, in 1892. The moment he glimpsed the 73,000-acre expanse of Owens Lake, he saw the Owens River that fed it as LA's best hope for a copious and reliable future water supply. From 1896 to 1904 long dry spells oscillated with erratic rainfall in Southern California, prompting Eaton and Mulholland to visit the Owens Valley in 1904 and formulate the aqueduct project in earnest. The following year Eaton began to purchase land and water rights in the Owens Valley—though he gave the false impression that he was working for the US Reclamation Service on a public irrigation project that would have benefited local farmers. Eaton was abetted in his efforts by a crony named Joseph B. Lippincott (1864–1942), the Reclamation Service's regional engineer, who supplied him with valuable inside information about Owens Valley water rights in return for private consultant's fees. When Owens Valley farmers and ranchers realized that Eaton's plan was to usurp their water for use elsewhere, they were understandably enraged but there was nothing they could do to stop the aqueduct. For his part, Mulholland downplayed the amount of water locally available for Los Angeles' growth in order to "sell" aqueduct bond issues to the city's citizens. He also misled residents of the Owens Valley, claiming that LA would only divert a portion of the flow of the Owens River, while he was secretly planning on using the full water rights to fill San Fernando Valley's giant aquifer.

On 29 July 1905, the *Los Angeles Times* announced the conclusion of "preliminary negotiations securing 30,000 inches of water, or about ten times our present supply, enough for a city of 2,000,000 people." The front-page box announcement was just the start of a relentless public relations campaign by the *Times* (and, to a lesser extent, by the *Los Angeles Herald*) that lasted 700 days, right up to the bond vote on 12 June 1907. *Times* publisher Harrison Gray Otis was investing heavily in San Fernando Valley land that would become much more valuable from an aqueduct so his paper zealously promoted the project. Almost every day for twenty-three months the *Times* ran news items, editorials, and cartoons refuting nay-sayers and exhorting Los Angelinos to vote for the bond issue. On the appointed day the citizens complied, voting 22,063 to 2,135 in the affirmative: a margin of almost ten to one that the *Los Angeles Times* trumpeted "as emphatic enough to satisfy the most cautious of investors" (13 June 1907, p. 20). But the *Times* neglected to note that 24,200 votes comprised less than 20 percent of the city's 135,000 eligible voters—hardly a resounding mandate. Perhaps the protracted daily drumbeat had had an effect opposite of the one intended, breeding apathy, perhaps even disgust in some quarters. Other factors in the low voter turnout might have been the end of a long drought in 1904, new pumping stations tapping underground sources, and Mulholland's successful efforts to get city residents to reduce per capita water consumption by one third.

At any rate, the bond passed, construction began in 1908, and moved rapidly thereafter. Over the next six years, 100,000 men worked on the aqueduct but only about 4,000 at any given time; the arduous work, much of it over mountainous terrain or in the Mojave Desert, resulted in extremely high worker turnover. The aqueduct was completed on 5 November 1913, ahead of schedule and under budget. Ironically, what seemed to be an abundant water supply drove higher and higher levels of demand as the population of Los Angeles continued to explode and capacity was soon reached. Mulholland tried to obtain additional water from the Colorado River but was initially blocked, so he decided to take all available water from the Owens Valley. A devastating drought in 1923–24 further taxed water from that source. Valley farmers and ranchers formed an irrigation cooperative in 1923, but the City of Los Angeles managed to acquire some of its key water rights and diverted the remaining inflows to Owens Lake, which dried up by 1924. At this point, the farmers and ranchers rebelled. They seized the Alabama Gates at Lone Pine, California, where the aqueduct diverted water from the Owens River and temporarily rediverted the city's water supply back into the dry Owens River to publicize their predicament. There were also incidents of sabotage by dynamite. In August 1927, when the conflict was at its height, the Inyo County Bank that funded the cooperative collapsed, and Owens Valley resistance effectively ceased.

Employing cinematic shorthand, *Chinatown* represents the unrest in Owens Valley in a single, early scene: the Water Board public hearing scene.

Right after Hollis Mulwray refuses to authorize the proposed VanderLip Dam, a shepherd (played by Rance Howard) disrupts proceedings by ushering his bleating flock down the aisle of the hearing room (much to Jake Gittes's amusement). The shepherd angrily shouts at Mulwray, "You steal water from the Valley. Ruin their grazing. Starve the livestock. Who is paying you to do that, Mr. Mulwray? That's what I want to know!" What was a protracted and complicated struggle between the Owens Valley and the city of Los Angeles is rendered with just a few cinematic brush strokes.

Highly lucrative real estate speculation also occurred at the southern end of the aqueduct even before its inception. In late 1898 Henry Huntington (nephew of Collis Huntington, president of the Southern Pacific Railroad) began buying scattered parcels of cheap land on the city's margins. In 1901 Huntington founded the Pacific Electric Railway (PER) to tie his several scattered subdivisions together. For example, the "Old Mission Route" linked the San Gabriel Mission and Pasadena to Los Angeles. The PER's "Balloon Route" ran west through Hollywood, Santa Monica, and Venice before returning to LA through Culver City. The "Triangle Trolley" line went to San Pedro, Long Beach, south to Balboa, east to Santa Ana, and back to Los Angeles. By 1914, Huntington's electric cars took potential homebuyers to picturesque destinations in San Bernardino, Redlands, Santa Ana, Yorba Linda, and San Fernando (Waldie). Thus, rail transportation and power lines preceded the Owens Valley Aqueduct water as key infrastructure elements that enabled Los Angeles to expand northward into San Fernando Valley.

When he wrote his screenplay for *Chinatown*, Robert Towne constructed Noah Cross as a composite character of rather large proportions: not just a Fred Eaton figure, but really an amalgam of Eaton and a group of LA businessmen who made up two land speculation syndicates, both headed by General Harrison Gray Otis (1837–1917), the publisher of the *Los Angeles Times*. In 1904, in his role on the Board of Water Commissioners, Moses Hazeltine Sherman (1853–1932), a railroad magnate, real estate developer, and close associate of Otis, was privy to advanced notice of water rights purchases in the Owens Valley. The aqueduct's planned terminus in the San Fernando Valley aquifer northwest of LA meant that the introduction of a reliable water supply for irrigation and home use would combine with new power and light rail lines to make sparsely settled farmland in an otherwise semiarid region far more valuable. Accordingly, Otis and Sherman formed a real estate syndicate to take advantage of insider knowledge of the coming aqueduct and bought 16,000 acres in San Fernando Valley on the cheap. Once construction of the aqueduct commenced in 1908, Otis and Sherman formed a second syndicate that called itself the Los Angeles Suburban Homes Company.[5] Sitting on the five-man Board of Control of this second syndicate were Harrison Otis; Moses Sherman; Harry Chandler (1864–1944), Otis's son-in-law and protégé; Hobart Johnstone Whitley (1847–1931), "Father of Hollywood" and one of the nation's most successful land developers; and Otto F. Brant (1858–1922), head of Title Insurance and Trust Company. In 1909 the Suburban Homes syndicate purchased a 47,500-acre parcel from another syndicate: the Los Angeles Farming and Milling Company, owned by Isaac Newton Van Nuys (1836–1912) and his son-in-law, James Boon Lankershim (1850–1931). The price paid was $2.5 million, or just under $53 an acre for an enormous swath of real estate comprising 74 square miles or nearly the entire southern half of the San Fernando Valley: land annexed by the City of Los Angeles in 1923 that now includes North Hollywood, Sherman Oaks, Encino, Van Nuys, Tarzana, Burbank, and Studio City. As Noah Cross explains to J. J. Gittes, "You see, Mr. Gittes. Either you bring the water to L.A.—or you bring L.A. to the water . . . [J]ust incorporate the Valley into the city so the water goes to L.A. after all. It's very simple." Between 1900 and 1920, 22 new cities incorporated in Los Angeles County, and the county's overall population grew from 102,479 to 576,673 (Waldie).

In an early scene in *Chinatown*, Hollis Mulwray alludes to the ill-fated St. Francis Dam (called the Vanderlip Dam in the film) when he refuses to authorize the building of the fictional Alto Vallejo Dam and Reservoir at a public hearing.[6] Shortly after its completion, hasty construction and dubious geological siting caused the St. Francis Dam to fail on 12 March 1928: a catastrophe that unleashed an inland tsunami of twelve billion gallons of water and took some 450 lives. As chief engineer of the Water Works, William Mulholland took personal responsibility for the disaster, retired a year later, and lived in semi-seclusion the remaining six years of his life. By all accounts the failure of the St. Francis Dam weighed heavily on Mulholland's conscience. Hollis Mulwray shows similar remorse in *Chinatown* for authorizing the Vanderlip Dam and vows to never make the same mistake twice. Insofar as the movie elides the real reason for the falling out between its Eaton and Mulholland figures, it forfeits an opportunity to emphasize the actual consequence of the rift: the St. Francis Dam disaster. William Mulholland's refusal to pay Fred Eaton's price (and Eaton's refusal to lower his price) for the land at Long Valley forced Mulholland, many years later, to site a large storage reservoir much further south (at Francisquito Canyon, fifty miles north of LA): a location that would prove tragic.

In his screenplay for *Chinatown*, Robert Towne conflates the widely separated Owens and San Fernando Valleys and renames them Alto Vallejo. He also turns California Water Wars history on its head by having J. J. Gittes discover that the LA Water Department is diverting water from farmland in the "Northwest Valley" (i.e., the San Fernando Valley) during a drought so it can be bought by agents of Noah Cross on the cheap and then incorporated into the City of Los Angeles. In reality, all the water diversion happened in the Owens Valley to feed the aqueduct, not in the San Fernando Valley, which benefited hugely from the importation of Owens Valley water. As already noted, pre-WWI land speculation in the San Fernando Valley was based in part on insider knowledge that a proposed Los Angeles Aqueduct would soon bring massive amounts of water to the area—not on a manufactured water shortage that deflated land values for cheap purchase, as depicted in the film. William Mulholland was by no means a muckraking defender of the commonwealth. Nor was he murdered by Fred Eaton, of course. Though perhaps a schemer committed to enriching himself, Eaton was not a monster like his cinematic counterpart. In his zeal to make Noah Cross as evil as humanly possible, Robert Towne turns him into an incestuous rapist—and skews history toward myth and melodrama. As film scholar David Ingram notes,

> This doubling of the rape of the land with [Cross's] incestuous rape of his daughter turns the land grab into an exemplum of a wider, more pervasive evil ... [a] doubling [that] tends to depoliticize the film, in that the environmental crime becomes no longer specific to a particular time and place, but the consequence of a corrupt human nature that is universal and innate ... The specific history of the Los Angeles land fraud has, moreover, been turned into a more sensational melodrama of murder and sexual violence. (153)

Furthermore, the film's use of Chinatown as a synecdoche for a thoroughly corrupt, unfathomable, and iniquitous America seems to warrant charges of Orientalism for invoking well-worn racist stereotypes regarding inscrutable Asians. The effect is somewhat mitigated, though, by an early scene showing Jake Gittes embarrassing himself by repeating a tasteless sex joke featuring a Chinese couple and being overheard by Mrs. Mulwray, who is not amused. Jake's boorish racial insensitivity is further ironized in a key scene late in the film. An Asian gardener (played by Jerry Fujiyama) at the Mulwray estate notes that the salt water in a backyard pond is "bad for the glass" (i.e., grass). Gittes mocks the man's poor English pronunciation but then realizes that what he's saying constitutes a vital clue as to the real circumstances of Hollis Mulwray's death. Though Mulwray's drowned body was recovered from a freshwater reservoir, salt water was found in his lungs; Gittes suddenly intuits that Hollis Mulwray was likely drowned in his own backyard. With the gardener's help, Gittes also recovers a pair of bifocal eyeglasses from the pond. He assumes they belong to Mulwray until Evelyn tells him that her husband did not wear bifocals. Gittes then correctly surmises that they belong to Noah Cross, Mulwray's murderer. Jake Gittes solves the case but solves it too late to effectively intervene. His unexamined prejudices, fueled by smug egotism, show his ability to penetrate surfaces and correctly "read" Otherness, in other words, his cluelessness as to Evelyn Mulwray's real secret. In the end, Jake's perceptual and moral blindness result in tragedy and defeat. So perhaps Chinatown is not merely a stock symbol of inscrutability but also a legitimate interpretive challenge unmet by the observer-protagonist: a bitter lesson that is driven home by Gittes's dimwitted assistant, Walsh (Joe Mantell), who blithely advises resignation with the film's final line, "Forget it, Jake. It's Chinatown." Though a great work of cinematic art—visually stunning, well-acted, marvelously intricate in plotting, and emotionally powerful—*Chinatown* is unfortunately poor history: a misshapen pastiche that obscures more than it illuminates. Does it matter? Only if viewers mistake the film as a legitimate vehicle for historical representation.

Notes

1. *Chinatown* is set in the summer of 1937.
2. The screenplay for Robert Evans's 1974 film adaptation of *The Great Gatsby* was written by Francis Ford Coppola.
3. A 230,000-square-foot Art Deco building located at 3050 Wilshire Boulevard in Los Angeles, built in 1929.
4. Towne is referring to Los Angeles Union Station. The main railway station in Los Angeles and the largest railroad passenger terminal in the western United States, Union Station opened in May 1939. Its architecture combines Art Deco, Mission Revival, and Streamline Moderne style.
5. *Chinatown* conflates the two syndicates into one and associates it with the fictional "Albacore Club," an exclusive men's club that is based on the Los Angeles Athletic Club, to which many syndicate members and investors belonged.
6. The Vanderlip Dam references the name of Frank Arthur Vanderlip Sr. (1864–1937). President of the National City Bank of New York (now Citibank) from 1909 to 1919, assistant secretary of the treasury, and one of the founders of the Federal Reserve System, Vanderlip was a prominent real estate developer.

Works Cited

Andersen, Thom. "Los Angeles Plays Itself." *new filmkritik*, 15 March, 2005, http://newfilmkritik.de/archiv/2005-03/los-angeles-plays-itself/.

Brook, Vincent. *Land of Smoke and Mirrors: A Cultural History of Los Angeles*. Rutgers UP, 2013.

Chinatown. Directed by Roman Polanski, Paramount Pictures, 1974.

Ingram, David. *Green Screen: Environmentalism and Hollywood Cinema*. U of Exeter P, 2000.

Kirshner, Jonathan. *Hollywood's Last Golden Age: Politics, Society, and the Seventies in America*. Cornell UP, 2012.

Leopold, Todd. "'My Sister! My Daughter!' and Other Tales of Chinatown." Interview with Robert Towne, CNN, 29 September 2009, http://www.cnn.com/2009/SHOWBIZ/Movies/09/29/chinatown.towne.movie/.

McWilliams, Carey. *Southern California Country: Island on the Land*. Duell, Sloan & Pearce, 1946.

Piper, Karen. *Left in the Dust: How Race and Politics Created a Human and Environmental Tragedy in L.A.* St. Martin's Press, 2006.

Simon, Alex. "Forget it, Bob, It's Chinatown: Robert Towne Looks Back on Chinatown's 35th anniversary." Interview with Robert Towne, *The Hollywood Interview*, http://1carnomineevioladavis.blogspot.com/2013/02/robert-towne-hollywood-interview.html.

Towne, Robert. *Chinatown: A Screenplay*. Neville, 1983.

Waldie, D. J. "How We Got This Way (Los Angeles Has Always Been Suburban)." KCET, 12 December 2011, https://www.kcet.org/shows/lost-la/how-we-got-this-way-los-angeles-has-always-been-suburban. Accessed 20 May 2017.

The Cinematic Portrayal of
Water Wars in Bolivia and Ecuador

> All peoples, whatever their stage of development
> and social and economic conditions, have the right to
> have access to drinking water in quantities and
> of a quality equal to their basic needs.
>
> —"Action Plan," Mar del Plata
> UN Water conference, March 1977

> El agua es la sangre de los pueblos. No puede ser de nadie.
> [Water is the people's blood. It cannot belong to anybody.]
>
> —Óscar Olivera (in Limón)

THE NEOLIBERAL POLITICS of the late twentieth century resulted in large-scale privatization of common goods throughout the globe. One of the consequences was that public access to water became threatened because in the 1990s "some of the world's largest multinationals (Bechtel, Enron, Vivendi) began expanding operation and ownership of water supply systems on a global scale" (Bakker 2). Those who advocate for water privatization argue that governments have been shown to fail in their attempts at water management and allege that private companies "will be more efficient, provide more finance, and mobilize higher-quality expertise" (Bakker 2), as well as making the—one could say, condescending—claim that only by treating "water as an economic good" (Bakker 2) will society learn to treat it in an environmentally responsible way. On the other hand, those who oppose water privatization argue that "government-run water supply systems, when properly supported and resourced, are more effective, equitable, and responsive" (Bakker 2) and, maybe more importantly, identify the unethical factor of profiting from a human right. Water was in fact recognized as a human right in March 1977 during the Mar del Plata UN Water Conference. The fact that water is conceived as a basic human right may be why, in comparison with other neoliberal practices, water privatization has inspired exceptionally massive and furious protest.[1] Particularly noteworthy instances of such protest can be found in Latin America, including Bolivia, Ecuador, and Peru. There, demonstrations have turned into the so-called *guerras del agua* (water wars), which on a few occasions even resulted in violent clashes and have inspired the cinematographic representations that will be discussed here. The feature films that will be analyzed are *También la lluvia* (*Even the Rain*) directed by Icíar Bollaín, from 2010, the 2008 Bond movie *Quantum of Solace* by Marc Foster, and *A Dark Truth* by Damian Lee, from 2012. The first two reflect on the situation in Bolivia, while the last examines the struggles in Ecuador. Although all three directors are from a different culture than the one that is portrayed, the cultural appropriation is moral and necessary in the first film, defendable in the second, and debauched in the third.

To understand the portrayal of these water wars, it is imperative to grasp the historical context in which they arose. They are not the result of an isolated occurrence but rather of various factors: in Bolivia, the source of the issue can be traced back to 1985, three years after the end of the military dictatorships, when the then president Víctor Paz Estenssoro took neoliberal economist Jeffrey Sachs's advice to apply a "shock therapy" to control the hyperinflation. The shock therapy included multiplying gas prices, deregulating market prices, and drastically cutting public spending (Morales Peña and Klein 57). Paz Estenssoro finally sought the help of the International Monetary Fund and the World Bank to prevent an economic collapse, and "the country has since been handcuffed by the package of conditions imposed by the Bretton Woods institutions" (Roncallo 103). The reason Bolivia accepted the conditions, which, among others, required privatizing "the railways, the telephone system, the national airlines, [and] the great mines of Oruro and Potosí" (Finnegan), was to secure these mainly foreign investments as well as loans. In 1998, under the government of Hugo Banzer Suárez,[2] the International Monetary Fund approved a loan of $138 million that included the proviso that all remaining public services be privatized. The IMF press release accordingly cited the following planned "structural reforms": "The government plans to privatize all remaining public enterprises, including those owned by the armed forces. The most important action is to privatize the state oil company YPFB's refineries by June 1999" ("IMF Approves"). Although the statement points to the oil refinery as the most important action, for the Bolivian people the fact that SEMAPA (Municipal Services of Drinking Water and Sewage) was among those to be sold would have the biggest impact on their daily lives. In addition, one year later, the World Bank, in its *Bolivia Public Expediture Review*, recommended that "[n]o public subsidies should be given to ameliorate the increase in water tariffs in Cochabamba, which should reflect the full cost of provision by the Misicuni multipurpose project" (González and McCarthy 7).

A few months later, from June to September 1999, the water system was finally sold at auction to the only bidder, the multinational consortium Aguas del Tunari whose controlling partner was International Water, a British company owned by Bechtel (Finnegan). Finally, the Bolivian government, behind closed doors and with little leverage for negotiation because of the lack of other bidders, agreed to concede the consortium a 2.5-billion-dollar contract that would give it the right to provide water and sanitation services to the population of Cochabamba throughout the following forty years with the "exclusive rights to all the water in the district, even in the aquifer" (Finnegan).[3] The local peasants branded this sale as an attempt to "lease the rain," which, even though it might sound outrageous at first sight, is surprisingly accurate. The citizens were barred from collecting rainwater and had to ask for explicit permission from the superintendent if they wanted to do so (Olivera and Lewis 9); this absurd, almost authoritarian, clause is what, anecdotally, gave Bollaín's film *Even the Rain* its title. The direct consequences of the privatization were an increase of up to 300 percent in water tariffs (Olivera and Lewis 10), with the implication that water bills now constituted up to 25 percent of many families' incomes. In January of 2000, these price surges led to popular protests in Cochabamba, the third most populous city in Bolivia, with 600,000 inhabitants. The initially uneventful demonstrations involving road blocks turned into violent clashes in February "when President Banzer dispatched police with tear gas as thousands of protestors marched peacefully. About 175 marchers were injured and two were blinded by the gas" (Public Citizen 3).

In March 2000, the Coalition in Defense of Water and Life, called *La Coordinadora*, spearheaded by the activist Óscar Olivera, held a popular referendum, the first of its kind in Bolivia (Olivera and Lewis 36) in which the contract and the new law were rejected with 96 percent of voters and, therefore, the barricades and demonstrations continued. Hugo Banzer declared a state of siege, and in April an "army sniper killed seventeen-year-old Víctor Hugo Daza [as he] walk[ed] home from work. Daza was not even part of the battle; he had just stopped to see what was happening" (Olivera and Lewis 43). This homicide would make headlines beyond the national borders and cause protests to extend to other provinces, involving more bloodshed and violence.[4] Two days later, public pressure forced the Bolivian government to announce the end of the water contract with Aguas del Tunari, hand the control over to *La Coordinadora* (Public Citizen 4), and annul Law 2029 the next day.

In Ecuador, unlike in Bolivia, water privatization did not evoke the same media outreach. Here, the most infamous sale was conducted in Guayaquil, Ecuador's largest city and its economic capital: only a few months after the resolution of the Cochabamba contract, in 2001 the company Interagua—Bechtel is, again, part of the firm— signed a thirty-year concession contract with the local government to handle public water in which, allegedly, the needs of the poorest would be taken into account. Nonetheless, as the Food and Water Watch indicates:

> Guarantees and loans provided by the World Bank and the Inter-American Development Bank have ensured a profitable investment for one of the world's most influential corporations, Bechtel. But, similar to the experience of many other

cities across the world, water privatization has not solved water problems in Guayaquil. Instead, Bechtel has delivered water not suitable for drinking, refused to expand service, cut-off water to those unable to pay, and neglected responsibilities to provide wastewater treatment compromising the local environment and public health. (Food and Water Watch 2–3)

In other words, even though the more vulnerable parts of society were supposed to be protected, again, they are the ones who suffer most because of the water privatization. In addition, a reversion comparable to the one in Bolivia has not yet occurred, but Interagua is controlled and regulated by a government company, and calls for deprivatization regularly recur in parliament, newspapers, and the general population. There is one group, the Oberservatorio Ciudadano de Servicios Públicos (Citizens' Committee for Monitoring Public Services), which has diligently documented all "constitutional, legal, and contractual violations of Interagua and is working to ensure that action is taken" (Food and Water Watch 3). Finally, in March 2016, the government has taken legal action against Interagua on grounds of environmental crimes ("Gobierno").

This historical context puts into perspective how water wars are portrayed in the three aforementioned films of contemporary cinema. The first one, the Spanish feature *Even the Rain*, is a metafilm that depicts the shooting of a motion picture about Christopher Columbus's arrival in America, which is critical of Columbus and the Spanish enterprise in the Americas. The protagonists, the director Sebastián (Gael García Bernal) and the producer Costa (Luis Tosar), choose their location, the city of Cochabamba and its surroundings, because of the beautiful, lush landscapes and the low wages (two dollars a day) that extras are paid in Bolivia. Nevertheless, shortly after filming begins, they encounter the demonstrations against water privatization, and the two characters who initially had seen it as essential to defend the indigenous cause in their film, now dismiss the new form of oppression to which the Bolivian people are being subjected to; this time not by colonizers but by Western capitalism and globalization. Sebastián and Costa seem to worry only about the interruption of shooting, because their film is more important to them than anything else. In addition, the choice of location had also been motivated by capitalist considerations, such as the possibility of financing a superproduction at a minimal price.[5] Although the film crew does not take part in it, the other important parallelism that will become evident by visually correlating the story of the "invaders" now and then is that five hundred years ago, they came for gold and now they are coming for water. In his book *The New Imperialism*, David Harvey describes new forms of the capitalist machine and its imperialistic strategies, one of them being the privatization of public utilities, which he defines as "a new wave of 'enclosing the commons'" (148) that leads to "accumulation by dispossession" (149). That is, the Bolivian people, for the Western eyes, the weak opponent, easy to betray or subjugate, are being dispossessed of their own natural resources. These include not only water but also oil, the two liquid golds of modern times and, of course, the resource of cheap labor that the film producers are after. As neoliberal economists would judge the matter, this occurs "for their own good," since without Western "help" they'd be doomed to economic collapse, just as the earlier colonizers pretended to "Christianize" the "barbaric," whereas the genuine interest for both lay in the profits that would result from the resources of the country they were subjugating.

These new capitalist intruders intend, moreover, to "[expand capital] by incorporating resources, peoples, activities, and lands that hitherto were managed, organized, and produced under social relations other than capitalist ones" (Swyngedouw 82). In other words, again, just as the colonizers tried to impose their rule(s) on the people of the Americas when Christopher Columbus "discovered" the continent, capitalist imperialism will subdue those who do not accept its playbook by choking them economically until the country in question has no choice but to oblige:

> The credit system and finance capital became, as Lenin, Hilferding, and Luxemburg all remarked at the beginning of the twentieth century, major levers of predation, fraud, and thievery. The strong wave of financialization that set in after 1973 has been every bit as spectacular for its speculative and

predatory style. Stock promotions, Ponzi schemes, structured asset destruction through inflation, asset-stripping through mergers and acquisitions, and the promotion of levels of debt incumbency that reduce whole populations, even in advanced capitalist countries, to debt peonage, to say nothing of corporate fraud and dispossession of assets . . . by credit and stock manipulations—all of these are central features of what contemporary capitalism is about. (Harvey 147)

This quotation underscores how Jeffrey Sachs's "shock therapy"[6] and the quest for help from the World Bank and the International Monetary Fund were not Bolivia's salvation but only the commencement of a horrible historic reiteration: as Marx put it, adding to the Hegelian assertion, important historic events repeat themselves, "the first time as tragedy, the second as farce."[7] If one interprets thus both the invasion in quest of water and the effort to exploit its people as the farce of the five-hundred-year-old tragedy of the invasion of America, it is very difficult to imagine a better way to juxtapose these two events than Bollaín's metafilm. In witnessing a film about a film, the spectator does not need to be told explicitly about these parallels, but can deduce them and as the chronologically remote event gains distance, the current injustices feel even closer, making us sensitive to our shared responsibility. The director's assistant, who is making a documentary about the production, highlights this feeling in a scene in which she proposes to change the focus of the documentary and shift it to the *water war* instead. The suggestion is rejected in the film, revealing Bollaín's interest in decrying the entertainment industry's indifference (epitomized by Sebastián and Costa) to the people's real, and particularly present-day, problems even though they pretend to be politically committed with their historical films. By using this approach Bollaín distances herself from commonplace mainstream productions: for them, documentaries address a very specific audience that they are not interested in, while Bollaín, on the contrary, succeeds in incorporating the documentary contribution within a feature film that targets an extensive audience and thereby finds a way of drawing attention to Bolivia's specific water problem, on the one hand, and to the global water crisis, on the other. As Paszkiewicz points out, this scene also comments on the role of female directors in the cinematographic industry: on the one hand, the female assistant, María, is overshadowed by the male director and the producer and, on the other, it is through her that Bollaín "changes the oppressive and one-directional, dominating 'gaze' for the 'looking relation', a process that, according to Kaplan, denotes curiosity about the Other"[8] (235), plus it is María and her subjective camera with whom the film seems to identify.

The film's cast also exemplifies the unequivocal effort to acknowledge the importance of portraying what the Bolivian people had been exposed to: one of the actors, Bolivian Juan Carlos Anduviri, had the explicit desire to make the issue known beyond his country's borders and stated in the newspaper *La Jornada* that it represents his compatriots without stereotypes and that Bolivians who will see the film will be proud because of the respectful way it treats them ("En *También*"). Politically committed as he is, he felt that the assertion of the rights of the indigenous population was very important, and he explained that this largest indigenous community in South America which resides in Bolivia is standing up to take back their land, their country and to start to govern themselves ("En *También*"). This portrayal, which avoids stereotypes and always looks at its subjects from a respectful point of view, is a very important aspect of a film that criticizes the arrogance of characters such as the producer, who laughs at how little the extras are paid but is shown trying to convince Anduviri's character, Daniel, not to participate in any more demonstrations because without him they could not continue the film:

> COSTA (laughs): This is fucking great. You know what? It's cheaper to get a man to sit on the light stand than buy a sandbag. Yeah, yeah, two fucking dollars a day and they feel like kings. You can throw in some water palms and give them some old trucks when you are done, and, *listo*, two hundred fucking extras. (32:45)

The excerpt is part of a phone conversation between Costa and another producer to whom he speaks in English, therefore not paying attention to the fact that Daniel is right next to him, who, to his surprise reveals his knowledge of English by answering "This is fucking great, man" (34:31).

The scene illustrates the general tone of the film and how Bollaín exposes in a subtle and intelligent manner the behavior of those who could be called invaders or neo-colonizers, in lockstep with neoliberal politics, those who believe themselves to be superior, morally superior even, but continue the exploitation of the indigenous community even when they precisely allege that the reasons why they chose the film's subject is their ethical commitment. However, their dismay diminishes over the course of the film: some protagonists begin to understand the importance of the fight for water. They also start to feel empathy toward the locals, and this learning process is expressed by sincere attempts to help them, as, for example, when Costa carries a wounded girl to the hospital despite the danger of being unable to get out of the conflict zone.

Costa's drastic transformation suggests, at a minimum, the criticism that Schenker has leveled, that the film relies on the oppressor suddenly aiding the oppressed instead of focusing the climatic act on "the far more heroic efforts of the local resistance fighters, [which leads one] to wonder how closely the filmmakers have studied their Zinn after all" (Schenker).[9] Though his criticism is certainly valid, this part might also be interpreted as another piece of the reenactment of history. It would then make sense that Bollaín would recreate a modern-day Bartolomé de las Casas who gradually becomes aware of the injustices, as de las Casas did during the "conquest," to finally turn into a spokesman for the indigenous people. Costa, and even the name suggests a resemblance to the Dominican friar, now realizes his own oppressive behavior. Nevertheless, that does not mean, and here Schenker might have been a bit too harsh with his criticism, that it is represented as more heroic than the efforts of the local resistance fighters, but seems rather motivated by narrative coherence. Moreover, the representation of the clashes and the degree of violence is plausible and cinematographically well resolved. In other words, there is no overdose or overexploitation of violent images but they only appear, on the one hand, if it makes sense within the story as a whole and, on the other, if they follow an internal narrative logic that conveys the development of the water protests with Anduviri portrayed as the movement's leader who, even though he does not embody Óscar Olivera, the real-life water activist, directly, certainly is reminiscent of him. The only feature a viewer might miss is that the larger context, such as the role of the World Bank, is not integrated nor is explained how the country came to the point of deciding to privatize water.

The 2008 James Bond feature, *Quantum of Solace*, also takes the Bolivian water privatization issue as its subject, although seemingly less out of political engagement than as a device to further its plot: the crisis and the protests are limited to peripheral references. Although the director, Marc Foster, has said in an interview that the issue was fundamental for him and declared his awareness of the global problem of water shortage (Bergendorff), it seems that the film has no intention of ensuring that viewers without a broad background knowledge can understand the real problem nor that it was inspired by actual events. Joshua Clover, in his *Film Quarterly* review even criticizes the fact that the plot is "wholly plagiarized from the archives of reality," a fact which, according to him, got "lost on every major national critic", as for example the reviewers of the *New York Times*, the *Los Angeles Times,* and the *New Yorker*. The villain, Greene, and his company ironically named Greene Planet (he advertises his firm as environmentally and ecologically committed and even runs an eco-hotel in Bolivia, most likely to mislead possible clients) form part of *Quantum*, a consortium that clearly reminds one of Bechtel and that constitutes a shady criminal group that is after global power. It tries to achieve this power through financial and geopolitical tactics, such as supporting a coup d'état to get rid of the current Bolivian government and to put the ex-dictator General Medrano in charge, in exchange for a piece of apparently barren land. As is foreseeable, it turns out that this territory is not desert, but contains all the country's water, and Greene will be able to supply it with ease, and with consequent profit for him and hikes in water prices for the Bolivians. Not only has water privatization and its geopolitical ins and outs nurtured Foster's imagination but also the fact that a previous dictator would again win control over the country, even though in the film that did not happen through democratic elections. Greene's plan is described only vaguely, and the images with citizens who suffer because of the water shortage are so fleeting that they almost go unnoticed. Notwithstanding, if one compares the film not to another that focuses primarily on water shortage but to other action-superhero movies, it could be argued that this example at least offers evidence of the existence of a serious problem. A case study about the audience of *Quantum of Solace* claims to prove that, indeed, "many also engaged (in an unsolicited manner) with the geopolitical context of the movie" (Dittmer and Dodds 82). In this spirit, Marc Foster might even have made the conscious choice not to provide more details about the case of Bolivia because, though he used real facts as a fulcrum, his aim was not to comment on a specific occurrence but rather on the global problem of water privatization and how multinationals convert a basic human right into a lucrative commodity. If that was his rationale, it would be logical and coherent to choose the Bolivian setting, given that here the people went from victims of neoliberal politics to winners who imposed popular democracy.

In the last scene of *Even the Rain*, Costa opens a present from Daniel that turns out to be a miniature bottle filled with water, which at a first glance might seem to play at one's heart's strings or to be melo-dramatic, but proves endearing and shows that the movie is everything the last film, *A Dark Truth* is not. This film looks at Ecuador's water problem from a Hollywood perspective of a former CIA-agent who tries to soothe his guilty conscience, tinting the atmosphere with a sensationalist flair. It is not only not based on real facts, but the story is invented from beginning to end: that is, in the film, a multinational called Clearbec tries to cover-up a typhoid outbreak in Ecuador, caused by an error during water sanitation, to be able to sign a similar contract in Africa. Therefore, the solution they find, together with the Ecuadorian government, is to get rid of, that is, kill, those who contracted the disease and the only existing witness, Francisco Francis (Forest Whitaker). The sister of the head of the company finds out because a young Ecuadorian man, a former employee of Clearbec whose mother was murdered by soldiers, tracks her down to kill himself in front of her by gunshot. Once her attention is drawn in this bizarre way to the problem, she hires the protagonist, Jack Begosian, the CIA-agent (Andy García, who was also executive producer of the picture) to find out what happened in the Latin American country.

Admittedly, one could argue that it is legitimate to create a completely fictional story for a fictional movie. Nevertheless, the cultural appropriation that occurs here can be considered problematic within its context. In this case, had the purpose of the production been to create a fictional story, there was no reason to choose a place like Ecuador with a real-life problem regarding water privatization instead of creating a fully fictional context as well. The situation is further complicated if one takes note of the final credits, which assert that the spectator assisted a "dramatic interpretation of true events based upon hundreds of media accounts of these events, as well as interviews with many of those involved" (1:45:35). These credits further state that a large part of the dialogue is based on recorded conversations, while only conceding that some of the "actual names have been changed, certain events and characters have been fictionalized and some timelines have been condensed for dramatic purpose" (1:45:35). This is aimed at making the spectator believe that the core or the events remained faithful to what happened rather than being a loose inspiration for a crime thriller. More importantly, the way the plot unfurls shows, rather than dramatic purpose, the director's indifference toward the real situation and how he took advantage of it to provide a mere framework in which to place a hero repentant of wrongdoings he committed during his time in the CIA. His indifference is emphasized by the lack of attention to detail: the military wear Bolivian instead of Ecuadorian flags, which seems to suggest the presence of a guerrilla army; the cars' license plates are Peruvian, and every time credits indicate a specific place, the images do not seem to correspond, as for example in the case of Quito, a city of more than one and a half million inhabitants that looks rather like a tiny peaceful village in the film.

Damian Lee also tried to profit at the expense of those who had and keep having to live these dramatic circumstances by overshadowing them: a viewer who learns that there were no deaths nor clashes similar to the ones in the film will likely be tempted to feel that the real conflict was less significant because compared to an unrealistic Hollywood story the struggle for water seems like a minor issue. Likewise, he distorts the story of La Via Campesina: in the film, the leader and founder of the movement is Francisco Francis, "a San Francisco native with a PhD in environmental studies who came to South America as a Greenpeace activist" (Achtenberg), while in the real world a "group of farmers' representatives—women and men—from the four continents founded La Via Campesina in 1993 in Mons, Belgium" (La Via Campesina). Similar to the misrepresentation of La Via Campesina, the history of the water wars is falsified. In addition to these historical misrepresentations, the protagonist shows an exaggerated heroism throughout the film, which is used to lecture the viewer about the crimes committed in the name of neoliberalism. The director seems to forget that this type of film and the representation of the white man as savior of the native people is not far from its own criticism. The difference between Bollaín's Costa and Lee's Jack becomes evident: though the first might change surprisingly quickly, his development is reasonable, while the second is overloaded with Hollywood-style inflated bravery. To say nothing of the preposterous amount of violent images, false drama, and extreme sensationalism to which the viewer is subjected to in *A Dark Truth*, along with mediocre acting and grandiloquent speeches. Even the film's teaser, "Escape the jungle, expose the truth," that appears on the official poster summarizes all these problematic elements: the sensationalist way in which the incidents are looked at, the inflated tensions, as well as the attempt to present the film as exotic. This Latin American exoticness is conveyed by including the idea of a tropical jungle, therefore increasing the detrimental cultural appropriation.

The three films show that the discourse changes depending on the intentions of the directors. On the one hand, there is what could be called the internal perspective, represented by Bollaín, who tried to accurately portray the water wars, collaborating with Bolivian actors and trying to understand the problem from within. On the other hand, there is the external perspective, that can be found in both Hollywood films, in which a cultural appropriation with no attempt of including reliable research or collaboration of those affected by the water privatization is observed. While the Bond feature is just negligent of details and does not aim at understanding the intricacies of the water wars but stays within its action hero genre, *A Dark Truth* could be characterized as inappropriate and unethical, given that it pretends actively to depict real events. The distinctive cultural contexts in which these films were produced lead not only to different perspectives, but also to unequal quality: if judged as films that look at neoliberal politics and privatization, there is no doubt that *Even the Rain* is far more effective than the other two, and even as works of art, the Spanish film is the only one that achieves a satisfactory result. Viewer numbers would seem to corroborate that Bollaín told a compelling story relative to Lee's fiasco.[10] To compare those numbers to an offering from the B nd franchise would be unfair, of course. Finally, the different perspectives of Bollaín's and Lee's films are evident in their very titles: while the latter chose the CIA agents' radio show, called *The Truth* modified with the melodramatic adjective, *dark*, the former carefully identified the essence of what would turn the scandal into a popular uprising, that is, the unbelievable injustice that bars farmers from using rainwater. Bollaín, on the other hand, chose a title that focuses on the people from the very beginning, acknowledging their fight and their victory.

Notes

1. For possible reasons of this stronger response concerning water compared to housing or health care, for example, particularly interesting is her concept that water privatization works as "a microcosm of contemporary struggles" (3), see Karen Bakker, "Introduction" in *Privatizing Water: Governance Failure and the World's Urban Water Crisis*, Cornell UP, 2013.

2. The same Hugo Banzer Suárez who had been Bolivia's dictator from 1971 to 1978 and was democratically elected in 1997. For a detailed account of his rise and fall as well as election during the democracy and years in-between, see *El dictador elegido: biografía no autorizada de Hugo Banzer Suárez* by Martín Sivak, La Paz, Bolivia: Plural Editors, 2001.

3. In order to legalize this situation, the Bolivian government passes Law 2029 one month later, in October of 1999, which "governed drinking water and sanitation [and] eliminated any guarantee of water distribution to rural areas" (Olivera and Lewis 8) and thereby contradicting the UN Action Plan that the access to water is a basic human right.

4. For a detailed report on the events in April see "The April Days" in Óscar Olivera and Tom Lewis, *Cochabamba! Water War in Bolivia*. Cambridge, Massachusetts, South End Press, 2004.

5. For a detailed analysis of the parallelism between the exploitation of the indigenous people now and then as well as of the symbolism of the cross, see Katarzyna Paszkiewicz's essay "Del cine épico al cine social: el universo metafílmico en *También la lluvia* (2010) de Icíar Bollaín." *Lectora*, no. 18, 2012, pp. 227–40.

6. In his 2005 book *The End of Poverty: Economic Possibilities for Our Time*, though Jeffrey Sachs defends his plan, he also admits that Bolivia's situation is far from resolved.

7. It seems rather anecdotal to point out that even though Marx earned fame for this quote from his introduction to *The Eighteenth Brumaire*, it "was most likely inspired by a letter [he] received from Engels in December 1851 as he was composing the work" (Hunt 388) that read "as though old Hegel ... were directing history from the grave and, with the greatest conscientiousness, causing everything to be re-enacted twice over, once as grand tragedy and the second time as rotten farce" (Hunt 388).

8. The original reads: "Bollaín cambia la mirada opresiva y unidireccional («gaze») dominante por un tipo de mirada llamado «looking relation», un proceso que, según Kaplan, connota la curiosidad por el Otro."

9. The film is dedicated to the memory of Howard Zinn, an American historian and activist who "first introduced many a previously miseducated reader to Christopher Columbus's true legacy of enslavement and genocide, a heritage central to Icíar Bollaín's film" (Schenker).

10. *Even the Rain* grossed $5,810,300 while *A Dark Truth* grossed $5,750, both calculated worldwide and in total lifetime grosses (www.boxofficemojo.com/movies/?page=main&id=eventherain.htm and www.boxofficemojo.com/movies/?id=adarktruth.htm. Accessed 15 January 2016).

Works Cited

Achtenberg, Emily. "*A Dark Truth* Disrespects Latin American Struggles for Water Rights." *NACLA: Rebel Currents*, 2013, nacla.org/blog/2013/1/4/%25E-2%2580%259C-dark-truth%25E2%2580%259D-disrespects-latin-american-struggles-water-rights. Accessed 22 April 2017.

Action Plan, "The Human Right to Water and Sanitation", UN-Water Decade Programme on Advocacy and Communication (UNW-DPAC), p. 1. www.un-.org/waterforlifedecade/pdf/human_right_to_water_and_sanitation_milestones.pdf. Accessed 15 January 2017.

Bakker, Karen. *Privatizing Water: Governance Failure and the World's Urban Water Crisis*. Cornell UP, 2013.

Bergendorff, Chris. "James Bond's New Water War Is Real." *Science Central*, 2008, www.youtube.com/watch?v=bNHbRznN9Qo. Accessed 22 April 2018.

Clover, Joshua. "Cinema for a Grand New Game." *Film Quarterly*, vol. 62, no. 4, Summer 2009, www.filmquarterly.org/2009/06/cinema-for-a-grand-new-game. Accessed 22 April 2018.

A Dark Truth. Directed by Damian Lee, Vortex Words Pictures, 2012.

Dittmer, Jason, and Klaus Dodds. "The Geopolitical Audience: Watching *Quantum of Solace* (2008) in London." *Popular Communication*, vol. 11, no. 1, 2013, pp. 76–91.

"En *También la lluvia* los bolivianos aparecen sin estereotipos, comenta Juan Carlos Aduviri." *La Jornada*, 10 January 2011, www.jornada.unam.mx/2011/01/10/espectaculos/a13n1esp. Accessed 20 January 2017.

Finnegan, William. "Leasing the Rain." *The New Yorker*, 8 April 8 2002, www.newyorker.com/magazine/2002/04/08/leasing-the-rain. Accessed 22 January 2017.

Food and Water Watch. "Bechtel Profits from Dirty Water in Guayaquil, Ecuador," www.foodandwaterwatch.com, November 2007. ciel.org/Publications/MurkyWaters_Background_15Apr08.pdf. Accessed 15 January 2017.

"Gobierno anuncia demanda contra Interagua por delitos ambientales." *El Telégrafo*, March 12, 2016, www.eltelegrafo.com.ec/noticias/guayaquil/10/gobierno-anuncia-medidas-judiciales-contra-interagua-por-delitos-ambientales. Accessed 15 January 2017.

González, José Antonio, and Desmond McCarthy. *Bolivia–Public Expenditure Review*. Washington, DC: World Bank, 1999, http://documents.worldbank.org/curated/en/689781468768283970/Bolivia-Public-Expenditure-Review. Accessed 15 January 2017.

Harvey, David. *The New Imperialism*. Oxford UP, 2003.

Hunt, Tristram. *Marx's General: The Revolutionary Life of Friedrich Engels*. Holt Paperbacks, 2010.

"IMF Approves Three-Year Arrangement under the ESAF for Bolivia." www.imf.org, no. 98/41, 18 September 1998, www.imf.org/en/News/Articles/2015/09/14/01/49/pr9841. Accessed 15 April 2017.

La Via Campesina, "The international peasant's voice," viacampesina.org, n.d., https://viacampesina.org/en/international-peasants-voice. Accessed 22 April 2018.

Limón, Raúl. "El agua es la sangre de los pueblos. No puede ser de nadie." *El País*, April 6, 2011, elpais.com/diario/2011/04/06/ultima/1302040802_850215.html. Accessed 15 January 2017.

Morales Peña, Carlos, and Naomi Klein. *Entrevista con la globalización: América Latina en la encrucijada de la mundialización a comienzos del siglo XXI*. Plural editores, 2008.

Olivera, Óscar, and Tom Lewis. *Cochabamba! Water War in Bolivia*. South End Press, 2004.

Paszkiewicz, Katarzyna. "Del cine épico al cine social: el universo metafílmico en *También la lluvia* (2010) de Icíar Bollaín." *Lectora*, no. 18, 2012, pp. 227–40.

Quantum of Solace. Directed by Marc Foster, Metro-Goldwyn-Mayer, 2008.

Roncallo, Alejandra. *The Political Economy of Space in the Americas: The New Pax Americana*. Routledge, 2014.

Schenker, Andrew. "Even the Rain." *Slant Magazine*, 14 February 2011, www.slantmagazine.com/film/review/even-the-rain. Accessed 15 January 2017.

Swyngedouw, Erik. "Dispossessing H2O: The Contested Terrain of Water Privatization." *Capitalism Nature Socialism*, vol. 16, no. 1, 2005, pp. 81–98.

También la lluvia. Directed by Icíar Bollaín, Paramount Home Entertainment, 2011.

PART 3

Arid and Awash

High Pollution, High Energy Demands, and High Waters

Troubled Waters

Unveiling Industrial Negligence in Three Deepwater Horizon Films

ILA TYAGI

ON 20 APRIL 2010, an accident occurred in the Gulf of Mexico that culminated in the largest US oil spill in history, to date. Late that Tuesday, seawater shot up onto the derrick of BP's Deepwater Horizon drilling rig, located 50 miles off the coast of Louisiana. A mixture of methane, mud, and water then erupted 250 feet into the air, followed by an explosion that instantly set the rig alight. Two days later, the burning rig crumpled into the water, snapping the mile-long pipelines connecting it to the well on the ocean floor. Roughly 170 million gallons of oil and gas were subsequently released into the Gulf at high pressure over 87 days, affecting 35 percent of the Gulf Coast (Watts 189).

BP managed the disaster not just by attempting to cap the source of the spill and clean up the crude oil it was spewing directly into the water, but also by turning the area of the spill into a blind spot for media and the public. It was not until three weeks after April 20 that the company released the first images of the disaster (Peters). In collaboration with the Coast Guard and the Federal Aviation Administration, BP issued a moratorium on aircraft flying over the spill zone. As a result, ordinary citizens resorted to extraordinary tactics to monitor the company's cleanup activities in the Gulf, including attaching point-and-shoot cameras to balloons or kites that were stabilized using empty soda bottles and then floated over the area of the spill (Groner). These amateur digital cameras' aerial images were among the earliest to be gathered independently of BP, puncturing the protective carapace that the company had tried to draw over itself.

Once they leaked out, images of the disaster flowed everywhere, including into a number of feature documentaries and narrative films. I will examine three such films: *Vanishing Pearls* and *The Great Invisible*, both documentaries released in 2014, as well as *Deepwater Horizon*, a 2016 docudrama starring Mark Wahlberg as the rig's real-life chief electronics technician, Mike Williams. I am interested in the three films' relationship to vision, as I believe vision to be a key issue when studying the oil industry and its representations. BP's attempt to ensure that no one outside the company could see the true extent of the spill suggests that BP, and by extension the oil industry in general, regards vision to be a dangerous, transgressive tool: useful if it remains within industrial control, but dangerous if relinquished to journalists or laypeople. They might see too much.

I argue that *Vanishing Pearls*, *The Great Invisible*, and *Deepwater Horizon* do see too much, piercing BP's blind spot more successfully than the company would like. Theirs is a superlative vision, meaning that the three films function as eyesight powerful enough to make visible to their viewers what BP strenuously sought to hide, from the corner-cutting that had increased the likelihood of the disaster in the first place, to the company's ham-handed failure to cap the spill in a timely manner or clean up the wasted oil effectively. Through visual strategies like aerial footage and animated sequences, the films reveal the oil industry to be a skilled manipulator of the naked eye's weaknesses, serving as pleas to their audiences to beware of bewilderments to their eyes and to look as closely and clearly as they can instead. Toward the end of the essay, I contextualize the films by considering an earlier representation of oil drilling in the Gulf of Mexico, in the narrative Hollywood film *Thunder Bay* (1953), illustrating how cultural attitudes to the oil industry have changed as a result of industrial negligence and pollution in the intervening half century.

The Deepwater Horizon spill, though unprecedented in scale, was only the latest in a string of Gulf disasters that have unfolded over the past fifty years. The year 1970 witnessed the first two major accidents off the Louisiana coast, the Chevron Oil Company's spill in Main Pass and the Shell Oil Company's in Bay Marchand. The 1970s marked "a turning point in the history of oil in the United States when two national imperatives—the need to increase energy supplies and the desire to protect the environment—collided" (Theriot 187). Expanding domestic petroleum production from the Gulf competes with protecting and restoring the Gulf Coast's sensitive tidal marshlands, with ecology frequently losing out. *Vanishing Pearls*, a documentary centering on African American oystermen in Pointe à la Hache, shows an animated map of 3,500 offshore oil and gas platforms spreading across the Gulf since the postwar era, the red dots standing in for them blooming like a measles epidemic. Between 2001 and 2011, according to one of the film's intertitles, there were 948 explosions and fires in Gulf oil drilling, claiming not just human lives but also killing off its extraordinary habitat and species diversity.

Rising sea levels, partially caused by burning fossil fuels, also mean that the Gulf is swallowing up the wetlands at the rate of one football field-sized area of land per *hour*. Per a recent *New York Times* article, each day the state of Louisiana "loses nearly the accumulated acreage of every football stadium in the N.F.L. Were this rate of land loss applied to New York, Central Park would disappear in a month. Manhattan would vanish within a year and a half. The last of Brooklyn would dissolve four years later" (Rich). Apart from their ecological significance and immense beauty, the Louisiana coast's disappearing wetlands also buffer the impact of hurricanes threatening cities like New Orleans and the port of South Louisiana. This port is the nation's largest, encompassing 10 percent of the country's oil reserves, a quarter of its natural-gas supply, a fifth of its oil-refining capacity, and serving as a gateway to its internal waterway system. "The attenuation of Louisiana," as the *Times* points out, "like any environmental disaster carried beyond a certain point, is a national-security threat" (Rich).

The director of *Vanishing Pearls*, Nailah Jefferson, is appalled by the devastation the oil industry wreaks, devastation poised to backfire on even its own infrastructures along the Louisiana coast. Though Jefferson never appears onscreen, the viewer hears her voice interviewing people from behind the camera. Her environmentalism is occasionally at odds with her interviewees' viewpoints. Wes Tunnell, a marine biologist whom BP gave under two weeks to produce a report on oyster damage caused by the Deepwater Horizon spill, takes a "nature is resilient" view during his interview in the film. "I always try to preach the kind of spatial perspective," he says. "It would be like standing in the top of the Superdome full of seawater, and somebody spilled a Coke can of oil in the top." His statement is accompanied by a sweeping aerial shot of the Mercedes-Benz Superdome in New Orleans. Minimizing the scale and seriousness of the spill by comparing it to a soda can spilled in a stadium, Tunnell glibly portrays the Gulf as "a limitless environmental sink—or at least too big to harm" (Colten 92). This, as may be expected, is a popular oil-industry view. "That's the philosophy that many polluters use, that it was only a drop in the bucket," says Ed Cake, another marine biologist interviewed on-screen. "While that may be volumetrically, it has literally damaged and destroyed many of our seafood resources." By disavowing oil-industry impact on the environment, Tunnell imagines nature as capable of repelling the ravages of human activity.

Tunnell seems at a remove from nature, which results in a willful blindness and corresponding decrease in knowledge. He shields himself with ignorance. When Jefferson asks him whether oyster mortality, the subject of his report, can be traced to BP's use of the dispersant Corexit, he equivocates, "I've told people it wasn't applied. The nearest it was to shore was about 75 miles, and others say 50. And others say, 'oh, no, I saw the planes flying right over the oyster reef.'" Raising his hands in a helpless gesture, he adds, "So, I don't know about that." Tunnell is surrounded by some nods to the natural world in his office, including a potted plant, glass vases filled with seashells, and a wooden statue of a pelican. These accouterments bespeak a calcified nature studied from a distance, rather than a living one interacted with dynamically. Perpetuating the myth of an infinitely resilient nature, as Tunnell does from inside his office, makes any environmental damage the oil industry brings about through its activities appear trifling and temporary. The industry regards taking a "spatial perspective" as a useful tool for rejecting allegations that it is causing pervasive ecological injury.

Since obtaining "spatial perspectives" from the air has hitherto been expensive, requiring flying up in a helicopter or plane, bird's-eye views are usually limited to individuals and industries that can afford them. Restricting outside entities' access to aerial perspectives takes on especial urgency at moments of crisis like April 2010, when flying over the Deepwater Horizon rig would have exposed more about the true extent of the spill than BP cared to divulge. "What was just shocking was the expanse of it," says Bonny Schumaker in *Vanishing Pearls*, "Even when you would go as high as 3,000 feet, it was as far as you could see." Schumaker is introduced as a pilot and the founder of On Wings of Care, a nonprofit organization that aims to protect natural ecosystems through constant visual survey "in flight, at sea, and on land" ("About"). Footage of the Deepwater Horizon spill gathered by On Wings of Care and included in *Vanishing Pearls* punches holes in BP's blind spot, making plainly apparent what the company strove to obscure.

Since BP could not conceal the spill indefinitely from digital cameras fastened to balloons or from organizations like On Wings of Care, the company next tried manufacturing an illusion that the spill had magically evaporated. It sprayed Corexit onto the Gulf in order to break the slick up into smaller droplets that would then sink below the water's surface. "Out of sight, out of mind," says John Wathen of the Waterkeeper Association in *Vanishing Pearls*, followed by a series of intertitles outlining Corexit's harmfulness to sea and human life. Wathen goes on to explain that BP was penalized by the barrel for the amount of oil it lost, making dispersants useful for blurring out just how much that total quantity was. The Corexit portion of the film features aerial footage of planes pouring it onto the Gulf in a "chemical death rain," as well as an animated underwater sequence showing Corexit and oil droplets descending onto oyster beds and killing them with their combined toxicity (Carson 12).

The animated sequence, in particular, sheds light on what BP would sooner keep in the dark: that while "terminating a spill is often synonymous with making it less visible," a less-visible spill is still carrying out its deadly destructiveness out of sight (LeMenager 23). Naomi Klein visited the spill site on a research vessel in 2011, writing, "One of the things I am learning aboard the *Weather Bird II*, watching these scientists test for the effects of invisible oil on invisible organisms, is not to trust my eyes. For a few months last year, when BP's oil formed patterns on the surface of these waters that looked eerily like blood, industrial society's impact on the ocean was easy for all to see. But when the oil sank, it didn't disappear" (17). By successfully dispersing the oil but failing to make it disappear, BP mitigated its own accountability while simultaneously ensuring that everything alive in the Gulf, from oystermen to microorganisms, would continue suffering the spill's consequences for years to come.

Temporally protracted events elude the eye, as it is difficult to continually monitor them unfolding over periods as long as several years, but animated sequences can compress them into a few seconds, making them easier to visualize. Knowing that BP is a skilled manipulator of the sense of sight, and knowing that sight is fallible, *Vanishing Pearls* commits to visually overwriting the company's obfuscations as much as possible. The naked eye can confuse oil's absence from the surface of the water with its removal, and the naked eye has a hard time seeing anything occurring over long periods without the help of time-lapse footage, or animation. Post–Deepwater Horizon films, however, have access to the same technological enhancements for the naked eye that were only the oil industry's preserve earlier. *Vanishing Pearls* contains aerial footage of the spill obtained independently by On Wings of Care, rather than from the oil industry, which clearly shows how much oil was on the water's surface, despite BP's attempts to displace it. The film's animated oyster sequence makes visible a process that BP was also counting on being difficult to see, because the oysters are underwater, and because their death by the Corexit-oil cocktail is distended in time.

If the animated sequence reminds viewers that oil has not disappeared from the Gulf as conveniently as BP would have us believe, other parts of *Vanishing Pearls* draw attention to oil inconveniently showing up where the company claimed it was not. Hurricane Isaac made landfall in Louisiana in August 2012, washing tar balls from the bowels of the Gulf onto beaches, blatantly demonstrating BP's claims that the spill had been cleaned up to be false. *Vanishing Pearls* overlays images of oil-blanketed beaches with sound bites claiming that "the people of BP made a commitment to the Gulf, and every day since, we've worked hard to keep it" or that "our beaches and waters are open for everyone to enjoy." In one scene, Byron Encalade, an oysterman, is seen roaming these beaches. They are deserted, posted with signs marked "closed until further notice," directly refuting the company's assurances. He picks up oil clumps and says, "You can smell the petrol. You can smell it in the mud." Encalade, unlike Tunnell, clearly sees that nature does not have an infinite capacity to absorb the oil industry's sloppiness. Joel Waltzer, an environmental lawyer, says, "We're seeing all the time BP claiming that they have restored the Gulf, that things are better, that the fisheries are back. If you say something enough times, people believe it." His words overlap shots from BP television advertisements offering a rosy picture of the Gulf's health.

This sequence interspersing Waltzer's interview—in which he argues that BP has fallen far short of fixing the considerable damage it did to the Gulf—with BP commercials claiming the exact opposite serves as a warning to *Vanishing Pearls*'s spectators to pay closer attention to the source of the images they look at. Since BP is invested in tricking the public eye, images originating from the company are not to be trusted. The film juxtaposes images showing the company's version of reality with others depicting a different reality, such as Encalade disconsolate on the sand. In *Vanishing Pearls*, the oil industry assumes a blinkered view of reality. The documentary takes it upon itself to acquire the full picture instead. Cynthia Sarthou, the executive director of the Gulf Restoration Network, points out in her *Vanishing Pearls* interview that "BP, very quickly, after the oil was shut down and the cameras were turned off, turned from this proactive 'We are going to do the right thing' into that defensive posture that industry goes into." *Vanishing Pearls*, like *The Great Invisible*, turns the camera back on. It reveals that what the oil industry's cameras show is frequently different from what other cameras might show. It applies the same tactics—like taking to the air—that the oil industry used to collect evidence supporting its version of reality to propose alternate versions of that reality. By doing all of the above, the film extends its viewers' vision, helping us see better and thus know more than we would otherwise. Extending our vision is crucial, the film seems to say, given that the oil industry is perpetually trying to pull the wool over our eyes.

Like *Vanishing Pearls*, the documentary *The Great Invisible* is interested in moments when BP tries to censor the public's vision, as well as in hampering the company's efforts by making visible what it seeks to cover up. In the immediate aftermath of the spill, BP initiated a "Vessels of Opportunity" program, hiring fishermen now out of work to use their nets to "catch" the escaping oil. An unnamed fisherman interviewed on camera bemusedly notes the futility of this project: nets have holes in them, making them useless for holding oil. His interview is cut short when an unseen man calling to him beyond his boat says, "They ain't supposed to be on that boat," referring to the camera crew. "We signed the thing, you can't talk to no media." "I didn't sign that," the fisherman replies, unsure. The unseen man emphatically repeats, "I signed a contract sayin' I can't talk to them. Get 'em off the boat." The fisherman returns making his apologies, and we catch a brief glimpse of the boom mic as the camera is lowered and the screen cuts to black. An intertitle flashes onto the screen saying that BP declined to participate in the making of the film.

As this sequence illustrates, BP is not a company accustomed to transparency. This is partially justifiable for safety reasons. Doug Brown, a chief mechanic on the Deepwater Horizon, says in one of his *Great Invisible* interviews that no visitors or family members of the rig crew were ever allowed onto it, as curious crowds wandering about would have been a hazard. However, as he observes, this embargo on extraneous eyes also had the effect of shrouding the rig in mystery. "A lot of us lived in a secret world," he says. Cloaking rig conditions in secrecy worked to BP's advantage, as the company had consistently been cutting corners to save time and money in the months leading up to the spill. Deteriorating safety standards made a catastrophe more likely, something that BP was understandably anxious to suppress. The company's resistance to transparency makes viewing the home-video footage that Brown took on the rig and that he shares in *The Great Invisible* an unexpectedly thrilling experience.

Brown's camera in the home-video footage is shaky and the image quality grainy, but it serves an important function nonetheless, giving its audience a window into a forbidden domain. Just as the On Wings of Care aerial footage makes available to a mass audience a view of the spill that BP would have preferred was limited to specialized eyes affiliated with the company, Brown's footage provides widespread access to a rig that would normally have been restricted to a small group. His footage helps level the visual playing field between the oil industry and everybody else, allowing us to see, and therefore know, as much as BP does.

Us seeing and knowing as much as BP does makes the company's public professions of ignorance seem all the more mendacious. *The Great Invisible* incorporates footage from a Congressional hearing with the heads of five major oil companies, including Lamar McKay, the chief executive officer (CEO) of BP America, and Rex Tillerson, the CEO of ExxonMobil. When Ed Whitfield, a Republican representative from Kentucky, asks McKay whether he was aware of any of the problems that existed with the Deepwater Horizon well before it blew, McKay simply replies, "No, I was not." As we saw with Tunnell, taking refuge in ignorance after an accident is useful, since it absolves the agent of responsibility. Democratic representative Ed Markey points out to Tillerson that Exxon Mobil's printed oil spill response plan for the Gulf of Mexico lists walruses as sensitive biological resources. "As I am sure you know," Markey concludes cuttingly, "there aren't any walruses in the Gulf of Mexico, and there have not been for three million years." "It's unfortunate that walruses were included," Tillerson waffles, "and it's . . . it's an embarrassment that they were included." Tillerson and his fellow boardroom executives are so out of touch with nature that they need to be reminded that there are no walruses in the Gulf.

McKay's willful ignorance during the Congressional hearing in *The Great Invisible* is mirrored by the willful ignorance of BP executives in *Deepwater Horizon*. *Deepwater Horizon* is a lightly fictionalized dramatization of the events of 20 April 2010. The film strongly suggests that BP's cavalier attitude toward maintaining the rig properly made a catastrophe more or less inevitable. BP was leasing the rig from Transocean. In an early scene, *Deepwater Horizon* shows BP executives sending Schlumberger employees who were supposed to run a cement test on the rig home early, despite warnings from Transocean's Offshore Installation Manager Jimmy Harrell (Kurt Russell) that the cement is all that stands between the rig and a blowout. Harrell asks Wahlberg's Mike Williams, also a Transocean employee, to outline for the benefit of BP's well site leader Donald Vidrine (John Malkovich) how many machines on the rig need repair. "390," says Williams, "almost 10 percent of all the machinery aboard." He goes on to recite a comically long litany of horrors: everything from the telephone system to the toilets, the salt-water service pumps to the smoke alarms are out of order. He points out that the reason why the BP representatives are sweating bullets into their shirts is because the air-conditioning is down, too.

Shortly before Williams delivers this dismal report to his bosses, he has been playing an eye-blinking game in his office with his wife Felicia (Kate Hudson) over Skype. The game involves staring deeply into each other's eyes, with whoever blinks first losing. They stare at each other through his computer screen until she breaks and covers her eyes with her hand. Still staring fiercely, Williams exults in victory. On his way out, Williams's eagle eyes spot something strange: the labels on a row of plastic jars on his top shelf are facing the back wall rather than the front, which is how he knows that someone on the rickety rig has been rummaging through his personal belongings. The audience infers an important element of Wahlberg's character from this scene. Being able to literally keep his eyes open longer than his wife illustrates that his eyes are figuratively open all the time as well: he is consistently vigilant, meaning he notices what might escape a less observant person's attention.

Noticing more than the average person translates into knowing more than the average person, represented here by Vidrine and his BP colleagues. Williams is much more intimately knowledgeable about the rig's many flaws than BP is. Being the film's noble hero, he shares this knowledge freely with the company's executives, and is dismayed when they seem not to register that the "well from hell" is held together with "bandaids and bubblegum." Vidrine runs a negative pressure test on the rig, and finds, to his satisfaction, that the pressure on its kill line is zero pounds per square inch (PSI). Choosing to ignore that the pressure on its drill pipe is 1,395 PSI, even though that figure should read zero as well, Vidrine orders Transocean to press on. They are forty-three days and $50 million behind schedule, and cannot afford to waste time on maintenance. Harrell chides Vidrine for refusing to spend $125,000 on a vital cement test even though BP is a $180 billion company. "That's why we're a $186 billion company," Vidrine replies unctuously, "we worry about those bills!" Turning a blind eye to festering problems is good for business. Money-hungry corporations smugly opt for the convenience of ignorance, rather than the hardship of fixing the messes that watchfulness uncovers.

The contrast between Williams, the film's hero, and Vidrine, its main villain, is underscored in a scene where Vidrine comes to visit Williams in his office. Vidrine spots a photograph of Williams, an avid fisherman, on Williams's desk showing him holding a sixty-five-pound fish that he caught. "That a catfish?" Vidrine asks uncertainly. "What y'all call that? Nibblin'?" "Noodlin'. We noodle for catfish," Williams corrects him. Vidrine's unfamiliarity and discomfort with the natural world serves to exhibit his villainous character, much the way unfamiliarity with the natural world works during the CEOs' Congressional hearing in *The Great Invisible*. Closeness to nature in the Gulf is proof of sound morals, according to contemporary oil films set there, as well as, interestingly, in oil films made much earlier. The ecological ignorance of CEOs in *The Great Invisible* is a significant reason why they come off as evil. *Deepwater Horizon*'s Williams, in contrast, is a hero, much like Jimmy Stewart's character Steve Martin in *Thunder Bay*. It is instructional to compare *Deepwater Horizon* with *Thunder Bay*, another film about oil drilling in the Gulf of Mexico, but released half a century before.

In *Thunder Bay*, Stewart plays an entrepreneur who constructs the Gulf's first offshore oil rig. *Deepwater Horizon* feels like a direct descendent of *Thunder Bay*, a funhouse mirror distortion in which everything that went right in the earlier film goes wrong. Martin's crew warns him in *Thunder Bay* that if he hits a high-pressure area at the rate at which he is drilling into the Gulf seafloor, the whole rig will blow out, just as Williams warns Vidrine in *Deepwater Horizon* that he is dangerously relying on "hope as a tactic." Like Vidrine, Martin chooses not to heed the warning and urges them to proceed full speed ahead. Salt water gushes out of Martin's drill onto his rig, as it did on the Deepwater Horizon just before it caught fire. Momentarily rattled, he deploys his blowout preventer quickly and effectively, to cries of "I think we got her licked!" Despite his many trials and tribulations over the course of the film, he successfully strikes oil by the end. Conversely, in *Deepwater Horizon*, careless drilling spells disaster.

Thunder Bay is sympathetic to the oil industry, whereas *Deepwater Horizon*, like *Vanishing Pearls* and *The Great Invisible*, is dismayed by it. Nevertheless, both *Thunder Bay* and *Deepwater Horizon* cast their heroes as rugged outdoorsmen. *Thunder Bay*'s Martin is first seen walking down a seashell-encrusted road thickly fringed with shrubs and trees as he makes his way to Port Felicity, a small fishing village in Louisiana. He turns out to understand the fishermen's work better than they do themselves, eventually leading them to the mythical "golden shrimp" they have fruitlessly sought for years. *Deepwater Horizon*'s Williams, as we have seen, is a skilled fisherman. He talks about his love of fishing at length to BP's Vidrine. The fact that Williams is thus shown to be comfortable interacting closely with nature for prolonged periods, means that he—unlike Vidrine—is fundamentally honorable, and that the film's spectators are right to trust him when he informs the executive that the rig is on the brink of calamity.

That impending blowout is augured by some superb foreshadowing in the film, including Williams's daughter's rehearsal of her school show-and-tell presentation going awry just before he leaves for work on the rig. Her presentation models the process by which the Deepwater Horizon drills into pressurized oil under the seafloor using a shaken Coke can and a metal tube. She pours honey down the tube to prevent the soda from shooting out, mimicking the mud used in real life. The Coke can unexpectedly explodes later in the scene, just as the rig's blowout preventer eventually would. Even though its sympathies lie resolutely with ordinary workers on the rig who were betrayed by BP's corner-cutting, *Deepwater Horizon* applies similar strategies to educate its audience about the complexities of offshore drilling that films sympathetic to oil companies used at midcentury.

Williams coaching his daughter through her presentation in *Deepwater Horizon* resembles the way Martin uses a model to demonstrate to his investor (and, conveniently, also to the film's audience) how he will build an offshore platform in *Thunder Bay*. *Deepwater Horizon* showcases the seamy underbelly of processes that half a century ago seemed purely innovative and exciting. The shaken Coke can exploding in *Deepwater Horizon* is reminiscent of the way Johnny Gambi (Dan Duryea), Martin's sidekick in *Thunder Bay*, shakes a beer bottle and unleashes its contents in a spray of foam to mimic a gusher coming in: the moment is wholly celebratory in *Thunder Bay*, but ominous in *Deepwater Horizon*. Gambi complains more or less continuously to Martin about the long odds they face as the nation's first offshore oil riggers, and Martin good-naturedly replies that he only worries about Gambi when he stops beefing. This dialogue is virtually identical to the *Deepwater Horizon* scene in which Felicia good-naturedly tells Williams, grousing about unsafe conditions on his rig, that "the only time you start worrying about a Marine is when he stops bitching." Gambi's fears prove to be unfounded; Williams's turn out to have been justified.

Studying the cultural construction of the offshore American oil industry at midcentury and at present reveals that the industry has gone from all-seeing and all-knowing to shunning knowledge via deliberate blindness. Sociocultural perceptions of a natural setting within which the offshore oil industry operates, the Gulf of Mexico, have also gone from imagining it as a hardy frontier rich in resources ripe for seizure to a vulnerable ecosystem battered by routine industrial pollution. These two developments in how we think of the oil industry, and in how we think of nature, are interlinked. The supposed hardiness of nature was a useful myth for the oil industry to circulate when establishing itself in the Gulf, in order to override ecological concerns and subsidiary economic activities there, like fishing. Furthermore, these subsidiary interests, misaligned with the oil-industry target of setting offshore platforms up across the Gulf, were more likely to yield to the industry's objective if the latter positioned itself as knowing the Gulf better than them, and knowing best what the nation at large really needed. At the end of *Thunder Bay*, Port Felicity's fishermen revolt against being ordered around by an oilman, and storm Martin's offshore rig. As they approach him, brandishing weapons menacingly, Martin snarls:

> You may put me out of business, all of you. But that isn't important. The important thing is that there's oil under this gulf, and we need it. Everybody needs it. You need it. Without oil, this country of ours would stop! And start to die. And you'd die. Now, it doesn't make any difference what you do to me, Dominique, you can't stop progress. Nobody can.

Abashed, the fishermen fall back, clearing the way for Martin to continue drilling and eventually strike a gusher. Oil's enormous economic and geopolitical importance are seen as trumping fishing's comparatively small value, despite its greater ecological sustainability.

Midcentury petrocinema is engrossed by the concept of "progress," as Martin's dialogue illustrates. Progress means harnessing the power of science and technology to amplify the American economy. Hidden amid the fog of *Thunder Bay*'s pro-oil propaganda is a remarkably clear-eyed moment about the tradeoffs that are made while pursuing the profit motive. Dominique (Antonio Moreno), a fisherman who is one of Martin's primary adversaries throughout *Thunder Bay*, sends for a specialist from the Department of Wildlife and Fisheries to determine if his dynamiting the Gulf to find the best place to drill has done any damage to fish and shrimp, since they are "among Louisiana's chief natural resources." Martin outfoxes them, saying that he has already finished dynamiting, and that he hopes for the same "conscientious protection" from the Department in the future, because "as I recall, oil is also one of this state's great natural resources." "Progress is not without faults, my friend," the Department man says ruefully to Dominique. At midcentury, "faults" like a shrinking livelihood for fishermen and environmental pollution are considered acceptable sacrifices to make for the sake of a fuel that keeps America alive.

Perhaps because too much pollution has accumulated in our sea, air, and soil in the past half century, contemporary films about offshore oil drilling are much less indulgent about economic progress' "faults." A shrinking livelihood for fishermen becomes an incalculably bitter cultural loss in *Vanishing Pearls*, whose interviewees mourn a disappearing way of life that has supported their families for generations. While midcentury films argue that tradeoffs are necessary because oil serves the greater good, the main purpose oil seems to serve at the moment is the personal enrichment of the oil executives in *Vanishing Pearls*, *The Great Invisible*, and *Deepwater Horizon*. Midcentury films, in other words, think in terms of generalized abstractions like "progress" and "this country of ours" and "luck"—as Martin says in *Thunder Bay*, even if the fishermen force him out of business, someone else will come along to take his place, as individual actors are secondary to the unstoppable march of collective "progress." In contrast, contemporary films take an atomized approach, bringing specific people (and other species) both profiting from and suffering at the hands of the oil industry into focus.

This initially has the effect of making oil-industry mismanagement seem more egregious, since it seems more intent on the particular goal of turning $180 billion companies into $186 billion companies than in maintaining basic safety standards, let alone serving a collective good. Moreover, while the suffering fishermen in *Thunder Bay* are a noisy rabble difficult to separate out into distinct faces, the fishermen bearing the brunt of Gulf oil spills in *Vanishing Pearls* and *The Great Invisible* receive faces, names, backstories, and dignity. Midcentury films suggest that energy, standing in for the economy as a whole, is locked in a zero-sum game with ecology, with the advancement of one interest corresponding to a diminishment of the other. Rather than economy-ecology, contemporary films are more interested in eyesight-empathy, positing that the enhancement of one leads to an enhancement of the other. In a context in which the oil industry expediently pretends to be blind to disavow its responsibility for industrial accidents and subsequent cleanup costs, these films help their audiences see more through aerial shots, animated sequences, home-video footage, and sharp-sighted characters like Wahlberg's Williams, which together draw attention to phenomena that would otherwise elude the eye. By ameliorating our vision, the films seek to augment our empathy for the agents involved in and affected by the oil industry—even oil executives, who, we understand, behave the way they do because they have to answer to shareholders hoping for the maximum return on their investments. Empathy has no economic value, and little direct effect on improving the natural world's health. However, its relationship to eyesight—sharper vision, greater empathy—offers a roadmap for rethinking economy and ecology as not mutually exclusive, but as compatible.

Works Cited

"About." *On Wings of Care*, www.onwingsofcare.org/index.php/ mission. Accessed 13 November 2016.

Carson, Rachel. Silent Spring. 1962. Mariner Books, 2002.

Colten, Craig E. "An Incomplete Solution: Oil and Water in Louisiana." *Journal of American History*, vol. 99, no. 1, 2012, pp. 91–99.

Deepwater Horizon. Directed by Peter Berg, Summit Entertainment, 2016.

The Great Invisible. Directed by Margaret Brown, Motto Pictures, 2014.

Groner, Anya. "Healing the Gulf with Buckets and Balloons." *Guernica*, 6 September 2016, https://www.guernicamag.com/anya-groner-healing-the-gulf-with-buckets-and-balloons/.

Klein, Naomi. "After the Spill." *Nation*, 31 January 2011, pp. 11–18.

LeMenager, Stephanie. *Living Oil: Petroleum Culture in the American Century.* Oxford UP, 2014.

Peters, Jeremy W. "Efforts to Limit the Flow of Spill News." *New York Times*, 9 June 2010, www.nytimes.com/2010/06/10/us/10access.html?pagewanted=all&_r=0.

Rich, Nathaniel. "The Most Ambitious Environmental Lawsuit Ever." *New York Times*, 14 October 2014, www.nytimes.com/interactive/2014/10/02/magazine/mag-oil-lawsuit.html?_r=0.

Theriot, Jason. "Building America's First Offshore Oil Port: LOOP." *Journal of American History*, vol. 99, no. 1, 2012, pp. 187–96.

Vanishing Pearls. Directed by Nailah Jefferson, Perspective Pictures, 2014.

Watts, Michael. "Oil Frontiers: The Niger Delta and the Gulf of Mexico." *Oil Culture*, edited by Ross Barrett and Daniel Worden, U of Minnesota P, 2014, pp. 189–210.

The River as Character
in Niger Delta Poetry

IDOM T. INYABRI

> The Oil Rivers are chiefly remarkable among our
> West African possessions . . . for the exceptional facilities
> which they offer for penetrating the interior by means of large
> and navigable streams and by a wonderful system of natural
> canalization which connects all the branches of the lower
> Niger by means of deep creeks.
> —Sir Harry Johnston in 1888.
> Qtd. in Dike, *Trade and Politics in the Niger Delta*, 19

LOCATED AT THE WASH PLANE of the River Niger, the Niger Delta occupies an area which stretches southwest and southeast of what is now known as Nigeria. Although there are many contentious claims with regard to the specific area of the Niger Delta, which are sometimes conditioned by political geography, the definition of the area as given by K. Onwuka Dike, one of Nigeria's earliest historians of the region, seems more apt to capture the region's historical imperative, its cultural nuances, and complex geography. It is for these reasons that Dike sees the Niger Delta as "the region bounded by the Benin river on the west and the Cross River in the east, including the coastal area where the Cameroon mountains deep in to the sea." Perhaps to be more precise about this stretch, Dike goes further to state that "[i]t covers an area of some 270 miles along the Atlantic coast and is 120 miles in depth" (19).

This complex geographic continuum is defined by dense mangroves, tortuous creeks, canals, streams, and thick rain forests.

From the sixteenth century, when European adventurers and slave merchants began to make incursions into the region, to the nineteenth century, when the British began to sign treaties to enforce "legitimate trade" in palm oil, historians have shown that the Niger Delta has held strong attraction to Europeans. As it is obvious in the prefatory note above, the reason for the pull to the Niger Delta is unmistakable; the rivers of the Niger Delta and the natural resources that they held for imperialism and British commercial monopoly are at the center of the grand narrative of Western encounter with the "natives." Indeed, the rivers still remain at the center of the tragic story of the region and by extension of the Nigerian postcolony. But it is not only the West that has been dazzled by the rivers of the Niger Delta, even if the legacies of their encounter with the Niger Delta have left indelible scars on the entire region, the aboriginals themselves have had a primordial relationship with the ubiquitous rivers that have been part of them and defined their lives for centuries. In this paper, my aim is to prioritize the creative representation of the rivers by Niger Delta poets, through a subtle application of postcolonial ecocriticism. I will also show that the narratives of the region which have configured the rivers as background or at best an ecological canvas upon which to read the ramifications of imperialism and post-independent contradictions is actually the narrative of the fate of the rivers in the region. By implication, for the eco-poets discussed here, successful resolution of the Niger Delta tragedy must implicate nonhumans, especially some of its most famous rivers namely: Forcados, Nun, Ethiope, Brass, Benin, Bonny, Kwa-Ibo (Qua Iboe), Cross, and Abeb Rivers among many others. My discourse will facilitate a robust appreciation of the creative representation of the rivers within the context of the life imbued nonhumans by an organic/animistic worldview expressed by the poets under study, and the inexorable connection that exists between them and humanity. Given this quality of interconnection that is a guiding principle in this chapter, it also becomes imperative to see the health of the rivers and other nonhumans generally as a sine qua non to sociopolitical peace.

In presenting rivers as characters, my study challenges the Aristotelian prescription for literary appreciation. In his classical aesthetics, Aristotle categorizes nonhumans at the periphery of literary discourse as *milieu* or setting, while humans and human actions are given priority. This ontology is, of course, a precursor of the (post-) Enlightenment duality that sustains the Otherness of woman, nature, emotion, and what is considered the subaltern. However, in the context of palpable contemporary ecological threats, the discourse of what is now known as the "Anthropocene" (Clark 1) and the vulnerability of humans, the Classical egoistic representation of man becomes problematic and unsustainable. Hence, Cheryll Glotfelty sees the nonhuman as "actor" ("Introduction" xxi) in the same way as Glen Love wants us to appreciate it as "an indispensable participant and leading character" (90) in the narrative of life. Therefore, in the spirit of this subversive logic, one recognizes the agency of nonhuman elements, including rivers and streams in texts where they come alive in their active pristine forms. In this perspective, as DeLoughrey and Handley would have it, "place encodes time, suggesting that histories embedded in the land and sea have always provided vital and dynamic methodologies for understanding the transformative impact of empire and the anti-colonial epistemologies it tries to suppress" (4). With this method of reading, we have to be more contemplative of narratives that include and prioritize the place of the often ignored nonhumans in human experiences. Again, DeLoughrey and Handley urge us to open up the implicit meanings from nonhuman life and take seriously that which have been trivialized as mere symbols in literary analysis.

To this end, I derive critical principles of analysis from the precolonial agrarian ethos of the Niger Delta poets under discussion to retrieve the true value of the rivers in their minds and landscape. Within this agrarian pre-industrialized culture, Wangari Maathai tells us that humans "retain a close, reverential connection with nature, and their life style and natural resources are not yet commercialized" (174). It is the same period of African ecological history that Mikhail Bakhtin calls the "folkloric time" (210). In this folkloric time as he also explains, "[t]he agricultural life of men and the life of nature (of the earth) are measured by one and the same scale" (208). In other words, in such societies there exist an ornate, mutually dependent relation between humans and nonhumans. The life patterns of society in terms of ritual, rites of passage, festivals, and everyday living are equally defined by the ritual of planting and harvesting, animal husbandry, and diverse encounters with nonhumans in the environment.

Within this paradigm of the organic agrarian life, my perspective is also conditioned by what has been referred to as an ecological "commons" (Adamson and Ruffin 2), a biotic community where nonhuman nature, including rivers and streams are seen as "ecological citizens" (Adamson and Ruffin xvii). While my idea of ecological citizenship derives from a postmodern interrogation of life and rights to belonging in a hegemonic globe, my perspective also finds validity in the postcolonial ecocritical attempt at drawing attention to the subtle insights that "marginal" entities can offer us in the project of attending to the wrongs inaugurated by colonialism.

Although the theories of postcolonialism and ecocriticism come from two different ontologies, where the former is anthropocentric and the later ecocentric, postcolonial (ecocritical) scholars have uncoupled an ideological synergy that connects the two theories. In this regard Huggan and Tiffin have worked through the environmental history of Alfred Crosby and Richard Grove to show that nonhuman beings are equally witnesses to the colonial adventures of the west all over the world. For them, postcolonial ecocriticism is attentive to "the historical embeddedness of ecology in the European imperial enterprise" (Huggan and Tiffin 3). The ideological disposition within which colonialism is validated and sustained wells from a dualistic thinking which does not only discriminate against non-Europeans as inferior Others but, as Val Plumwood has argued, also marginalizes and places women, subalterns, "animals and animalized humans", and other aspects of the physical environment in the same stereotypic category. It is this post-Enlightenment epistemology that continues to structure human attitude to the environment, sees them "as being either external to human needs, and thus effectively dispensable, or as being in permanent service to them and thus an endlessly replenishable resource" (Huggan and Tiffin 4).

For nineteenth-century European adventurers and administrators, the beauty of the Niger Delta rivers lies in their natural connectivity to one another, which also creates natural access to the interiors for palm produce (palm oil and kennel), the new money spinner at that time. But as Richard and John Lander, who are credited with the discovery of the River Niger saw it, the rivers also provide another route to Central Africa. No wonder Sir Johnston would praise the rivers of the Niger Delta in such glorious terms as we see in the quotation that opens this paper. Indeed, the discovery of the Niger, as Dike documents, was greeted with much euphoria and triumph in Britain—the imperial metropolis. But what should also intrigue us here is the objectification that also characterizes the British colonial encounter with the rivers of the Niger Delta. For the colonizers, the rivers became immediately one of "our West African possessions" for penetration of the hinterland and indeed farther into the heart of Africa (Quoted in Dike 19). Thus, to consolidate this possession, several British expeditions from the early nineteenth century made sure that, by all means possible, treaties were signed for the protection of waters and rivers, which were borders and entry points into the Niger Delta. Local monarchs or "princes," who opposed the British offer of "protection," faced exile and imprisonment, which were common instruments used by British consuls to dispossess stubborn princes of their authority over ancestral borders. Through the possession of rivers, the entire Niger Delta became a British protectorate, which was subsequently amalgamated to Northern Nigeria to be known as the protectorate and colony of Nigeria. In an animistic ecocritical sense, through which nonhumans are characterized and made subjects, it could be said that the rivers and land first encountered and experienced annexation and colonization before humans in the Niger Delta. It is in this context, perhaps, that one understands Edward Said when he asserts that "the actual possession of land is what empire in the final analysis is all about" (78).

Discussing the colonial engagement with the rivers and peoples of the Niger Delta enables us to better appreciate the indigenous relationship with the same rivers. As a source of livelihood, recreation, and spirituality in the Niger Delta, the rivers are intertwined with the people's lives. The ubiquity of rivers and streams, and their centripetal pull to the people have given them a prime place in the entire literary expression of the region. In poetry, water (represented as streams, ponds, and rivers) has continuously possessed the imagination of poets. Born in the 1920s and 1930s respectively, Gabriel Immomotimi Okara and J. P. Clark (Bekederemo) are two notable modern pioneers of Niger Delta poetry. Both poets offer Nigerian poetry as a whole the most memorable poems on water.

Although water remains a motif in the poetic oeuvre of Clark (Bekederemo), his "Stream Side Exchange" (*A Decade of Tongues* 20) is a popular piece that, though has been seen as pastoral, triangulates the inexorable ecological connectedness of the human (the child persona bemoaning his mother's demise), the river-side bird that the child supplicates, and the stream (the serene body of water) that provides a tryst for the contemplation of existential realities. To the pondering question of the sorrowing child the bird consoles:

> You cannot know
> And should not bother;
> Tide and market come and go
> And so has your mother. (20)

Just like Clark (Bekederemo), Okara's poetry is also suffused with the water motif. This is evident in his "The Fisherman's Invocation" and "Piano and Drums." His "The Call of the River Nun" (*The Fisherman's Invocation* 16) illustrates his poet persona's sentiments toward the river at that time. It is also in this poem that he celebrates the Nun, that famous ancient river, "one of the two mouths of the Niger" (Dike 19). Found in the heart of the Niger Delta, River Nun is in present day Bayelsa State, south of Nigeria. As one of the major rivers of the Niger Delta, River Nun was also one of the major routes for the trade in palm oil. For this reason, it is one of the most famous among what was known in colonial times as the "Oil Rivers."

The poem "The Call of the River Nun" is perhaps made memorable for its magnetic feel and spiritual "call" that the river makes to the estranged poet persona who declares:

> I hear your call!
> I hear it far away;
> I hear it break the circle
> Of these crouching hills. (*The Fisherman's Invocation* 16)

But more than this strong call, the river becomes a vehicle for the poet persona's introspection on his life and the inevitability of death; a rite of passage, which he begins to contemplate more seriously at this point of surreal connection with the river. In this situation, the archetypal river bears a complex personality as the poet introspectively immerses himself in the transcendent possibility of that ever-present body of water. Although Okara is one of Nigeria's most surrealistic, if not mystical, poets, this poem like many of his other poems is a tangible expression of place-consciousness and be/longing. In stanza two, which is worth quoting at length, the poet persona does not hide his child-like desire to indulge and reconnect with his beloved river:

> I want to view your face
> again and feel your cold
> embrace; or at your brim
> to set myself and
> inhale your breath; or
> Like the trees, to watch
> my mirrored self unfold
> and span my days with
> Song from the lips of dawn. (20)

The dense imagery of self-discovery and recuperation is an ecological logic that the reader cannot ignore in the lines above. Though the romanticism in the poem is obvious, its imagery is realistic to the extent that it captures the vitality that the riverine environment holds for the persona, who is suffering from estrangement. Indeed, the river has a psychological therapy because the poet persona thinks that it has a certain purity and ecological association that is revitalizing. This therapeutic potential can be seen in the river's "cold embrace," its life-giving "breath," and clear "silver-surfaced flow" (20). More so, around the river is ample evidence of life displayed by the "trees" and "sea-birds," part of the river's identity or ecological "personality" that the persona desires to reconnect with.

A closer reflection on Okara's "The Call of the River Nun" and Clark's (Bekederemo's) "Stream Side Exchange" would reveal that, though the poems are written with slightly different themes, there is imagery that connects them. Generally, the body of water in both poems provides a venue to contemplate deep philosophical issues with regard to existence, rites of passage, and the mystery in-between. But, again, one finds out that the river and the stream in both cases attract life forms that define the tonality of the waterscape namely, "river-bird" and "grass" (in the case of Clark [Bekederemo]) and "sea-bird" and "trees" (in the case of Okara). This obvious expression of ecological kinship implies a healthy freshwater context around which flora and fauna interconnect symbiotically and mutually harness a natural synergy that sustains the rhythm of riverine life. This subtle connection should help us see each element, especially the river and stream, as complex characters in an organic environment, where each life form has its value and enlivens others. The subtle representation of water, its ambience and inexorable connection with the flora and fauna in Clark (Bekederemo's) and Okara's poetries creatively capture Larry Commoner's first law of ecology: "everything is connected to everything else", which, in turn, is a fundamental guiding principle of ecocritics (Ruecket 108). Although the pastoral accent that we observe in Okara's and Clark (Bekederemo's) poems can be seen in the poetry of Tanure Ojaide, another prodigious Niger Delta poet, its ideological lining in his creative oeuvre gives water (in the form of rivers, streams, and ponds) a different quality.

Born in the late 1940s, Ojaide displays palpable imagery of water in his Urhobo homeland. The ubiquity of water that he specifies in his childhood memoir has a lush feeling that also goes beyond sheer pastoral romance. In his essay "I Want to Be an Oracle," Ojaide tells his reader that he "was born into an age of innocence" (*Poetic Imagination in Africa* 121). In that golden age, which suits the definition of Bakhtin's agrarian/folkloric time and Maathai's preindustrial society, the ponds, streams, and rivers around the homestead exuded life. It was a period when on rainy days, fish could be seen jumping out of the streamside onto the road or as it often happened during rainstorms fish were thought to fall from the sky (*Great Boys* 84–85). This paradisiacal imagery is reflected in his early collection of poems *Children of Iroko and Other Poems* where the poet persona showed that the environment was conducive for the propitiation of a river god. In the poem "Map of Time" (*Children of Iroko* 1), the poet persona, obviously an acolyte, invites his people to join him to the river where they would offer sacrifices of thanksgiving to the benevolent river god.

In the study of modern Niger Delta poetry, Ojaide is a bridge between the "old" and the "new" wave of Niger Delta poetry. I make this assertion with regard to his age and the fact that, by association, he is closer to the poets who emerged after him—those who began to find their voices in the 1980s. This, however, is not to infer that by the rise of these poets, whom I often classify as third generation, the older poets namely, Clark (Bekederemo) and Okara have stopped writing or do not dwell on contemporary issues. This point has to be made here, because in engaging a subject matter such as water, it is only necessary to see its dynamics and complex character in terms of "generations." To this extent, apart from Ken Saro-Wiwa, Ojaide has applied himself much more to the scholarship of providing us with insight into what Rob Nixon has referred to as "environmentalism of the poor" (2011), a concept which consists in the manner in which global capitalism in league with the establishment think of and treat poor indigenous peoples and their ecologies as disposable (Nixon 4). Nixon's elastic conceptualization of the poor as "a compendious category subject" (4) is apt when applied in the Niger Delta environment. Given the indigenous animistic world view and the people's strong connection with their nonhuman environment, the humans become a vital embodiment of the flora and fauna that share their ancestral homeland. In this sense, defiled elements such as the Niger Delta rivers identified in this discourse are located in one dispossessed space and condition as objectified humans, who suffer the same fate of exploitation and abandonment. In this paradigm, the rivers of the Niger Delta are implicated in that impoverished "compendious category" that Nixon talks about.

Although Ojaide indicates that the discovery and use of the chemical Gamalin 20 by fishermen in his homeland to maximize profit was one of his earliest exposure to injury on aquatic life ("Nativity and the Creative Process" 33), it was the exploration and exploitation of crude oil by multinational oil companies that would traumatically disrupt the ornate rhythm of life of his people and mar the ever-vibrant rivers and streams in a more extensive, tragic, and irretrievable manner. Ike

Okonta and Oronto Douglas give us a graphic picture of the scientific and technological processes of crude oil exploration in the Niger Delta, and its implication on the water sources for the indigenous people of the delta. From seismic surveys to blowouts, primitive ancestral forests, farmlands, and above all rivers, streams, and ponds were mowed down, drained, and dugout. This horrific process, which started in the early 1950s, became a continuous reality for the people and the nonhuman environment of the Niger Delta even into the millennium. Indeed, this process marks the transition from preindustrial bliss to the nightmarish experiences engendered by the connivance of successive predatory post-independence governments and multinational oil companies.

As a boy growing up in the 1950s, Ojaide remembers the euphoria with which his people welcomed the promise of crude oil at first. But with time, he also tells of the shock felt by his people when they first saw the effect of crude oil on water and its impact on the rivers, streams, and, inextricably, their life pattern in general. In a narrative that is at once mythical and innocent, the child narrator in *Great Boys: An African Childhood* says:

> Fishermen and women soon discovered that they couldn't catch as many fish as they used to. Rumors had it that Mammy Water or the water goddess had withdrawn to the sea with her retinue of fish from rivers over which the black oil light shone. Even gods and goddesses, we realized, needed privacy. Within months a pipe broke and the streams were covered with thick seams. The fish floated belly-up, and no one would eat dead fish. (*Great Boys* 126–27)

Thus, began the swan song for the ancient, awe-inspiring, and ever-vibrant rivers and streams of the Niger Delta poets. From the late '70s and '80s to the millennium, poets from the region began to sing of rivers that are dead, sickened, or vulnerable. It is interesting that some of the historic rivers that were important to the British colonial enterprise and which were also fascinations to a precursor poet such as Okara still remain important to the third-generation Niger Delta poets. In his *Oily Tears of the Delta*, Ibiwari Ikiriko bemoans the woeful condition of the great River Nun. In a mournful tone, the poet persona announces the tragedy of that same river in his time:

Now
Crude-surfaced
It Lumbers
Along lifeless,
Like dead wood.

Lifeless like
The dead woods
That border
Its crude soiled banks. (25)

Unlike the days of Okara when the Nun was exuberant, attractive, and gave life to the flora and fauna that were typical of its ecology, today, because of the reality of insensitive profiteering, the river "lumbers, / ... Reflecting nothing / invoking nothing / Except ghosts / Of tall tales / Of spillage / And pillage . . ." (25). In his own thoughts over the River Nun, Ikiriko creates a human persona who does not have the luxury of meditation on the essence of life. Rather, the reader encounters a poet persona who shows that the archetypal ambience that is associated with such introspection is defiled by greed.

In "To Dappa-Biriye on the Jubilee," Ikiriko seizes the opportunity of an ethnic nationality's jubilee celebration to show that the fate of the River Nun is not limited to it. Capturing the awful pollution that has taken over the "omnipresent" bodies of water, as Ojaide would have it, Ikiriko rhetorically asks Dappa-Biriye—the celebrated Ijaw monarch for whom the poem is dedicated:

When you make the salt-windy trek
On that boa constrictor jetty seawards
In your native Ayama
Only an eye cast from the bight

How do you feel, Delta Warrior? (22)

In the string of rhetorical questions that characterize the poem, the poet persona hopes to impress on the reader the depressing impact of despoliation that is prevalent in his time on account of crude oil exploitation. In the stanzas that follow, he inscribes the time-specific nature of the effect of mindless desecration of the waterscape in his generation as different from the organic simple life of his riverine forbears:

What do you see on the seascape?

The fish-folk's fish-mine of yore?
The canoe and paddle, hook and net hive of yore?
Or a face-lift exclusion zone,
A desert-sea, oarless and uncameled? (22)

In the scheme of then-and-now, the poet persona shows how horribly defiled and terrorized the seascape has become in his time; a time in which the "sea-sky" has become "pollution-stricken" and "[b]ereft of the gull's intricate flight-dance" (22). The dispossessed imagery that we see here sharply differs from the imagery of serene riverine environment recreated in Clark's (Bekederemo's) "Stream Side Exchange" and Okara's "River Nun," where the stream and river have a natural force that attracts life forms to themselves. In fact, at that time, these bodies of water have an admirable life; one that only has meaning in an agrarian culture where there is a subtle connection between humans and nonhumans. In the "now" of Ikiriko, the myth surrounding the rivers, streams, and ponds have been successfully overturned, while the logic of the Enlightenment is enthroned. In this new (enlightened) globalizing regime, development implies the demystification of all taboos and spirituality attached to rivers and streams.

The objectification and victimhood of the river and people in Ikiriko's poetry have a deeper dramatic expression in Ogaga Ifowodo's *The Oil Lamp*. The collection of poems itself is a masterpiece of ecopoetry made so by the deftness of its dialogic and intertextual qualities. Utilizing Dante's apocalyptic "Inferno" as a subtext, Ifowodo shows that the history and daily life of the Niger Delta is hellish. Divided into five parts and a postscript entitled "The Agonist" (dedicated to Ken Saro-Wiwa and the Ogoni eight) the collection narrativizes major traumatic incidences in the recent history of the Niger Delta. As it is with all other poets in the region, Ifowodo does not make any distinction between humans and nonhumans in his drama of abysmal living in a late modern era.

From the prologue (entitled "A Waterscape") to the Postscript ("The Agonist"), the life of water as a character in an organic world is brought into one category of Otherness with that of humans. "A Waterscape" opens with an imagistic representation of a dead river or seascape that has become scum. The poet persona describes the oddity as a "massive ink-well, silent and mute"; a ". . . black water" that is devoid of life for impoverished fishermen who only "glide / home to the first meal" (xi).

All through the collection, as the poet persona recounts the experiences of the region, the dispossessed rivers, creeks, and streams face the same threat of annihilation and extinction as other characters or to use the word of Glotfelty, their fellow "actors" in the bioregion. In Part 1 called "Jesse," the poet presents the real but unfortunate experience of the inferno which consumed a whole community in 1998 as they were driven by deep-seated poverty and ignorance to scoop gas (PMS) from a cracked pipe, one of many that run through their homestead and farmlands. At the height of the consuming bolts of fire, the poet persona tells us that even "[t]he creeks and ponds" were at the verge of "boil[ing] dry" and that "the rivers, now on fire, rushed / to the sea for a dip, floating / along the land's burning question" (13). Thus, in what looks like a ritual sacrifice to a vampire god (the state in conjunction with transnational oil companies), the rivers like humans, flora, and fauna become victims. This victimhood is made palpable by the characterization of the rivers as seen below:

> The land burned, the trees burned, the rivers burned,
> the smoke unrolled endless bolts of cloth
> to wrap naked grief and shield the world. (14)

It is indeed difficult to think of the fate of the rivers in isolation from the environment in which they are an intrinsic part. It is for this reason that in Part III entitled "Ogoni" the poet includes the rivers in a fictive rhetorical face-off with the occupying forces of the neocolonial state armed by the usurping multinational oil companies. In what one may describe as a townhall meeting with the military representative dispatched to enforce peace in the troubled Ogoni land, voices from the fringes of society: an old man, a woman, and a little schoolboy with his peasant father engage Major Kitemo (nicknamed "Kill-them-All" for

his brutishness) on the validity of the state to exercise control over their
land. Through a smart official history of the country, Major Kill-them-
All argues that the state derives its justification of ownership from colonial cartography (39) and "by decrees and edict" (40). However, the
old man, who remains nameless, poses his own challenge to the establishment claims of the state:

> ... So tell me, my son, [he asks the soldier]
> How long do you think we have been on this land,
> how long the oil, the trees, the creeks and the rivers? (39)

In the rhetorical question above, the poet through the instrumentality of the nameless old man uses aboriginal logic to invalidate what
Saro-Wiwa has tagged "domestic colonialism" (*A Month and a Day* 18).
But what is more intriguing here, is not just the fact that the old man
holds his own against the totalizing force of the state. It is rather the
poet's signification of the ecological right of belonging to a place that
nonhuman elements like humans possess. This sense of "ecological citizenship" (Adamson and Ruffin 3) is specified through what Duncan
Brown, in a similar postcolonial context, calls "an unofficial cartography
of knowing, belonging and growing" (129). Implicit in Brown's assertion
is the specification of an indigenous and alternative expression of root-
edness and territoriality or a sense of place that is encoded in people's
mores, myths, narratives, rituals, and other performative significations
of identity that may not be recognized by the hegemony of the establishment. In this aboriginal logic, nonhumans, especially the rivers, which
in evolutionary and creationist terms predate humans, are respectfully
included in place and consciousness despite their seeming vulnerability.
More so, through the old man's argument, as it is with the posers from
the little boy and the woman, the poet gives voice to marginality. Here,
this marginality consists of the objectified indigenes and their vulnerable
nonhuman environment. Again, through the engagement between the
people and the military (the coercive agent of the state), the poet persona
metaphorically indicates an encounter between two unequal forces in his
homeland. These forces are his marginalized people (represented by the
nameless personae in the poem) and their equally endangered environment on the one hand and the exploitative multinational oil companies

in league with the neocolonial Nigerian state on the other. Through the nameless personae in the poem, the poet speaks germane ecocentric lessons to a country that has become blind by corruption.

It should be noted though, that not all rivers are marred by the factor of crude oil in the poetry of the third-generation Niger Delta poets; some are affected by other human activities. For instance, Joe Ushie, who comes from Bendi, northern Cross River State of southeastern Nigeria, tells how his homeland is threatened by avaricious logging, mowing of the hills and mindless bush burning, and public sector corruption among several other inimical practices. Within this circumstance, the streams and ancient rivers that provided much life for the ecosystem and once placed Bendi in the map of colonial palm oil enterprise, have also met misfortune. From his first collection of poems entitled *Popular Stand and Other Poems* the poet displays a strong connection with the streams and rivers that run through his birthplace. It is this strong attachment to these bodies of water that forms part of the rationale for the constant journey home that is a dominant motif in Ushie's poetry. As in Clark's (Bekederemo's) and Okara's early poetry, Ushie's *Popular Stand* presents a poet persona who muses over the serenity, vitality, and awesomeness of the rivers and stream in Bendi. This is what comes through when we read poems such as "Begwang River" (*Popular Stand* 29–30) and "A Trip Home" (*Popular Stand* 26–28).

As a twist of fate and in the context of the lachrymal nature of the poetry of his generation, Ushie shows that in recent times "[t]he streams of [his] bloom" (*Hill Songs* 10) and the "River[s] that nursed our grandsires" (*Hill Songs* 29) have been "burnt" (*Hill Songs* 10) and are at the verge of extinction:

Old now, the Abeb River goes
Wearily bearing bundles of woes.
Like it, our yams are going
Like it, our grains are going
Like it, our gods are going
And gone, are our baked children
Whose loud names echo here from hill
To hill like fiction from afar. (*Hill Songs* 29)

It is interesting to note the overall ecological and cosmic implication of the fate of the streams and rivers as indispensable characters in Ushie's poetry and in his Bendi environment as a whole. The
poet persona shows that the tragic fate of the rivers in contemporary
time foreshadows subsequent disaster for the entire environment and
indeed the people's spirituality. Therefore, he seems to say that the
essence of life and its sustenance are embodied in the waters of the
homeland that are now under enormous pressure. The poet persona in
the poem above does not equivocate about the sources of threat to this
life-giving streams and rivers. For him, they derive from "greed-fanned
flame / greed-clad axe and greed-brewed death" (*Hill Songs* 10); the life
pattern of unguided living in a dysfunctional state where, as the poet
persona would decry in "Back to Kugbudu," "Bona fide members are
re-membered only / during ballot season." (*Hill Songs* 29).

Although a mournful note pervades the musings over the rivers in
contemporary Niger Delta poetry, there are some rivers that are still
celebrated for their grandeur and gracefulness. This sensibility is what
we encounter in Ebi Yeibo's first poetry collection *Maiden Lines* where
the River Forcados—one of "two mouths of the Niger" (Dike 19) and
Ethiope are celebrated in the two poems that are entitled after them.
The River Ethiope is a clear-water spring, one of nature's wonders be-
queathed to the Delta and located in the present Delta State of Nigeria.
Little wonder then that Ojaide's child narrator tells us that it is one of
the domains of Olokun, the goddess of water, and that his people "once
in a year . . . went to the big river . . . to make sacrifices to the Queen
of Fortune" (*Great Boys* 79). As riverine people, the river goddess is
a deity that is associated with fertility, riches, and peace. To honor
this "Queen of Fortune" is to show gratitude for her benevolence or
to seek for blessings from her bounty. This explains the significance of
the people's annual propitiation of the goddess of the river. More so,
this annual ritual symbolically establishes the strong bond that Bakhtin
theoretically specifies as the quality of an agrarian, preindustrial life
pattern, where the "life of men and the life of nature (of the earth) are
measured by one and the same scale" (208).

For Yeibo, the Ethiope is a goddess who attracts to herself "bridal
fishes . . . / Radiating sleepy seaweeds . . . / . . . suave ladies with smooth

sportive hips / ... white and black folks" (61–62). But as the poet would have it, the Ethiope like its kin, the Forcados, is a beautiful goddess with an "awesome ambivalence" (63). Both rivers harbor within their bowels hideous sharks, reptiles such as pythons and crocodiles lurking around for "those ill-fated preys" (62). Though Yeibo recreates this imagery within his modern pastoral, for us the sharks and reptiles within the Ethiope and Forcados are worth celebrating. They give us hope for a region whose rivers, some of the most important and indispensable "participant[s] and leading character[s]" (Glotfelty 90) in West African history, are bedeviled by mindless human activities such as crude oil exploitation, deforestation and mindless fishing activities. Indeed, their celebration here, as we also have in Iquo Eke's praise of the Kwa Iboe (Qua Ibo) river (*Symphony of Becoming* 3), which echoes Okara's "The Call of the River Nun," underscores the import of Edward Glissant's idea that "passion for the land where one lives is a start, an action we must endlessly risk." (Quoted in DeLoughrey and Handley 27). Perhaps, these aesthetic representations of the rivers in Niger Delta poetry will draw attention to the fate of its waters, which are some of the most important elements in the ecosystem.

In this study of water in the poetry of Niger Delta poets, I have decided to historicize the imagery of the river because it is only within that rubric that one can appreciate the subtle characterization of such nonhuman elements. More so, this heuristic model helps us to locate the nonhuman environment within the overall reality of life in the Niger Delta. By foregrounding the narrative of rivers in this discourse, I show that the Niger Delta poets invest much more agency and personality to bodies of water that are their subject matter. In this context, I offer the reader a more ecocentric reading that avoids the unconscious duality present in many studies on the environment in Niger Delta poetry.

Works Cited

Adamson, Joni, and Kimberly N. Ruffin. "Introduction." *American Studies, Ecocriticism and Citizenship: Thinking and Acting in the Local and Global Commons*, edited by Joni Adamson and Kimberly N. Ruffin, Routledge, 2013, pp. 1–17.

Bakhtin, M. M. *The Dialogic Imagination: Four Essays*. Edited by Michael Holoquist, translated by Caryl Emerson and Michael Holoquist, U of Texas P, 1981.

Brown, Duncan. *To Speak of This Land: Identity and Belonging in South Africa and Beyond.* U of KwaZulu Natal P, 2006.

Clark, J. P. *A Decade of Tongues.* Longman, 1965.

Clark, Timothy. *Ecocriticism on the Edge: The Anthropocene as a Threshold Concept.* Bloomsbury Academic, 2015.

DeLoughrey, Elizabeth, and George B. Handley. "Introduction: Towards an Aesthetics of the Earth." *Postcolonial Ecologies: Literatures of the Environment,* edited by Elizabeth DeLoughrey and George Handley, OUP, 2011, pp. 3–39.

Dike, K. Onwuka. *Trade and Politics in the Niger Delta 1830–1885: An Introduction to the Economic and Political History of Nigeria,* OUP, 1956.

Glotfelty, Cheryll. "Introduction: Literary Studies in an Age of Environmental Crisis". *The Ecocriticism Reader: Landmarks in Literary Ecology,* edited by Cheryll Glotfelty and Harold Fromm. U of Georgia P, 1996, pp. xv-xxxiii.

Huggan, Graham & Helen Tiffin. *Postcolonial Ecocriticism: Literature, Animals, Environment,* Routledge, 2010

Ifowodo, Ogaga. *The Oil Lamp.* Africa World P. 2005.

Iquo, Eke. *Symphony of Becoming.* Image, 2013.

Love, A Glen. *Practical Ecocriticism: Literature, Biology and the Environment.* U of Virginia P, 2003.

Maathai, Wangari. *The Challenge for Africa.* Arrow, 2009.

Nixon, Rob. *Slow Violence and the Environmentalism of the Poor.* Harvard UP, 2011.

Ojaide, Tanure. *Children of Iroko and Other Poems.* Greenfield Review P, 1973.

———. *Great Boys: An African Childhood.* African World P, 1998.

———. "I Want to Be an Oracle: My Poetry and My Generation." *Poetic Imagination in Black Africa: Essays on African Poetry.* Carolina Academic P, 1996, pp. 121–33.

———. "Nativity and the Creative Process: the Niger Delta in My Poetry." *Ordering the African Imagination: Essays on Culture and Literature.* Malthouse P, 2007, pp. 23–40.

Okara, Gabriel. *The Fisherman Invocation.* Ethiope, 1978.

Okonta, Ike and Oronto Douglas. *Where Vultures Feast: Forty Years of Shell in the Niger Delta.* Environmental Rights Action / Friends of the Earth, 2001.

Ruecket, William. "Literature and Ecology: An Experiment in Ecocriticism." *The Ecocriticism Reader: Landmarks in Literary Ecology,* edited by Cheryll Glotfelty and Harold Fromm. U of Georgia P, 1996, pp. 105–23.

Said, W. Edward. *Culture and Imperialism.* Vintage, 1994.

Saro-Wiwa, Ken. *A Month and a Day: A Detention Dairy.* Spectrum, 1995.

Ushie, Joe. *Hill Songs.* Kraft, 2000.

———. *Popular Stand and Other Poems.* Scholars P, 1992.

Yeibo, Ebi. *Maiden Lines.* Kraft, 2004.

Water and Mental Health in Three British Climate Fiction Novels

GIULIA MILLER

THIS CHAPTER CONSIDERS the representation of water and mental health in three British Climate Fiction novels: Martine McDonagh's *I Have Waited and You Have Come* (2006), *Cold Earth* (2009) by Sarah Moss, and Liz Jensen's eco-thriller *The Rapture* (2009). More specifically, it examines the relationship between time, weather, and mental well-being that is manifest in various permutations in each of the three novels. This relationship, also reflected etymologically in the Latin "tempus" (meaning both "time" and "weather"), but also related words "temporary," "temperature," and "tempest," as well as words pertaining to state of mind and behavior such as "temper" and "temperament," has been described by sociologist Barbara Adam as follows: "As living beings we are permeated by rhythmic cycles which range from very fast chemical and neuronal oscillations, via the slower rhythms of heartbeat, respiration and circadian rhythms, to menstrual and reproductive cycles, and to the very long-range recurrences of seasonal and even climactic change" (*Timewatch* 43). In other words, diverse temporalities underpin the workings of nature and humanity; these are further affected by the notion of an absolute, invariable, and linear time, also known as "Newtonian" or "industrial" time, which governs our daily lives in the form of clocks and imposes notions of being early, late, or punctual as well as contributing to positive and negative experiences of time such as deadlines or routines (*Timewatch* 24–29). The interplay of these various temporalities—biological, environmental, social, seasonal, planetary—constitutes a vast and complex web.

This temporal complexity is pertinent to attitudes regarding nature, climate, and environmental sustainability. Adam argues that the "invisible" nature of time—we cannot for instance physically see the life span of radiation—has led to an overly spatial perspective with serious consequences for the environment, and by extension, for the physical and emotional well-being of the individual (*Timescapes* 9–11). Adam uses the example of water drilling to demonstrate this shortsightedness: during times of shortage water companies bore deep into the earth to access ancient water supplies. However, while surface water is renewable, these ancient supplies can take thousands of years to regenerate, which means that from the perspective of human time they are not a renewable resource (144–47).

Indeed, the function of water, and its use and misuse, are excellent examples of time's complexities and the hazards of a predominantly spatial and linear perspective. Water is vital for human survival and this is temporally defined: we take it for granted that water will be there in our daily lives, for us to drink when we are thirsty, to wash with when we are dirty, and to water our crops at the right time. We also take it for granted that, depending on location, a period of rainfall will eventually be punctuated by dry or sunny periods. Yet water's importance also transcends human timespans in the formation of oceans, icebergs, glaciers, and soil. While humans can, for instance, harness the energy of flowing water to produce hydroelectric power, they cannot control or predict the absolute potential power of water, including water that is situated 700 kilometers deep in the earth's core or thousands of feet below the surface of the ocean. Thus, the threat of natural water disasters such as tsunamis and tidal waves can be roughly monitored but not prevented.

The relationship between water and diverse temporalities is central to all three novels under discussion, though this relationship manifests itself in different ways in each text. *I Have Waited and You Have Come* and *The Rapture* revolve around the implications and consequences of water-related climate change and environmental crises—storms, drought, and tsunamis– and both posit a relationship with temporality that leads to deteriorating mental health. In the former, it is the ceaseless rain that tortures the protagonist and stunts her emotional and psycho-logical development. In the latter, the protagonists, who live in an over-heated world of extreme drought and violent storms, anticipate a colossal tsunami and respond in different ways. In both novels, the link between weather and mental health is evident, suggesting that climate change will seriously impact upon humanity's psychological well-being.

In *Cold Earth* the relationship between water, time, and mental health is represented in a slightly different way from *The Rapture* and *I Have Waited and You Have Come*. In *Cold Earth*, which is set on a modern-day archaeological dig in Greenland, it is the proximity to the river and the sea that triggers paranoid delusions relating to the fate of the Norse Vikings during the cold snap known as the Little Ice Age. In this case, the significance of time is situated in water, in the flow of the river and the tides of the sea that hold memories of the past—invasions, migrations, fishing for survival, and the Little Ice Age. It is also situated in the approaching Arctic winter that brings with it water in its many guises—ice, snow, and heavy fog—and which also forces the archaeol-ogists to remember and relive the fate of the Vikings. Indeed, in *Cold Earth* it is the multifaceted nature of water that informs the protago-nists that time is complex and not a simple case of linear chronology. This knowledge, which is revealed to them through powerful visions and experiences, has a profound effect upon their psyches.

Fundamentally, all three novels depict, directly or indirectly, a world in which climate change has a profound influence upon our psychological and emotional well-being. It is not simply that dwell-ings, habitats, or infrastructures are destroyed, causing us distress, but we too are essentially altered. In each of the three novels, characters carry out murder, perform sadistic violent acts, fantasize about sav-age attacks, succumb to extreme paranoia, and become obsessed by irrational thoughts. Even when the weather-related events—the storms, the tsunami, the frenzied murder, and the nightmares—have passed it is clear that the mental health of the protagonists has not recovered. Nature, on the other hand, in these texts, rapidly adapts to environ-mental change and prevails. Moreover, as previously stated, in each of the novels the profound psychological transformation is related to the effect and experience of multitudinous temporalities, including the passing of the seasons, the gradual trajectory of climate change, disrupted rain cycles, halted personal development, as well as the desire to understand chaotic weather systems.

McDonagh's *I Have Waited and You Have Come*, is set in the rural Midlands. With one exception, a brief diary entry dating back to 1937, the entire narrative supposedly—we only know the dates from the aforementioned diary—takes place in 1943, roughly between the seventh and nineteenth of September. The setting is apocalyptic: England has been beset by drought and plague; millions have died. After the drought there came storms, gales, and hurricanes and now large swathes of the country are flooded. The weather system has changed too; the country is permanently waterlogged. There is no sunshine; there is only drizzle or rainstorms, and variations thereof. Survivors live in scattered communities surrounded by debris and there is almost nothing in the way of communication. Rachel is the principal narrator, though her narrative is punctuated by diary entries believed to be authored by a man named Jez White who is stalking her. Rachel, who chooses to live alone, is repulsed by Jez, yet senses a kindred spirit. Her actions begin to mirror his, the stalked now become stalker.

At the start of the narrative it is apparent that there is nothing in Rachel's life beyond the rain. Her daily life consists of surviving the weather. She has to protect her home—an old water mill—from storms and use soaked wood for kindling; she has to travel over sodden terrain in order to get anywhere and she has to find ways to collect rainwater for drinking. Constant rain and clouds imply there are no clear breaks between night and day and the lack of sun means that there are no rain cycles. It is evident that the incessant rain disrupts all notions of time: days, months, seasons, and, by extension, memory and identity. The waterlogged and stagnant environment and the ceaseless rain lead to, and are reflected in, Rachel's similarly stagnant approach to life: she avoids all human contact and shuns everyday routines. She sleeps constantly; she makes no effort to make her house habitable; and she barely washes or cleans or looks after herself. Time is barely recognizable.

The erosion of temporal markers is evident from the very start of the novel. *I Have Waited* begins out of time, describing actions that do not appear to have a known beginning or end. The opening sentences depict a narrative and environmental sluggishness:

> Overhead the heron beats in. The full stretch of his wings rakes the air. His skinny legs dangle over the pond, which is too clogged with algae to offer up anything but a place to go, then drop him to his vigil at the water's edge. He folds his snake-neck into its watchful grey hunch and I move on. (McDonagh 1)

In this scene, the pond is stagnant and the heron that can no longer fish simply stands and watches. It is notably the heron's legs that "drop" him off rather than the heron himself landing or choosing to land, as though there is a disconnect between the heron's mind and its body. The heron's actions are passive, and sluggish like the pond. The word "vigil" suggests that this is an act that has been repeated, though we do not know for how long. It is also unclear what the protagonist has been doing up to this point—has she been watching the pond too—all we know is that she moves on.

Rachel's precarious mental state is made clear in the opening paragraphs and portrayed through rain and rain-related imagery. She approaches a slippery gate on either side of which there is no wall; yet she insists on climbing over it using her old umbrella, because "she is a stickler" and needs to get to the other side (1). Though she is sufficiently self-aware to realize that she is a "stickler," this characteristic has also stagnated, stubbornly reiterated at a time when it is not needed—she could easily "cross" the gate by walking around it. In this sense, the external *tempus* (that is, the disrupted weather cycles and stagnant pond) and the internal *tempus* (Rachel's stunted personal development), appear to be symbiotic.

Rachel's paranoia also becomes evident during these first paragraphs: she does not want to be seen by anyone, though the reader does not know why. Nature is described here, and throughout the novel, as out to get her: raindrops "dive" and "dodge" and "sneak" and clatter against windows like "a million marksmen" (42). The unending sound of rain, the ceaseless drip-dripping on the windows also impacts negatively on Rachel's psyche and she is "tormented by the constant rhythm of the rain" so that her "thoughts are stuck in a loop" (134). The lack of sunshine and the constant clouds impact her eyesight and heighten her paranoia: "One day I'll go blind from living so long in the half-light. Would my life really be so different? The unknown is the unknown whether you can see or not" (43).

In this sense, the function of the incessant rain is not one of pathetic fallacy, or an illumination of the internal character of the human protagonist as it battles with love and life. On the contrary, her only battle is the weather and the rain, which never stops. It is not surprising, perhaps, that even Rachel's vicious murder of Jez at the end of the novel is carried out using the sharp end of an umbrella as though there is a natural path from repelling the rain to repelling people. In this scene, Rachel plunges the metal point of the umbrella through Jez's earhole and grinds it, "entranced," until she is completely worn out. Disturbingly, her only concern after the attack is that the umbrella is now "bent and useless," though of course we no longer know what "useless" refers to—the umbrella as waterproof accessory or as murder weapon.

Cold Earth by Sarah Moss takes place in late summer on the west coast of Greenland on the site of an ancient Viking settlement. This settlement is bound by rocky terrain and the Arctic sea. Six archaeologists have gathered as part of a university-funded project to examine the site and unearth any material or data that they find. While they are there, they learn that a deadly pandemic is sweeping the globe but due to their isolated location, access to news is restricted. They set up camp across the river from the ruins of a farmstead and a burnt-out church. The river winds down to the sea, which is visible from the campsite. As the novel progresses, four of the archaeologists succumb to delusions that the site is haunted by dead Vikings. *Cold Earth* is narrated in turn by each of the archaeologists, though the principal narrator is Nina.

In *Cold Earth* water in its many forms—river, sea, ice, snow—functions as the nexus of three timespans. As the narrative progresses the protagonists experience a disorienting conflation of these timespans and this leads to acute paranoid delusions, nightmares, and violent fantasies. The first timespan, which is explicit, is the period of time that the archaeologists spend on the settlement, initially six weeks, which extends to an additional unspecified number when no one comes to collect them. This period is characterized by the gradual change of seasons—warm summer to freezing Arctic winter—and by the team leader's desire to collect as much data as possible before the six weeks is up. During this period, the team's relationship to water consists of washing in the river and admiring the beauty of the sea. Even though there are chunks of ice in the sea, the weather is warm and provisions are plentiful which means that there is no need to fish or worry about storms or thick sea fog. Nevertheless, the archaeologists meditate on the importance of water for the medieval Greenlanders. Nina muses: "I wondered how the Greenlanders had seen the sea. A highway, a source of food, a thing of beauty . . . the sea brought them everything from plague and terrorists to glass and the latest fashions" (Moss 74).

The second time span is implicit: as the late summer months turn to bleak Arctic winter the archaeologists remember that the same thing happened on the same spot, to the Greenlanders, five hundred years ago during the Little Ice Age. During the Little Ice Age, as the Arctic cooled, the amount of the ice in the sea increased and impacted fishing; meanwhile the colder temperatures also affected agriculture. Allegedly, those Vikings that did not die from the cold or from starvation, or the imported plague, were murdered by fishermen that entered the settlement from the sea. These violent images are present in Nina's recurrent and grisly nightmares where pirates arrive by sea and slaughter everyone; furthermore, in these nightmares, the ground is too icy to bury the dead victims.

These nightmares articulate the fear that time is not simply linear and that the events of five hundred years ago still play out in the present. This fear goes against the logic of archaeology which categorizes time into separate and distinctive periods. Nina is convinced that the archaeological remains on the site—bodies included—return to life each night and scenes of violence and death are reenacted. The sea becomes an obsessive focal point: she stares at it throughout the day, believing that pirate ghosts will return to haunt her. As previously stated, Nina's conviction that the horror and violence of the past still exists in the present suggests a nonlinear perception of time and it is arguably the timeless quality of the sea that triggers these delusions. During the narrative, the sea barely changes; sometimes it is dark blue, sometimes black, sometimes there are waves, and sometimes it is completely still. There is an understanding that it looks the same as it did five hundred years ago. While the rest of the world is gripped by a deadly pandemic, the sea does not reflect these changes. By way of comparison, when Catriona, one of the archaeologists, describes her research on the Atlantic she argues that it has not changed much in eight centuries. It is perhaps no wonder that in such a remote and isolated setting the archaeologists' experience of the immediate present merges so easily with that of the past.

While the timeless quality of the sea encourages Nina to imagine the return of the past, for others it is the river, which is also depicted as an unchanging entity that has not altered in five hundred years. For Yianni, the team leader, it is the river that forces him to confront the life and fate of the Greenlanders and to relive its brutality. Toward the end of the narrative when he is on the verge of death, he visualizes going to the river and violently smashing Nina's head with a rock. His gruesome reveries incorporate the presumed fate of the Greenlanders, namely death at the hands of vicious pirates and inadequate burial due to the icy weather:

> Came on her down by the river, breaking ice for snow. . . . Hit her face, again. And then again. And then what I cannot say. . . . After that, it was the cleaning up. . . . Blood and worse. . . . There's nowhere to hide a body here. The river is frozen, the beach too exposed, the snow not deep enough. (264–65)

This passage, which constitutes a section of Yianni's farewell letter to his parents, reveals the extent of his mental frailty. He is confessing to an attack that never occurred; yet, the language is frenetic and anxious, and the imagery graphic, as though he really believes that it has taken place. He does not even offer a motive for the imagined attack, suggesting that he simply gave in to mysterious forces.

Interestingly, throughout the novel, Yianni is the only one, other than Ruth, who does not succumb to Nina's delusions. While the others gradually believe her, he stubbornly focuses on the dig and on his academic deadlines and commitments. Yet, as we have just seen, he is also the only one to entertain vicious and sadistic thoughts and inadvertently incorporate the former brutality of the pirates, who putatively attacked over ive hundred years ago, with his own desires for the future. Moreover, there is no previous evidence in the narrative that Yianni is violent by nature; his grisly visions only emerge in the closing chapters when he is lying on the ground freezing to death. There is a suggestion that Yianni is not immune to his surroundings and that the proximity to the remains, and the water have all had a profound influence on his psyche.

The timeless quality of the sea and the river therefore triggers a conflation of two timespans: the present-day archaeological dig and the experience of the Greenlander Vikings as they prepared for an Arctic winter five hundred years before. This curious unchanging quality of the sea and river also evokes and recalls a third timespan, namely, the gradual trajectory of climate change that begins with the previously mentioned Little Ice Age, which was first recorded in the 1300s, and ends with the aftermath of a twenty-first-century global pandemic where the victims were "deadly as plutonium to everyone who saw them" (277). There is a period of roughly five hundred years between the Little Ice Age that wiped out the Greenlanders and the global pandemic described in the text. While this timespan could never be comprehensively chronicled and detailed within the confines of the novel, it nevertheless haunts the present tense of the narrative in curious ways; and yet again this haunting is inspired by the sea. As the archaeologists ponder the fate of the medieval Greenlanders, they reflect that the sea was a means of importing and exporting disease between the settlement and the outside world: "There must have been ships, we know they had external contact right through the plague era, so some farms must have had it" (65).

As the weeks pass and the weather gets colder, the team entertains the possibility that they will be stuck on the settlement because of the pandemic. Nina, forever fixated on the sea, also panics that gulls landing on the shore will bring the virus to them, further exacerbating her feeling that the present and past are intimately connected. However, when the snow begins to fall and the team face hyperthermia and death they consent to eating the sea gulls: "The beach is the only place to look for food, now, and we found some. A dead gull. One good thing about the cold is that dead fauna doesn't rot. I don't know what it died of but I know what we'll die of if we're picky" (269). This passage, which occurs toward the end of the novel, represents the final stage of the protagonists' relationship with the sea. This relationship begins at the start of the narrative when Nina and the others have plenty of provisions. They enjoy the beauty of the sea and enjoy meditating on its significance for the Greenlanders. Later, as the Arctic winter approaches Nina becomes more paranoid and imagines invading pirates. The others resist this paranoia but gradually give in. Finally, as in this passage, all supplies have run out and the archaeologists are forced to do what the Greenlanders would have done in their situation: to scavenge the beach for food even if it means risk of contamination. Notably, at this point in the novel the protagonists are so weak from hunger that they no longer care if the site is haunted.

The relationship between time, weather, and mental health is a complex one. McDonagh's *I Have Waited and You Have Come* and Moss's *Cold Earth* represent this relationship in different ways. In the former, Rachel, the neurotic and unreliable narrator describes a world where night and day cannot be distinguished and where she is tormented by the ceaseless rain. Rachel's narrative is interspersed by Jez's equally unreliable diary entries. In the latter novel, six narrative voices chronicle the psychological effects of water in its various guises. Both texts engage with climate change in experimental and nonrealist ways.

The question of realism and climate change is an interesting one. In his article "Ecothrillers: Environmental Cliffhangers," Richard Kerridge asks why it is that the realist novel deals so rarely with environmental issues (242). He suggests that the complex interplay of long-term and short-term timespans—instantaneous transmission of disease, activities of the nervous system, ozone depletion—is difficult to represent within the confines of a novel (243). It is partly for this reason, argues Kerridge, that the eco-thriller has become a popular means of engaging with environmental concerns. The eco-thriller focuses on one time span only: the feared-for-future made present. Consequently, such texts are action packed; there is literally not enough time to dwell on past mistakes or even on the future and the main aim is to *beat the clock* and *fight time* before the situation gets any worse. The protagonists have to act quickly to deal with the catastrophe at hand, whether it is deadly marine worms (Frank Schätzing's *The Swarm*), disturbing butterfly activity (Barbara Kingsolver's *Flight Behavior*) or a lethal plague (*The Windup Girl* by Paolo Bacigalupi).

Unlike *I Have Waited and You Have Come,* which envisages a world that is already irrevocably changed by weather, or *Cold Earth,* which dwells primarily upon climate change from another era, Liz Jensen's *The Rapture* focuses on the race against time to save the planet from a tsunami of biblical proportions. The novel is set in the near future in a familiar overheated world of melting ice caps, food shortages, terrorism, web crime, twenty-four-hour news, and crude reality shows. Global warming is taking its toll on the planet and Britain swelters under merciless temperatures. Contrary to the waterlogged landscape of McDonagh's novel, or the ice and snow of *Cold Earth,* in *The Rapture* people long for rain; and when it does come it is devastating and destructive. The weather swings erratically and unpredictably between drought, floods, and powerful electric storms.

The narrator-protagonist, Gabrielle Fox, an art therapist, is attempting to rebuild her life following a car accident that has left her wheelchair-bound. After relocating she starts a new job and is assigned patient Bethany Krall, a violent teenager who has killed her own mother by stabbing her repeatedly in the eyeball with a screwdriver, and who can also predict natural disasters. It is certainly no coincidence that Gabrielle's new job is in the British coastal town of Hadport at the Oxsmith Adolescent Secure Psychiatric Hospital, which used to be a hotel "for convalescents prescribed sea air" (6).

The novel's opening paragraph immediately links Bethany to the weather, and to climate, and more importantly to the lack of a restorative "sea air":

> That summer, the summer all the rules began to change, June seemed to last for a thousand years.... It was heat to die in, to go nuts in, or to spawn ... Down at the harbor, the sea reflected the sun in tiny, barbaric mirrors. Asphyxiated, you longed for rain. It didn't come ... But other things came, seemingly at random. The teenage killer, Bethany Krall, was one of them. If I didn't know, back then, that turbulence obeys certain rules, I know it now. (3)

In these opening lines, the intensity of the heat offers only three options: death, madness, and sex. Gabrielle suggests that Bethany Krall— and by extension, her violent behavior, and remarkable abilities—are not random. She suggests that they fill an atmospheric vacuum, as though restoring some form of balance. Instead of the longed-for downpour, there is Bethany and aggression and bloodshed. The overheated earth is disturbed and unhinged; "turbulence" in this opening paragraph applies to both weather and mental health.

This link between turbulent weather and turbulent behavior is further complicated in the narrative by other factors, including the violence Bethany experiences at the hands of others, such as her parents, and the mental health profession. Significantly, out of the three novels, *The Rapture* is the only one that is set within the world of institutional mental health care, in this case, the Oxsmith Adolescent Secure Psychiatric Hospital. It is also therefore the only one where the protagonist's mental health issues are given a psychiatric diagnosis: Cotard's Syndrome, a condition where the sufferer believes that he or she is already dead. Bethany's symptoms, which develop only after two years at Oxsmith, include self-harm, suicide attempts, refusal to eat or drink, and a refusal to speak.

Medical interventions are described in detail: "Antipsychotics and antidepressants, plus drugs to counteract the side-effects: Prozak, Cipramil, Lustral, Risperdal, Zyprexa, Trazodone, Effexor, Zoloft, Tegretol" (35). Several passages highlight the negative impact of Bethany's psychiatric treatment: "Increasingly experimental drug combinations were applied, some of which made her state of mind worse, and led to side-effects such as trembling, dribbling, lethargy" (11). The novel, in this sense, can be understood alongside other texts that deal with the mentally ill and their treatment. Such texts frequently consider incarceration from within the contexts of power structures and issues of autonomy (Baker et al. 90).

The interplay of power structures is pertinent to Bethany: the daughter of a radical preacher, she has been locked away for murdering her mother. Yet, we learn that her parents subjected her to terrible physical and emotional abuse, all in the name of religion, though we do not know what her supposed sins were. Bethany's act of murder is a rebellion, both against this abuse, and the Church that allowed it to happen. Notably, at Oxsmith, the clinical director is a hyper-masculine sportsman, who shows no interest in Bethany's well-being, and his male assistant, who is more interested in controlling Bethany than treating her. The central female characters are Gabrielle, who is stigmatized because of her disability, and Gabrielle's predecessor, Joy, who was fired for believing Bethany's premonitions, in other words, for sharing the madness.

Within this complex, gendered, power structure in which Bethany is let down by the Church, the Law, and the health profession, is the question of meteorological sensitivity. Bethany's ability to predict environmental disasters is a direct consequence of electroconvulsive therapy (ECT). In several novels dealing with mental health, ECT is administered as a punishment, a means of controlling the difficult patient (Baker et al. 80–82). Bethany, is given ECT when she refuses to eat (symptomatic of Cotard's Syndrome), in other words, as a means of control. Each dose that she receives lasts ten whole seconds, or more. It is this medical form of abuse which triggers her abilities; she no longer suffers from Cotard's Syndrome and the belief that she is dead; instead she feels very alive and hypersensitive to the world around her.

Although Bethany's predictions are initially dismissed as the ranting of a mad woman, it becomes clear that they are accurate to the very day and hour, and she is able to give precise dates. Gabrielle's lover, Frazer Melville, a fluid physicist, declares that this ability can be scientifically explained: ECT causes epilepsy and this may cause increased sensitivity to invisible turbulence. The trajectory from Bethany's abuse at the hands of her God-fearing parents, to her vicious attack on her mother, to the onset of Cotard's Syndrome, to ECT, and finally to her extraordinary abilities outlines an experience that is always outside conventional social timespans. We learn that Bethany's abuse constituted being locked away for days at a time, unable to eat or sleep; her subsequent incarceration, where she was cut off from the outside world, subjected her to enforced medical routines. Most significantly, her initial dose of ECT, which lasted ten seconds, clearly gave her access to nonhuman meteorological timespans. It is no surprise, then, when it becomes apparent that her response to impending catastrophes is alarmingly different from everyone else's.

For Bethany, the dates of a catastrophe are something to look forward to; she becomes more agitated and animated as each one approaches, and, as a consequence of ECT, her senses are further sharpened by electrical charges during storms. As lightning strikes she "wanders around turning her head this way and that, as though sensing the air's pulse" (60). When the events eventually take place, she relishes the elements; she literally lives for the moment. By contrast, Gabrielle dreads the dates and is overwhelmed by despair and helplessness when the catastrophes take place. Frazer and Gabrielle realize that they must use the information to warn the world. Bethany's calendar dates become a fixation for Gabrielle. Frazer is less interested in the dates, and more concerned with what they signify: the culmination of a process that has taken thousands of years to materialize. The point is not that something will happen on a specific date, but rather that the warning signs have been there for perhaps hundreds of years without anyone acting upon them.

The final date in Bethany's diary is October 12th when she predicts a "*Tribulation.*" While she conceives of this in theological terms, as the moment when the world ends and all believers will be saved by a giant wave, it transpires that the cause, though precipitated by human activity, is purely physical and geological. On this day frozen suboceanic methane will be suddenly released as a result of underwater mining—an experimental drilling company will inject hot water beneath the seabed in an attempt to access the methane. This will widen a pre-existing fissure on the ocean floor, leading to cataclysmic tsunamis and global devastation.

This final prediction is the one that the protagonists focus on as it is the only one that can be realistically averted or mitigated. It is also the only one that is clearly and directly accelerated by human gı ed and disregard for the environment. As Frazer explains to Gabrielle, cataclysms caused by suboceanic methane constitute "a part of geological history" (188). Consequently, the oil companies' shortsighted decision to drill underwater is an example of how humanity chooses to ignore these warning signs. He and Gabrielle, who are now in love, and optimistic for the future, believe that they have an ethical duty and responsibility to act upon the information provided by Bethany. They try to help everyone escape the tsunami, suggesting that their desire to survive supersedes their fear of a flooded world. Bethany, by contrast, is apathetic about helping others, and appears to conflate her painful history with a post-tsunami world that she calls "Bethanyland":

It's a completely fucked-up place. The trees are all burned.
Everything's poisonous. There's a lake there . . . You wouldn't
want to swim in it. All the fish are dead and there are mosquitoes buzzing around everywhere . . . (47)

The reference to swimming is a direct address to Gabrielle, who is paralyzed from the waist down, but goes to the pool every day and swims
using her arms. Bethany is telling her that defiance and hope will soon
be useless, because the earth will not be fit for humans. The trees, the
water, and the fish, all signs of life, will be no more. Significantly, there
will be mosquitoes, which of course indicate that other forms of life
may survive; but mosquitoes transmit disease to humans and are therefore considered to be irrelevant pests.

Gabrielle dismisses "Bethanyland" as a psychic projection, but
when the tsunami takes place, we see that it was entirely accurate. The
troubled teenager calls the post-tsunami world "Bethanyland," not because she is projecting herself onto the world, but precisely because she
is in tune with the world. In other words, Bethany's apathy regarding
the responsible use of information and her determination to literally
"go with the flow," is precisely because she understands that there is no
other option. Had there been no apocalyptic tsunami forecast, perhaps
Bethany would have had something to live for, in spite of her past.

The novel ends with a resolutely anthropocentric perspective: the
tsunami crashes across the earth leaving fire, destruction, and death.
Bethany commits suicide, leaping onto the "crest of the giant wave"
and disappearing into "a foul stew of water and gas and heat" (340).
Gabrielle watches the "burning waterscape" and realizes that the
earth is no longer a place she wants to be. Specifically, it will be nature without culture, the implication being that the earth can survive
without humanity; by contrast, humanity's ability or desire to adapt
to climate change is short-lived. And, more importantly, "there will be
no Bethany" (341). This final regret accentuates the idea that a human
perspective centers on human interaction, and love, and that humanity
is incapable of conceiving a world beyond these things. Thus, it is not
enough to inhabit the earth; life is not enough. There must be signs of
humanity—culture, love, affection, and friendship.

Each of the three novels—*I Have Waited and You Have Come, Cold Earth,* and *The Rapture*—depicts a world in which climate and climate change alter the psychological makeup of the protagonists. This alteration is related to the effects and experiences of multitudinous temporalities—industrial, seasonal, geological, and personal. In each of the texts, water functions as a medium through which the protagonists experience this complexity. In the case of *I Have Waited and You Have Come,* the ceaseless rain and clouds mean that night and day can no longer be distinguished. This relentless blurring destabilizes the protagonist's sense of time and impacts her behavior. Her sleep and waking patterns are disrupted leading to lethargy and stagnation, and a gradual erosion of self. In *Cold Earth* water in its many forms—seas, rivers, ice, and snow—functions as the nexus of numerous time spans; the protagonists no longer experience time as a clear linear chronology characterized by a succession of historical periods, but rather as an unsettling conflation of past and present. This experience, which contradicts the rationale of archaeology, is traumatic and leads to disturbed and violent visions.

Jensen's novel *The Rapture,* which centers on the consequences of a colossal tsunami, considers the disjunction between human and geological timespans and portrays a world where the human perspective is always shortsighted. While Bethany can predict environmental events, she does not use this knowledge responsibly because she knows that the final catastrophe will not be averted, and she sees no point in a world without humankind. Gabrielle, similarly, cannot see beyond a human timeframe and has no desire to inhabit a universe without culture, or without love. The race to stop the tsunami accentuates the tremendous gap between geological timespans—in this case, the million-year formation of underwater methane hydrates—and human time spans—represented by the hazards of industrial underwater drilling. The narrative is further complicated by episodes of abuse—personal and institutional—that Bethany suffers: first, at the hands of her religious parents, and later at the psychiatric unit where she is incarcerated and where she is administered ECT. This abuse separates her from the outside world and from normal routines; it also causes her extraordinary sensitivity to turbulence. This ability allows her to see, and feel, future environmental catastrophes; but her knowledge also means that she is pessimistic and consequently apathetic about using her knowledge responsibly.

A look at three British works of climate fiction uncovered intricate relationships between time, weather, and mental health with lasting effects on individuals. While the configuration between the three elements is different in each text, it is clear that multiple temporalities underpin the psychiatric health of the protagonists in all three. Climate and weather form a central part of these temporalities with regard to seasons, geological formations, rain cycles, and the flow of seas and rivers. These texts imagine a world where weather is no longer a pathetic fallacy, but a reality for everyone.

Works Cited

Adam, Barbara. *Timescapes of Modernity: The Environment and Invisible Hazards.* Routledge, 1998.

———. *Timewatch: The Social Analysis of Time.* Polity Press, 1995.

Baker, Charley, et al. *Madness in Post-1945 British and American Fiction.* Palgrave Macmillan, 2010.

Bate, Jonathan. *The Song of the Earth.* Picador, 2000.

Cold Earth. Directed by Sarah Moss, Granta, 2009.

I Have Waited and You Have Come. Directed by Martine McDonagh, Myriad Editions, 2006.

Kerridge, Richard. "Ecothrillers: Environmental Cliffhangers." *The Green Studies Reader: From Romanticism to Ecocriticism,* edited by Laurence Coupe, Routledge, 2000, pp. 242–48.

The Rapture. Directed by Liz Jensen, Bloomsbury, 2009.

There Will Be Blood

Water Futures in Paolo Bacigalupi's
The Water Knife and
Claire Vaye Watkins's *Gold Fame Citrus*

PAULA ANCA FARCA

ONE OF THE GOALS of post-apocalyptic works is to interrogate current social matters and explore certain societal fears and beliefs by presenting gloomy versions of not-so-distant futures. Ecological disasters as a result of climate change reveal people's struggles with resource depletion and elicit emotional responses from readers and viewers. María Pérez posits that cli-fi can inform the public about "scientific data or political discourses, by creating empathy, by fantasizing about future outcomes, by engaging audiences, and by offering alternative narratives" (61). Paolo Bacigalupi's *The Water Knife* and Claire Vaye Watkins's *Gold Fame Citrus* are two post-apocalyptic narratives that foretell extreme consequences of climate change and water-scarce futures. Their characters' survival stories instruct, terrify, or entertain readers and hopefully inspire them to take action against climate change.

Bacigalupi and Watkins seem to suggest that we should take aggressive steps to prevent a future of complete water scarcity and if this scenario is not possible, then violence and blood spilling are inevitable. However, creative technical solutions and collaboration among community members could alleviate some people's thirst. While I discuss water in connection to violence, tragedy, and survival, I also underline people's immense capacity for adaptation and creativity in the face of disaster. Watkins and Bacigalupi also show that the best creative solutions to environmental disasters emerge from multiethnic and gender equal collaborations.

Bacigalupi's thriller, *The Water Knife* (2015), centers on water scarcity and fights for water access from the Colorado River in three states of the American Southwest: Arizona, Nevada, and California. Within this triad, California is winning the water war due to its preventative and monetary investments; Nevada gains access to water through violence and cunning deals; and Arizona remains ravished by sand and thirst and left to suffer. With a weak federal government, the borders between states closed and guarded by militias, and corporations exerting their influence and control over water resources, the people of the American West literally have to bleed if they want to drink. The "huge, Donald Trump-like border walls [that] now separate semi-warring U.S. states and limit flows of climate refuges" (Pryor 5) turned people against each other and left them thirsty, hungry, and vulnerable.

People's survival in the West is dependent on the Colorado River, which used to serve the upper and lower basin states, but now is over-allocated and, in many areas, dry. Bacigalupi describes the Colorado River of the past as potent and alive—a river that generated a lush landscape and lively communities: "In its prime, the Colorado River had run more than a thousand miles, from the white-snow Rockies down through the red-rock canyons of Utah and on to the blue Pacific, tumbling fast and without obstruction. And wherever it touched—life" (12). The river, which symbolized life and progress during optimistic times of water abundance, represents death and destruction in Bacigalupi's not-so-distant future. Alliances shift in this fierce struggle for water and borders between American states or nations are closed as is people's access to water. Although Mexico had senior rights to water from the Colorado River as a result of the Mexican Water Treaty of 1944, in Bacigalupi's novel, Mexican children had never seen a drop of water from the Colorado River and think this river is a myth. If water, which is irreplaceable and foundational for human existence, has become a myth, something that is unseen and spoken about only in grandmothers' stories, then, Bacigalupi's characters who get water had to fight to death for the blue gold.

Bacigalupi humanizes the environmental disaster at the heart of the novel with characters directly affected by it; their stories of survival and their inner conflicts could possibly elicit emotional responses from readers who may wonder how they would survive the life and death situations presented by Bacigalupi. Against a parched landscape, a unique triumvirate emerges, one whose protagonists are initially unaware of each other but whose stories will intertwine. Angel Velazquez, an assassin, spy, and water knife, "cuts water" for his brilliant boss, Catherine Case who is in charge of the Southern Nevada Water Authority; fearless Lucy Monroe, an East coast Pulitzer Prize–winning journalist demonstrates an acute sense of social justice in Phoenix and throughout Arizona by uncovering facts about water plots; and Maria Villarosa, a young and street-smart Texan refugee, who tries to find a way out from a web of prostitution and violence. The three protagonists' mutual interests and actions intersect at a point from which they find themselves dependent on one another. Instead of presenting a wide array of people and conflicts, Bacigalupi zooms in and focuses only on a few characters representing different social, ethnic, economic, and cultural sides of the water debates. Bacigalupi's focus on three protagonists coupled with his use of alternating viewpoints and galloping stories of the three create a sense of suspense and underscore a dark reality: that the majority of people already lost the fight for water and the ones standing are the survivors, the ones who understand the rules of the new game. It is vision and courage that differentiate the winners from the losers in this dangerous new game. Fate favors the bold, so those who see clearly, anticipate well, act bravely, and make the right alliances stay alive and drink.

For the most part, Bacigalupi places his characters in difficult scenarios in which their daily survival and well-being are constantly threatened. And yet, it is these edgy situations that elicit reactions from readers and solicit their emotional engagement. Readers would want to know if and how the characters get out of the difficult situations they find themselves in and what creative solutions they find in their almost waterless lives. Like Maria, who learned to read the level of water at the pump and sell it to pay her rent, the inhabitants of Phoenix or Las Vegas had to adapt to a water-scarce reality. The poor, for instance, use their special plastic bags that filter urine and turn it into drinkable water. The rich live in massive infrastructures called arcologies that recycle water and minimize waste. In Nevada, Catherine Case's 007 agents, called the "water knives," blow up water treatment plants, make people offers they cannot refuse, and make deals with other states. In an interview on NPR's Science Friday, Bacigalupi himself admitted that in this fierce scenario "there'll be some winners and some losers . . . Different players will have certain amounts of power and certain people . . . will lose . . . but other people are going to consolidate their power . . . for every person who's losing, there's somebody else with opportunity." Bacigalupi sounds optimistic when he talks about Foucaultian power shifts that involve people's immense capacity for adaptation and ingenuity. His novel does show that individuals who possess intuition, courage, and vision will seize opportunities and be able to navigate this waterless terrain.

No one sees more clearly than the Queen of Colorado and Angel's boss, Catherine Case, whose actions drive the plot of *The Water Knife*. The unscrupulous water visionary hires water knives to cut water supplies for entire cities and communities in Arizona and Nevada so that the rich prosper and the poor vanish. Angel describes Catherine as a perfectionist dominatrix who manipulates larger patterns and arranges pieces of puzzle that happen to be rivers, streams, snow packs, tributaries, maps, dams, or pipes: "Her clothing was always perfect. Her makeup, her data, her planning—all perfectly analyzed and arranged. Case liked details, all details. She found patterns, fit them together, and then turned them to her use" (55). Catherine Case is the mastermind who turns cities into dust and deserts into oases. Those who serve Catherine well have a chance of surviving; those who betray her end up dead. The Vet, too, a character that looks like he came out of a bestiary, someone who "wasn't a person at all. . . . A demon, . . . Some kind of creature" (130), has a tenacious eye for opportunity achieved through violent means. Before he feeds Maria to hyenas because she sold water without paying him taxes, the Vet teaches Maria a lesson about vision: "You think I thrive because I fail to see? . . . You see it, don't you? We both see things, I think" (131–32). The Vet is right to praise Maria's vision and understanding of intricacies. Different characters throughout the novel compare Maria to Catherine Case more than once. Maria is a mini–Catherine Case running a small water operation because she needs to survive and make money. Unlike her father, who has old eyes, Maria sees clearly, survives, and even thrives.

The struggles for survival in *The Water Knife* open up ethical debates about humanity in general and our responsibility to our planet and to each other. Against characters that exhibit different ethical shades of gray, Lucy demonstrates a black-and-white approach and a sense of social justice for the disadvantaged. She gives up a comfortable life on the East coast for dusty Phoenix, which she now calls home. Lucy believes that the senior water rights that Maria got "will make Phoenix and Arizona the arbiters of their own fate instead of a place of loss and collapse" (363). In her mind, the "water rights are people's lives, . . . Phoenix can rebuild. With water, it doesn't have to be the way it is" (365). Lucy is in fact proposing a short-term solution for Phoenix that would annihilate California's and Nevada's water resources, but fails to see that Arizona is already doomed. Unlike Maria, Angel, and Catherine Case, Lucy lives in the past and advocates for a world prior to this climate change–induced drought, a world that no longer exists. While commendable, Lucy's devotion to Phoenix is shortsighted. People's lack of planning for a waterless future and their naïve belief that a desperate situation will improve in time shows blindness and inertia. Maria shoots Lucy at the end of the novel because she "had old eyes" (371) and she stands in Maria's way to a successful life in Nevada or California. Maria's extreme gesture ironically allows the three protagonists to survive and stick together. Lucy, who still adheres to pre-disaster ethical guidelines, intends to kill Angel to obtain the water rights and save Phoenix, a city which "ain't never getting better" (370). Maria recognizes instinctively that there are new rules and moral guidelines in this new world; she only injures Lucy and keeps everybody together in their journey forward.

Despite their disagreements, Angel, Maria, and the wounded Lucy move in tandem and solidarity forward to a wet future. Strangers at first, the three protagonists are brought together by chance and thirst. In their chase for senior water rights, they save each other more than once and help one another along the way. Their collaboration and mutual trust lead to innovative ideas, outsmart their enemies, and assure their survival and success. Toomie, Maria's older friend who is present with the three at the end of the novel, believes that people have an ethical responsibility to help each other in times of need: "'We're all each other's people. Just like we're all our brothers' keepers. . . . We're all in it together'" (250). In fact, Toomie risks his own life to ensure Maria survives. Toomie is convinced that individualism and isolation will bring America down while camaraderie, shared interests, and collaboration will contribute to the survival and prosperity of nations during crises. Pérez lauds Bacigalupi for presenting a successful "multi-ethnic coalition" (60) in which diversity, inclusion, and sustainable plans prevail over death and gloom. The coalition made of an American woman, a Mexican-American man and young woman, and an African American man does not propose grandiose plans such as saving the planet, delivering water to the American Southwest, or solving climate change and water scarcity. Instead, they choose to stay together and save themselves by taking the water rights to Nevada and to Catherine Case. They come up with the best solution for the dire situation they are in.

Bacigalupi offers his protagonists opportunities to work together and alleviate their thirst but puts forth a bleak perspective for America as a whole. He presents American states and citizens that pull in many directions and sabotage each other instead of channeling their energies toward a unified vision. The states on the East Coast witness the destruction and desperation of the American West and do nothing. The idea of "one nation under God, indivisible with liberty and justice for all" does not hold water any longer. And yet the author promises glimmers of hope when he underscores multiethnic collaborations among groups of people sharing common goals.

We see this kind of solidarity between human beings affected by climate disasters in Claire Vaye Watkins's *Gold Fame Citrus* (2015). Here, small groups of individuals stick together to survive extreme drought and water scarcity while armed militias guard state borders. The protagonists, lovers Luz and Ray, live in an abandoned mansion that once belonged to a forgotten starlet and ration their water. Other people that Ray and Luz encounter live in gangs, groups, or colonies because there is strength in numbers. Inside these groups, a patriarchal power structure emerges, one with a male leader at the top whose position is usually guarded by armed men and endorsed by subordinates among which there are many women.

Like Bacigalupi, Watkins envisions a divided America whose states and people do not come together in times of tragedy, but they still form small communities to avoid complete annihilation. Reliable political leadership to guide the general public toward decent living standards and a sustainable plan to address and combat climate change and water scarcity in California or parts of the US are absent from Watkins's novel as well. Instead of a coherent water plan for California, Watkins imagines a lifeless natural environment and a humanity driven by raw instinct. California is eaten up by rising temperatures and sandy winds; the Sierra snowpack is depleted, and the underground aquifer drained. Having finally won the fight against people, "nature had refused to offer herself to them" (7). This ardent, frightening refusal reads as nature's final warning that humans are doomed. Watkins herself roots for nature and confesses in an interview that "there's some poetic justice in the idea of nature reasserting itself. I like the idea of letting it wreak its revenge on people." Watkins's strong words both in her novel and the interview confirm nature's stamina and strength at the expense of human beings.

Fate takes its revenge on people, too. The greatest irony is that California, which attracted young people for its gold, fame, and citrus, has lost its magnetic allure and become a resource-depleted desert and a cemetery of lost dreams. Californians who avoided the government-imposed evacuation, Luz and Ray included, are survivalists, derelicts, religious fanatics, hippies, prophets, delinquents, or helpless dreamers. Stuck between a brutal water-scarce existence and a looming death by thirst or violence, the leftovers seem as broken as the landscape itself. Watkins manages to create an apocalyptic and captivating American West populated by characters who continuously erode and reinvent themselves like sand dunes. Their theories are equally mindless and quixotic. Ray's and Luz's friend, Lonnie, believes "there was no water crisis, ... Theirs was a human crisis" (77), so the money-hungry tourists should be eliminated and, after this cathartic process, pure cities will blossom in California. Levi Zabriskie, the leader of the colony in the Amargosa Sea Dune, concocts conspiracy theories about how the government threatens to annihilate the colony to deposit nuclear waste. Levi also puts together a catalogue of new species he claims to have observed in the desert, species that defy evolution, such as the dumbo jackrabbit with gigantic ears, the stiltwaker tortoise that walks on legs that look like stilts, or the blue-gray coyote. Having lost their firm grip on reality, Watkins's characters seem to oscillate between daydreaming and disillusionment.

Perfect candidates for lost dreams, Ray and Luz live in a mansion in ruins belonging to a Hollywood starlet, drink rationed glasses of coca cola, and eat food from the starlet's pantry. Their fragile love, fitting for California's attraction and its resource curse, mirrors the landscape itself: it is fiery, arid, lifeless, and aimless. Their relationship is predicated on their intentional avoidance of truth and the promise to each other not to talk about water. An AWOL soldier-turned-surfer in a waterless land, Ray spends his time building a half-pipe because he cannot skate in the mansion's pool. A former model and poster child for the Bureau of Conservation, Luz sleeps most days and tries on the starlet's dresses. As a baby and later as a child, Luz was used by the bureau to advertise the expansion of a new aqueduct and to announce the forthcoming water crisis. Her young life is linked to water depletion in newspapers headlines like: "EVERY SWIMMING POOL IN CALIFORNIA TO BE DRAINED BEFORE BABY DUNN IS OLD ENOUGH TO TAKE SWIMMING LESSONS.... BABY DUNN STARTS KINDERGARTEN TODAY WITHOUT GREEN FIELDS TO PLAY IN" (11). Even if her adult life is not documented in propaganda newspapers, Luz's existence is still linked to the Californian water disaster. Adult Luz Dunn remains in arid California to live a pointless life.

When Luz and Ray kidnap an orphaned toddler belonging to a gang because they want to alleviate the little girl's suffering and thirst, the couple seems to have found a renewed purpose and even laid a foundation for a family life. Baby Ig shakes their inertia and sets their lives in motion. Neither Bacigalupi nor Watkins populate their novels with children, so Ig becomes the exception that proves and completes the rule. For the most part, children and the elderly are absent from both novels because they would barely survive under such precarious circumstances. When Luz and Ray find her, Ig is thirsty, hungry, dirty, unsupervised, and in danger of being sexually abused. While Ig does represent hope and a promise for a future whatever that future may entail, she remains vulnerable. She requires constant attention and care in a world that lacks method and routine. She is kidnapped and passed on like an object among different adults, and she almost dies of thirst and tarantula bites. Her adoptive parents, Luz and Ray, love her and try to offer her a decent childhood, but such promises for happiness do not materialize.

Because they become parents overnight and are unequipped for parenthood, Ray and Luz are forced to ask for help. Their former friends, who barricaded themselves in an apartment complex, give the new parents gas, supplies, and water. Lonnie and his armed friends survive in the apartment complex by making conspicuous deals, stocking supplies, selling fake paperwork, and helping desperate people cross state borders. Loonie's gang in the apartment complex unveils a power structure conducive to violence, intimidation, subordination, and gender inequality. There is one leader at the top (usually an alpha male), who is able to provide water, food, and shelter, several members who endorse his vision and convictions through violent means, and the mob who follows orders and benefits from the supplies. Unlike Bacigalupi whose three protagonists find each other because of their intuition and savvy survival skills, Watkins creates characters whose lack of options forces them to gravitate toward powerful, violent, and corrupt male leaders. She suggests that survival and access to water are possible when groups or colonies of people come and stick together, but she also exposes the equity problems inside these power structures. Women are especially vulnerable and threatened by sexual violence and exploitation—scenarios present in *The Water Knife* as well. Lucy and Maria in Bacigalupi's novel are constantly threatened by rape and are subjected to extreme physical violence. Yet Bacigalupi also promises gender equality in his development of strong female protagonists like Maria, Lucy, and Catherine who act not as damsels in distress but as self-assured Wonder Women.

Watkins's Luz lacks the determination, insight, and resourcefulness of Bacigalupi's strong female leads and contributes to the perpetuation of one-sided patriarchal structures. Luz uses her sexuality to survive and becomes the lover and sexual partner of Ray, Levi, and Loonie. She is dependent on Ray who feeds her and gives her water; she sleeps with Loonie because he pays her a compliment; and she becomes Levi's lover when she and Ig cannot survive on their own. Failing to take care of herself and her adoptive daughter, Luz supports the patriarchal structures in the small communities described by Watkins and she strengthens the power and continued success of the male leaders in the pack. Her vulnerability and failure to come up with creative solutions

when she finds herself in dire circumstances make her dependable on
men and susceptible to violence and abuse.

Luz and Ig almost die of thirst before they are saved by Levi, a water
dowser-turned-prophet, and his colonists. Luz is indebted to the colonists before she even meets them all. Her position as a woman in need
of saving and saviors strengthens Levi's position as the leader of the colony and guarantees his control over Luz and Ig. Levi's position is also
solidified by his cunning ability to procure water even if his actions un-
veil corruption and unethical deals. On the surface, the colony, which
he runs, appears as a serene and peaceful community, but violence
and dishonesty creep in. At first, the town, which looks like a "Very
spiritual place. Very primal" (72), and the colony seem oases of hope.
And yet, as Luz discovers, the town, its inhabitants, and their leader,
Levi, are slippery and shifty as the sand dunes. The colonists, who are
mostly stoned, live in RVs or buses, meet at bonfires to exchange deep
thoughts, and place crystals in strategic places in the sand. They do
not question how they drink water from full and clean barrels and eat
vegetables, fruit, and bread tasting of fire. Ray, however, is convinced
that Levi is a charlatan who highjacks aid convoys instead of listening
to the call of water. The fact that nobody in the colony doubts Levi's
superhero powers or wonders about the source of their water suggests
that the disillusioned colonists adhere to doubtful ethical guidelines or
abdicated morality altogether.

When Luz refuses to use her adopted daughter as a propaganda tool
for Levi, the colonists keep Ig and ask Luz and Ray to leave for good.
Luz is strong in this refusal, but weak when she chooses to desert Ig.
While she takes care of Ig, Luz becomes a mother and even grows as
one, so she cannot return to a motherless existence when the colonists
take Ig. When she loses Ig, Luz loses herself altogether. She eventually
throws herself in the flood, which "came upon them like an animal, like
a vengeful live thing" (338) in front of Ray's desperate eyes. Ironically,
a flood that comes from an arid landscape kills Luz. The contradictions that abound in the novel (such as a flood in a waterless environment; the presence of water in the desert; or even an invented animal
like the dumbo jackrabbit) underscore disruptions in natural rhythms
and abnormal situations for characters. Perhaps Luz and motherhood

represent another contradiction. Had Luz been more assertive as a woman and mother, trusted herself to survive, fought for her existence and her daughter's, and defended her ideas, she would have created more options for herself and her family.

Ray and Luz remain travelers in an apocalyptic landscape and their love dissolves like any relief form eroded by the desert wind. So do their chances for a stable and happy family life. They pass by gangs, groups, or colonies, but choose naïvely to make their own home. It is a broken home, however. The couple live in a mansion they do not own; they kidnap a child; Ray abandons Luz and Ig because he cannot watch them die of thirst; Luz cannot take care of herself and Ig; Luz cheats on Ray; Luz and Ray are forced to leave Ig to Levi's colony; Luz commits suicide in front of Ray. Ray and Luz prove irrational and their actions are desperate. Watkins's characters do not collaborate to arrive at rational, constructive ideas and solutions; instead, they seek power individually, follow orders, or suffer harsh consequences.

Watkins tantalizes readers with a title that promises a Hollywood story and ending and she delivers the opposite. The originality of her novel lies not only in her presentation of a water-scarce environment, but also of the people who populate it. Watkins's American West, a mesmerizing place even in its devastation, is not sustainable and its people, who are the leftovers of a society in disarray, are predestined to anguish and a slow death. The only winner in this scenario is nature that takes back its resource-depleted territories and takes over.

Watkins's characters cannot find sustainable, long-term solutions for an equitable water future, and they are doomed to suffer. Like Bacigalupi, Watkins does show that groups of people have better chances of survival than individuals do, but unlike Bacigalupi, she is less concerned with constructive solutions resulting from multiethnic cooperation and more open to the idea that groups are formed out of necessity and are based on patriarchal leadership. Readers get the feeling that Levi's community in the desert will not last because the water trucks will eventually stop coming and Loonie's group in the apartment complex will dissipate when he cannot make any more deals to procure water. Bacigalupi's model promising beneficial collaboration,

vision, and street smarts proves more efficient than the inertia and disillusionment that characterize Watkins's protagonists.

In their post-apocalyptic novels, Bacigalupi and Watkins raise
awareness about the dangers of climate change and imagine people
in extremely difficult and dangerous situations generated by severe
droughts and water scarcity. In the scenarios presented in the novels,
the general public, political leaders, and government officials do not
plan for a water-scarce reality, which spirals down toward violence,
despair, and death rather quickly. Their lack of planning should shake
us, present-day readers, to the core, make us aware and determined to
tame climate change effects, and inspire us to demand political support. In an interview, Bacigalupi deplores the absence of organization
and planning:

> [W]hen I think about the future that *The Water Knife* rep-
> resents, it's one where there's a lack of oversight, planning and
> organization. That's really the disaster. There's the drought and
> there's climate change, and those things are horrible—and then
> there's how people react to it. And this is, this world is built on
> the assumption that people don't plan, don't think and don't co-
> operate—which makes for a pretty bad future! (Interview, 2016)

Interestingly, Bacigalupi argues that people's inertia and failure to
come together and change their present and future are bigger disasters
than climate change itself. To counter such disasters, Sandra Postel rec-
ommends that: "we need a water ethic—a guide to right conduct in the
face of complex decisions about natural systems . . . one that says it is
not only right and good but necessary that all living things get enough
water before some get more than enough. Because in the end, we're all
in this together" ("The Missing Piece"). Like Bacigalupi, Postel underscores the importance of collaboration, equality, and equity when it
comes to water problems.

Focusing on the water crisis in the US, Watkins posits that we need
to challenge the idea of an American West as a resource abundant
frontier: "I think that the American West is probably due for a reality
check. We're still under the impression that we deserve to be there in
whatever numbers we want, guzzling up whatever resources because

it's our manifest destiny. That's an uninterrogated idea that's run its course" (interview). Lester Snow, executive director, California Water Foundation agrees that individuals should regard water as a limited resource: "We need to move beyond that image, that mirage, that our water supply is endless" (*Beyond the Mirage*). The reality check that Watkins and Snow ask for would include both technical and social based solutions to solve water scarcity. Patricia Mulroy, who was also Bacigalupi's inspiration for Catherine Case, gives an example of water conservation in the West: "It is in everybody's interest to conserve early, leave that water in Lake Mead with no one's name on it. It's not a savings account for any particular municipal provider or for any agricultural provider, but it is there to preserve the system from crushing" (*Beyond the Mirage*).

All stakeholders involved should consider water issues exacerbated by climate change carefully and methodically and then implement technological, social, political, and ethical solutions to water depletion. Without planning and serious conservation efforts, the violent scenarios envisioned by Bacigalupi and Watkins could become harsh realities rapidly. As such, the line between civilization and savagery would become rather thin. Many writers have done their part and created compelling and thrilling stories about the human condition in the face of disaster, stories that prompt emotional responses from readers. Writers have instructed, entertained, and inspired audiences to imagine water scarce scenarios and possible solutions. Hopefully, readers' responses to these stories would translate into practical and valuable conversation and activism plans about water rights and water conservation. We are instinctual creatures, yes, but we should choose progress, civility, equity, social justice, and empathy to define us. We should show strength and diplomacy in our advocacy for water and we should continue to be loud and make waves.

Works Cited

Bacigalupi, Paolo. Interview by John Dankosky. NPR Science Friday, 8 April 2016, https://www.sciencefriday.com/segments/telling-the-story-of-climate-change-in-fiction. Accessed 15 December 2017.
———. Interview by NPR Staff. NPR All Things Considered, 23 May 2015, http://

www.npr.org/2015/05/23/408756002/what-if-the-drought-doesnt-end-the-water-knife-is-one-possibility. Accessed 10 December 2017.

———. *The Water Knife*. Alfred A. Knopf, 2015.

Beyond the Mirage: The Future of Water in the West. Directed by Cody Sheehy, Rhumbline Media, 2016.

Pérez Ramos, María Isabel. "The Water Apocalypse: Utopian Desert Venice Cities and Arcologies in Southwest Dystopian Fiction." *Ecozon@*, vol. 7, no. 2, 2016, p.44–64.

Postel, Sandra. "The Missing Piece: A Water Ethic." *American Prospect*, 23 May 2008, http://prospect.org/article/missing-piece-water-ethic. Accessed 15 December 2017.

Pryor, Roger Eardley. "Imagining Anthropocene Futures." *Endeavour*, vol. 41, no. 1, p.5–6.

Watkins, Claire Vaye. *Gold Fame Citrus*. Riverhead Books, 2015.

———. Interview by Steve Inskeep. NPR Morning Edition, 7 October 2015, http://www.npr.org/2015/10/07/446499515/californias-growing-dunes-in-gold-fame-citrus-force-residents-to-retreat. Accessed 23 January 2017.

Concluding Remarks

HUMAN EXISTENCE has been intricately connected to the presence of water on Earth. This sentence may sound trivial and yet we know that water has sustained our life and that without it, humanity perishes. Essential to human survival and prosperity, water has also been a rich symbol, which shaped our knowledge, culture, and history. The goal of *Make Waves: Water in Contemporary Literature and Film* is to capture symbolic qualities of water in contemporary settings and raise awareness of recent water challenges around the world. Through writing and critical inquiry, contributors of this edited volume celebrate water in all its forms whether as sea, oceans, snow, dew, lakes, moisture, rivers, streams, or rain. They investigate recent cultural meanings of water and focus on how water is a transformative symbol through which people address environmental concerns and a source of meaningful cultural interactions and political tensions. Creating relatable contexts for water dilemmas, contemporary authors and directors put human faces on water crises and provide possible solutions to these crises.

Several topics of the book include but are not limited to: water scarcity, droughts, high sea levels, water pollution, oil spills, dam constructions, floods, and water wars. Contributors of the collection analyze how these global water problems affect local communities around the world and intersect with social and cultural aspects such as class, gender, race, ethnicity, and citizenship. Designed to raise awareness on depleting water supplies due to climate change and increased demands from energy and industry sectors, *Make Waves* examines issues such as food security, energy security, and physical and mental health and suggests creative social and cultural solutions for a future of water scarcity.

The contributors of this edited book focused on a variety of water issues, starting with water as a cultural symbol and a medium for communication, recreation, and introspection, continuing with water which delineates borders, nations, and cultures, and ending with water pollution, wars, scarcity, and conservation. Their discussions revealed that water is obviously vital to human existence and that our relationships with oceans, rivers, and streams give us a renewed strength and purpose. We need water to survive and sustain our cultural existence.

In the first part, the authors convey the overall message that water is a rich symbol bridging fields as different as environment, politics, informatics, and economics and contributing to individuals' meaningful experiences and connections to the land outside of the necessities of modern, industrial life. Water's interactions to ecosystems, industry, and history, some contributors argue, produce new understandings of water landscapes and human presences in those landscapes. Its enormous capabilities for change (from rain to ice, snow, dew, etc.) open up different physical experiences with water. More so, water's imagery associations work powerfully to expose a rich repertoire of metaphors and to engage the audience's visual imagination. These enrichments that water promises, whether physical or intellectual, bring renewed understandings of our daily environments that are readily available to us but easily ignored or overlooked.

Contributors in the second part of the book expand on the individual-water relationship to include communities and nations. Physical water borders also imply political, cultural, and social interactions among citizens and these may be cordial or tense. The essays in this section capture the duality of these relationships mediated by water. When there are challenges, some opportunities present themselves. Difficult issues such as water wars, privatization of water, water as a weapon, or the forced control of water into dams and canals reveal unethical practices and environmental and political unrest. Capitalist systems rewarding profit and initiative may run counter to communal approaches to water management. Yet, contributors underscore the success of communities that nurture conservation, cooperation, and mutual thriving by promoting sustainable stewardship and equitable distribution of water. They also show that cooperative alliances among governments, environmental and local organizations, and indigenous people promote new visions of water conservation and restoration.

The third and final part looks at the future of water as portrayed by authors of post-apocalyptic texts, a future that includes violence but also chances toward new forms of adaptability and humanity. Here, water concerns exacerbated by climate change contribute to oil spills, water pollution, high sea levels, floods, and droughts that, in turn, affect the physical and mental health of individuals and threaten the social and cultural existence of communities. The authors under consideration suggest that people's adaptability, creative technical solutions, and equal collaborations could address and even solve dire water-related issues.

Contemporary literature and film are perfect venues for current debates on water because they instill empathy in readers and viewers who understand environmental problems through relatable and personable human experiences. Authors of literary text write powerful stories and characters whose familiarity and immediacy are recognizable to the readers. Scientific facts on water scarcity due to climate change may not be as effective as stories with farmers, immigrants, and children suffering from droughts and fighting for survival. By showing not telling, revealing, not scolding, and letting audiences learn about water issues and drawing their own conclusions, writers and directors personalize and contextualize their message. Readers' understanding and empathy could shift from a relatable situation to the environment or to water itself. In this shift lies the power of literature and film and the potential activism of individuals. Awareness and empathy could ideally lead to education, activism, and policy change. We should respect and conserve water and act ethically toward global water depletion. We should have great faith in our and future generations leading the fight against climate change and freshwater depletion. And we are lucky millennials and younger generations, who care deeply about sustainability, green energy, and water conservation, are leading the way—and they are ready to make waves.

About the Contributors

SOFIA AHLBERG is Associate Professor in American Literature at Uppsala University, Sweden. She has published widely on the contemporary novel. Her monograph *Atlantic Afterlives* (Palgrave 2016) explores the "afterlives" of transatlantic literature as it negotiates, distills, and translates technologically mediated modes of digital communication into new topographies of knowledge. Her current research is in the energy humanities with a focus on the responses of literature to our oil-made world.

ANDREW ANDERMATT currently serves as Associate Professor of English in the Environment and Society Department at Paul Smith's College in Paul Smiths, New York. He regularly teaches courses in environmental literature, writing, and philosophy. Dr. Andermatt earned his PhD in English from Indiana University of Pennsylvania in 2011, with a focus on literary theory and American environmental writers. His research interests include American environmental literature, ecocriticism, place studies, and pedagogy.

JULIENNE H. EMPRIC (PhD the University of Notre Dame) is Professor of Literature at Eckerd College, in St. Petersburg, Florida, where she teaches courses in English literature, Shakespeare, history of drama, Irish literature, and literature and the environment. Her research interests and publications are in literature and law, the scholarship of teaching and learning, and Irish literature, including *The Woman in the Portrait: The Transfiguring Female in James Joyce's* A Portrait of the Artist as a Young Man. Her professional contributions extend to regularly conducting seminars on law and literature at national workshops for federal judges, sponsored by the Federal Judicial Center.

PAULA ANCA FARCA is a Teaching Professor at Colorado School of Mines, where she teaches literature and environmental humanities courses. Her research and teaching interests focus on: contemporary and indigenous literature; women's fiction; and energy and the environment. Dr. Farca authored *Identity in Place: Contemporary Indigenous Fiction by Women Writers in the United States, Canada, Australia, and New Zealand* (2011) and edited *Energy in Literature: Essays on Energy and Its Social and Environmental Implications in Twentieth and Twenty-First Century Literary Texts* (2015). In addition to publishing numerous book chapters and peer-reviewed articles, she also coauthored a textbook and an anthology for students.

JAIMEY HAMILTON FARIS is Associate Professor of Art History and Critical Theory at the University of Hawai'i, Mānoa. She writes about global systems, infrastructure and ecologies. She has published widely on artists in the 1960s (*ARTMargins, Art Journal, October* and

In_Visible Culture). Her book *Uncommon Goods: The Global Dimensions of the Readymade* (2013) examines artistic representations of global trade structures. She edited a volume of experimental eco-criticism, *The Almanac for the Beyond* (Tropic Editions 2019), and her current book project *Liquid Archives, Liquid Futures* explores the aesthetics of water in contemporary art's representations of climate change and climate justice. Based in Honolulu, she also organizes artist residencies, events, exhibitions and the International Cultural Studies Research Group, Liquid Futures.

PAUL FORMISANO is an Associate Professor and the Director of Writing at the University of South Dakota, where he teaches courses in Western American literature, ecocriticism, and composition. His research focuses on water issues and their literary and rhetorical production with articles appearing in *The Journal of Ecocriticism, Landscapes: The Journal of the International Centre for Landscape and Language, Iperstoria,* and *Western American Literature.* He is currently working on a manuscript about marginalized discourses of the Colorado River Basin and an anthology of literature about dams.

REBECCA LYNNE FULLAN is a PhD Candidate in English at the Graduate Center, CUNY, working on her dissertation about decolonial imaginaries in the work of Louise Erdrich (Anishinaabe) and Tomson Highway (Cree). She has taught composition and literature at CUNY since 2011, and is currently an Instructional Technology Fellow working with the Macaulay Honors College. She has also recently participated in an interdisciplinary group focused on water justice and pedagogy, and thanks her colleagues for conversations that have stimulated and shaped the revisions of this essay.

CHRISTINA GERHARDT is Associate Professor at the University of Hawai'i, Mānoa. She is Associate Editor of *ISLE: Interdisciplinary Studies in Literature and the Environment,* the quarterly journal of the Association for the Study of Literature and the Environment (ASLE), published by Oxford University Press. She is author of *Atlas of Endangered Islands* and editor of *Climate Change, Hawaii and the Pacific.* She has been awarded grants by the Fulbright Commission, the DAAD, and the National Endowment for the Humanities. She has held visiting appointments at the Free University Berlin, Harvard University, Columbia University, and the University of California at Berkeley, where she taught previously. Her writing has been published in *Cineaste, Film Criticism, Film Quarterly, German Studies Review, Humanities, Mosaic, New German Critique,* and *Quarterly Review of Film and Video.*

LAURA HATRY received her PhD in Hispanic Studies from the Universidad Autónoma of Madrid in 2017 for her thesis, "Power, Violence and Politics in Latin American Film and Literature," as well as a MA in Contemporary Art History and Visual Culture in 2018 (Museo Reina Sofía, Madrid). Her research focuses mainly on cinematographic adaptations of Latin American literary works. Her work has been published in specialized journals, as well as academic research monographs. She is also a professional translator and has translated books and essays from and to Spanish, English, and German. She has participated as a speaker in international conferences in Spain, England, Germany, Italy, the United States, and Argentina, and her work as a visual artist has been shown in exhibitions in the United States, Spain, France, Germany, Canada, Austria, and the UAE.

IDOM T. INYABRI is a Senior Lecturer in the Department of English and Literary Studies, University of Calabar, Nigeria. He obtained his MA and PhD from the University of Ibadan and Calabar, Nigeria. His research interest ranges from Ecocriticism to African Poetry and Popular Culture. Dr. Inyabri is a Fellow of the African Humanities Program (AHP) with funding from the American Council of Learned Societies (ACLS) which has facilitated his research on Literature and Environment, including this study. His essay "Living the Weird: Apocalypses in Ogaga Ifowodo's *The Oil Lamp*" (2015), was published in Paula A. Farca's *Energy in Literature* and "Youth and Linguistic Stylization in Naija Afro Hip Hop" was published in *Sociolinguistic Studies*.

JEREMY LAROCHELLE is Professor of Spanish at the University of Mary Washington in Fredericksburg, Virginia, where he teaches courses on literature and environment studies. He has published articles in *Hispania, Review: Literature and Arts of the Americas, The Dirty Goat,* and chapters in edited volumes on Latin American literature and environmental issues. He published a critical anthology of recent poetry from the Amazon Basin entitled *¡Más aplausos para la lluvia!: Antología de poesía amazónica reciente* (2014) (More Applause for the Rain! Anthology of Recent Amazonian Poetry).

TRACEY DANIELS-LERBERG (PhD, University of Utah) is an Assistant Professor (lecturer). Her research includes nineteenth-century literatures and cultures of the US, multiethnic and posthuman rhetorics drawing on feminist and critical race theory, cultural studies, and animal and environment studies. Her publications include "To 'See with Eyes Unclouded by Hate': *Princess Mononoke* and the Quest for Environmental Balance," and "Science and Food Fictions: Agricultural Technologies, the Modern Industrial Diet, and a Food Revolution." She recently received a National Endowment for the Humanities grant to attend "On Native Grounds: Studies of Native American Histories and the Land" where she researched Native American ethno-history at the Library of Congress and National Archives and continues to work on projects that critically examine the intersection of race, gender, the environment, and power.

GIULIA MILLER is a Visiting Lecturer in English Literature at the University of Chester. She specializes in surrealism and modernism, with a particular interest in representations of climate, place, and landscape. She is the author of two monographs: *Studying Waltz with Bashir* (2017) and *Reconfiguring Surrealism in Modern Hebrew Literature* (2013).

ROBERT NIEMI teaches American literature, critical theory, film, and cultural studies at St. Michael's College in Colchester, Vermont. He is the author of books on Weldon Kees, Russell Banks, the Beat writers, Robert Altman, and film and history topics. His seventh book, on war films, is forthcoming from ABC-Clio.

EMMA TROTT is a Welcome Trust ISSF Early Career Researcher Fellow based in the School of English at the University of Leeds, where she is involved with the University of Leeds Poetry Centre. Her current project explores heart metaphors in contemporary literature and film, focusing on connections between cultural and biomedical conceptions of the heart. Her most recent publication is a short essay titled 'On Ken Smith's Heart' in Stand. Her PhD looked at the ecopoetics of Simon Armitage and Jon Silkin and she is interested in crossovers and dialogues between the environmental and medical humanities.

ILA TYAGI is a Lecturer at Yale-NUS College in Singapore. Her research and teaching interests include American cinema, the environmental humanities, science and technology, and twentieth-century literature in English. She completed a PhD in film and media studies and American studies at Yale University in 2018.

SUSAN J. TYBURSKI, JD, teaches courses concerning the interplay of literature, law, and society at the University of Denver, and has published numerous essays exploring this topic. She currently works as an administrative law judge for the State of Colorado.

Index